365

Favorite Brand Name ™

HAMBURGER

MEAT LOAVES, CHILIES & MORE

PUBLICATIONS INTERNATIONAL, LTD.

365

Favorite Brand Name™

HAMBURGER

MEAT LOAVES, CHILIES & MORE

Casual Snacks &
Party Tidbits

1 SPICY TACO DIP

1 pound BOB EVANS FARMS® Italian Roll Sausage
1 (16-ounce) can refried beans
1 (11-ounce) jar medium salsa
2 cups (8 ounces) shredded Cheddar cheese
2 cups (8 ounces) shredded Monterey Jack cheese
1 (2¼-ounce) can sliced black olives, drained
1 cup sliced green onions with tops
2 cups sour cream
1 (1-pound) bag tortilla chips

Preheat oven to 350°F. Crumble sausage into medium skillet. Cook over medium heat until browned, stirring occasionally. Drain off any drippings. Spread beans in ungreased 2½-quart shallow baking dish, then top with sausage. Pour salsa over sausage; sprinkle with cheeses. Sprinkle olives and onions over top. Bake 20 to 30 minutes or until heated through. Spread with sour cream while hot and serve with chips. Refrigerate leftovers; reheat in oven or microwave.

Makes 12 to 16 appetizer servings

2 HOT CHEESY CHILI DIP

1 pound lean ground beef
½ cup chopped onion
1 package (1 pound) pasteurized process cheese spread with jalapeño pepper, cut into cubes
1 can (15 ounces) kidney beans, drained
1 bottle (12 ounces) HEINZ® Chili Sauce
¼ cup chopped fresh parsley
Tortilla chips or crackers

In large saucepan, cook beef and onion until onion is tender; drain. Stir in cheese, beans and chili sauce; heat, stirring until cheese is melted. Stir in parsley. Serve warm with tortilla chips or crackers.

Makes about 5 cups

Spicy Taco Dip

CASUAL SNACKS & PARTY TIDBITS

3 CHILI CHIP PARTY PLATTER

- 1 pound ground beef
- 1 medium onion, chopped
- 1 package (1.48 ounces) LAWRY'S® Spices & Seasonings for Chili
- 1 can (6 ounces) tomato paste
- 1 cup water
- 1 bag (8 to 9 ounces) tortilla chips or corn chips
- 1½ cups (6 ounces) shredded Cheddar cheese
- 1 can (2¼ ounces) sliced pitted ripe olives, drained
- ½ cup sliced green onions

In medium skillet, brown beef until crumbly; drain fat. Add onion, Spices & Seasonings for Chili, tomato paste and water; blend well. Bring to a boil. Reduce heat to low; simmer, uncovered, 15 minutes, stirring occasionally. Serve over tortilla chips. Top with Cheddar cheese, olives and green onions. *Makes 4 servings*

PRESENTATION: Serve with a cool beverage and sliced melon.

4 COWBOY BEEF DIP

- 1 pound ground beef
- ½ teaspoon salt
- ½ teaspoon pepper
- ¼ teaspoon dried oregano leaves
- 1 can (11 ounces) nacho cheese soup
- ½ cup salsa
- ¼ cup chopped green onions
- ¼ cup sliced green olives
- ¼ cup sliced ripe olives
- 3 tablespoons chopped red bell pepper
- 2 tablespoons chopped green bell pepper
- 2 tablespoons chopped green chili peppers
- 1 teaspoon finely chopped jalapeño pepper
- 1 bag (16 ounces) tortilla chips
- 2 tablespoons sour cream
- ¼ cup shredded Cheddar cheese
- 2 fresh parsley leaves

1. Brown ground beef in skillet over medium heat. Drain and add salt, pepper and oregano. Stir in soup and salsa. Heat 5 minutes.

2. Reserve small amount of onions, olives and peppers for garnish; add remaining onions, olives and peppers to beef mixture. Heat 15 to 20 minutes.

3. Place dip and chips in separate bowls. Garnish dip with reserved vegetables, sour cream, cheese and parsley.
Makes 12 servings

*Favorite recipe from **North Dakota Beef Commission***

Chili Chip Party Platter

5 TIJUANA TACO DIP

1 can (16 ounces) refried beans
1 can (8 ounces) tomato sauce, divided
1¼ teaspoons TABASCO® pepper sauce,
   divided
1 large tomato, chopped
¾ cup (3 ounces) shredded Monterey Jack
   cheese
¾ pound ground beef
2 teaspoons chili powder
1 cup sliced ripe olives
1 cup (4 ounces) shredded Cheddar
   cheese
1 cup sour cream
   Sliced green onions, chopped tomatoes,
   chopped ripe olives and fresh cilantro
   for garnish
   Taco or tortilla chips

Preheat oven to 350°F. In medium bowl, combine refried beans, 3 tablespoons tomato sauce and ½ teaspoon TABASCO® sauce; mix well. Spread evenly in 1½-quart baking dish. Top with chopped tomato and Monterey Jack cheese.

In large skillet, cook beef with chili powder; stir frequently until meat is cooked. Remove from heat; drain off fat. Stir in remaining tomato sauce, sliced olives and remaining ¾ teaspoon TABASCO® sauce. Spread evenly over Monterey Jack cheese. Sprinkle with Cheddar cheese.

Bake 15 to 20 minutes or until cheeses melt and beans are hot. Remove from oven. Top with sour cream. Garnish with green onions, tomatoes, olives and cilantro. Serve warm with taco or tortilla chips.

Makes 12 appetizer servings

Tijuana Taco Dip

CASUAL SNACKS & PARTY TIDBITS

6 BEEFY NACHOS

1 pound ground beef
¼ cup chopped onion
⅓ cup A.1.® Steak Sauce
5 cups tortilla chips
1 cup (4 ounces) shredded Monterey Jack cheese
Dairy sour cream (optional)
1 cup chopped tomato (optional)
¼ cup diced green chilies, drained (optional)
¼ cup sliced pitted ripe olives (optional)

In large skillet, over medium-high heat, brown beef and onion; drain. Stir in steak sauce. Arrange tortilla chips on large heatproof platter. Spoon beef mixture over chips; sprinkle with cheese. Broil, 6 inches from heat source, for 3 to 5 minutes or until cheese melts. Top with sour cream, tomato, chilies and olives if desired. Serve immediately. *Makes 6 servings*

MICROWAVE DIRECTIONS: In 2-quart microwave-safe bowl, combine beef and onion; cover. Microwave at HIGH (100% power) for 5 to 6 minutes or until browned; drain. Stir in steak sauce. In 9-inch microwave-safe pie plate, layer half of each of the chips, beef mixture and cheese. Microwave at HIGH for 2 to 3 minutes or until heated through. Top with half of desired toppings. Repeat with remaining ingredients.

7 MINI BEEF TOSTADAS

1 pound ground beef
1 tablespoon instant minced onion
1 can (8 ounces) refried beans
1 can (4 ounces) chopped green chilies, drained (optional)
½ cup bottled taco sauce
4 dozen round tortilla chips
1 cup (4 ounces) shredded Cheddar cheese

1. Cook and stir beef and onion in large skillet over medium heat until beef is no longer pink, about 10 minutes; drain and discard drippings.

2. Stir in beans, chilies and taco sauce; cook and stir until bubbly, about 4 minutes. Spoon about 1 heaping tablespoon of the beef mixture on top of each tortilla chip; sprinkle with cheese. Place on baking sheets.

3. Bake in preheated 375°F oven until cheese is melted, about 2 minutes.
Makes 4 dozen

8 EGGPLANT APPETIZER

1 medium eggplant (about 1 pound)
¼ pound lean ground beef
¼ cup finely chopped onion
1 large clove garlic, minced
1 large tomato, chopped
1 small green bell pepper, finely chopped
¼ cup diced green olives
2 tablespoons olive oil
1 teaspoon white wine vinegar
1 tablespoon chopped fresh oregano *or*
    1 teaspoon dried oregano leaves
Salt and freshly ground black pepper

Preheat oven to 350°F. Pierce eggplant with fork; place in shallow baking pan. Bake 1 hour or until skin is wrinkled and eggplant is soft. Set aside until cool enough to handle.

Meanwhile, brown ground beef in medium skillet. Drain. Add onion and garlic; cook until tender.

Peel eggplant; cut into small cubes. Combine eggplant, ground beef mixture, tomato, green bell pepper and olives in medium bowl. Whisk together oil, vinegar and oregano in small bowl. Add to eggplant mixture; mix lightly. Season with salt and pepper to taste.

Serve with toasted pita wedges as an appetizer or serve on lettuce leaves as a first course.   *Makes about 8 servings*

9 CHINATOWN STUFFED MUSHROOMS

24 large fresh mushrooms (about 1 pound), cleaned and stems trimmed
½ pound ground turkey
1 clove garlic, minced
¼ cup fine dry bread crumbs
¼ cup thinly sliced green onions
3 tablespoons reduced-sodium soy sauce, divided
1 teaspoon minced fresh ginger
1 egg white, slightly beaten
⅛ teaspoon crushed red pepper flakes (optional)

Remove stems from mushrooms; finely chop enough stems to equal 1 cup. Cook turkey with chopped stems and garlic in medium skillet over medium-high heat until turkey is no longer pink, stirring to separate turkey. Spoon off any fat. Stir in bread crumbs, green onions, 2 tablespoons soy sauce, ginger, egg white and crushed red pepper; mix well.

Brush mushroom caps lightly on all sides with remaining 1 tablespoon soy sauce; spoon about 2 teaspoons stuffing into each mushroom cap.* Place stuffed mushrooms on rack of foil-lined broiler pan. Broil 4 to 5 inches from heat 5 to 6 minutes or until hot.   *Makes 24 appetizers*

Mushrooms may be made ahead to this point; cover and refrigerate up to 24 hours. Add 1 to 2 minutes to broiling time for chilled mushrooms.

Chinatown Stuffed Mushrooms

CASUAL SNACKS & PARTY TIDBITS

10 SOUTHWESTERN POTATO SKINS

6 large russet potatoes
¾ pound ground beef
1 package (1.0 ounce) LAWRY'S® Taco
　　Spices & Seasonings
¾ cup water
¾ cup sliced green onions
1 medium tomato, chopped
1 can (2¼ ounces) sliced ripe olives,
　　drained
1 cup (4 ounces) shredded Cheddar
　　cheese
2 cups Lawry's® Fiesta Dip (recipe follows)

Pierce potatoes with fork. Microwave on HIGH 30 minutes, turning over after 15 minutes; let cool. Cut in half and scoop out potatoes leaving ¼-inch shell. In medium skillet, brown ground beef until crumbly; drain fat. Stir in Taco Spices & Seasonings and water. Bring to a boil; reduce heat and simmer, uncovered, 15 minutes. Stir in green onions. Spoon meat mixture into potato shells. Top with tomato, olives and cheese. Place on baking sheet and heat under broiler to melt cheese. Spoon dollops of Lawry's® Fiesta Dip on each shell.

Makes 1 dozen appetizers

LAWRY'S® FIESTA DIP
1 package (1.0 ounce) LAWRY'S® Taco
　　Spices & Seasonings
1 pint (16 ounces) dairy sour cream

In medium bowl, combine ingredients. Blend well. Refrigerate until ready to serve.

Makes 2 cups

PRESENTATION: Sprinkle filled potato skins with additional sliced green onions. Serve with salsa.

HINT: Lawry's® Fiesta Dip may be served with tortilla chips and fresh cut vegetables such as carrots, broccoli, cauliflower or zucchini.

11 PIZZA–STUFFED MUSHROOMS

12 large *or* 24 medium fresh mushrooms
¼ cup chopped green bell pepper
¼ cup chopped pepperoni or cooked,
　　crumbled Italian sausage
1 cup (*half* of 15-ounce can)
　　CONTADINA® Pizza Sauce
½ cup (2 ounces) shredded mozzarella
　　cheese

Wash and dry mushrooms; remove stems. Chop ¼ cup stems. In small bowl, combine chopped stems, bell pepper, meat and pizza sauce. Spoon mixture into mushroom caps; top with cheese. Broil 6 to 8 inches from heat for 2 to 3 minutes or until cheese is melted and mushrooms are heated through.

Makes 12 large or 24 medium appetizers

Southwestern Potato Skins

12 BEEFY STUFFED MUSHROOMS

1 pound lean ground beef
2 teaspoons prepared horseradish
1 teaspoon chopped chives
1 clove garlic, minced
¼ teaspoon pepper
18 large mushrooms
⅔ cup dry white wine

1. Thoroughly mix ground beef, horseradish, chives, garlic and pepper in medium bowl.

2. Remove stems from mushrooms; stuff mushroom caps with beef mixture.

3. Place stuffed mushrooms in shallow baking dish; pour wine over mushrooms. Bake in preheated 350°F oven until meat is browned, about 20 minutes.

Makes 1½ dozen

13 CHEESEBURGER BITES

1 pound lean ground beef
1½ cups Corn CHEX® brand cereal, crushed to ½ cup
1 cup ketchup, divided
1 egg, slightly beaten
½ teaspoon seasoned salt
½ teaspoon prepared mustard
¼ teaspoon onion powder
⅛ teaspoon garlic powder
½ cup shredded Cheddar cheese
¼ cup real bacon bits or pieces (optional)
2 tablespoons packed brown sugar
Sliced green onion, olives and carrot (optional)
Fresh herbs (optional)

1. Combine ground beef, cereal, ¼ cup ketchup, egg, seasoned salt, mustard, onion powder and garlic powder; mix well. Add cheese and bacon; mix well. Form into 1¼-inch balls. Place in ungreased 13×9×2-inch microwave-safe baking dish. Cover with waxed paper. Microwave on HIGH (100%) 9 to 11 minutes or until no longer pink, rotating dish every 3 minutes and turning meatballs halfway through cooking time. Drain on paper towels.

2. Combine remaining ¾ cup ketchup and brown sugar in 2-quart microwave-safe baking dish; mix well. Add meatballs, stirring until evenly coated. Cover and microwave on HIGH 1 to 2 minutes or until heated through. Garnish with onion, olives, carrot and fresh herbs, as desired.

Makes about 24 meatballs

CONVENTIONAL DIRECTIONS: 1. Preheat oven to 350°F. Combine ground beef, cereal, ¼ cup ketchup, egg, seasoned salt, mustard, onion powder and garlic powder; mix well. Add cheese and bacon; mix well. Form into 1¼-inch balls. Place in ungreased 13×9×2-inch baking pan. Bake, uncovered, 15 to 20 minutes or until no longer pink, turning meatballs halfway through cooking time. Drain on paper towels.

2. Combine remaining ¾ cup ketchup and brown sugar in 2-quart baking dish; mix well. Add meatballs, stirring until evenly coated. Bake, uncovered, 5 to 10 minutes or until heated through. Garnish with onion, olives, carrot and fresh herbs, as desired.

CASUAL SNACKS & PARTY TIDBITS

14 CANTONESE MEATBALLS

1 can (20 ounces) pineapple chunks in syrup
3 tablespoons brown sugar, packed
5 tablespoons KIKKOMAN® Teriyaki Marinade & Sauce, divided
1 tablespoon vinegar
1 tablespoon tomato ketchup
1 pound lean ground beef
2 tablespoons instant minced onion
2 tablespoons cornstarch
¼ cup water

Drain pineapple; reserve syrup. Combine reserved syrup, brown sugar, 3 tablespoons teriyaki sauce, vinegar and ketchup; set aside. Mix beef with remaining 2 tablespoons teriyaki sauce and onion; shape into 20 meatballs. Brown meatballs in large skillet; drain off excess fat. Pour syrup mixture over meatballs; simmer 10 minutes, stirring occasionally. Dissolve cornstarch in water; stir into skillet with pineapple. Cook and stir until sauce thickens and pineapple is heated through.

Makes 6 to 8 appetizer servings

15 SWEET 'N' SOUR MEATBALLS

1½ pounds lean ground beef
2 cups Corn CHEX® brand cereal, crushed
1 can (8 ounces) water chestnuts, drained and finely chopped
½ cup milk
1 egg, slightly beaten
1 tablespoon soy sauce
1 teaspoon onion salt
½ teaspoon garlic salt
1 cup apricot preserves
½ cup chili sauce

1. Combine ground beef, crushed cereal, water chestnuts, milk, egg, soy sauce, onion salt and garlic salt; mix well. Form into 1-inch balls. Place in ungreased 13×9×2-inch microwave-safe baking dish. Cover with waxed paper. Microwave on HIGH 10 to 12 minutes or until no longer pink, rotating dish every 3 minutes and turning meatballs halfway through cooking time. Drain on paper towels.

2. Combine preserves and chili sauce in 2-quart microwave-safe baking dish; mix well. Microwave on HIGH 2 minutes, stirring after 1 minute. Add meatballs, stirring until evenly coated. Cover and microwave on HIGH 1 to 2 minutes or until heated through.

Makes about 4 dozen

CONVENTIONAL DIRECTIONS: 1. Preheat oven to 350°F. Combine ground beef, crushed cereal, water chestnuts, milk, egg, soy sauce, onion salt and garlic salt; mix well. Form into 1-inch balls. Place in ungreased 13×9×2-inch baking pan. Bake, uncovered, 20 to 25 minutes or until no longer pink, turning meatballs halfway through cooking time. Drain on paper towels.

2. Combine preserves and chili sauce in 2-quart glass baking dish; mix well. Add meatballs, stirring until evenly coated. Bake, uncovered, 10 to 15 minutes or until heated through.

16 MEXICALI APPETIZER MEATBALLS

⅔ cup A.1.® Steak Sauce
⅔ cup thick and chunky salsa
1½ pounds ground beef
 1 egg
½ cup plain dry bread crumbs

In small bowl, blend steak sauce and salsa. In separate small bowl, combine beef, egg, bread crumbs and ⅓ cup sauce mixture; shape into 32 (1¼-inch) meatballs. Arrange meatballs in single layer in shallow baking pan. Bake at 425°F for 12 to 15 minutes or until meatballs are cooked through. Serve hot meatballs with remaining sauce mixture as a dip.   *Makes 32 (1¼-inch) meatballs*

17 SOUTH–OF–THE–BORDER MEATBALLS

1¼ pounds ground beef
 1 package (1.0 ounce) LAWRY'S® Taco
      Spices & Seasonings
¼ cup unseasoned dry bread crumbs
¼ cup finely chopped onion
¼ cup finely chopped green bell pepper
 1 egg, beaten
1½ cups chunky salsa

In large bowl, combine all ingredients except salsa; blend well. Form into 1-inch balls. In large skillet, brown meatballs on all sides; drain fat. Add salsa to skillet. Bring to a boil; reduce heat and simmer, uncovered, 10 minutes.   *Makes 6 servings*

PRESENTATION: Serve with your favorite Mexican beer or sangría.

18 SAVORY APPETIZER PORK MEATBALLS

1 pound ground pork
½ cup soft bread crumbs
1 egg, beaten
2 tablespoons minced onion
1 tablespoon minced green bell pepper
1 clove garlic, minced
1 teaspoon salt
⅛ teaspoon pepper
1 tablespoon vegetable oil
1 can (8 ounces) tomato sauce
¼ cup apple jelly
¼ teaspoon curry powder

In large bowl combine ground pork, bread crumbs, egg, onion, bell pepper, garlic, salt and pepper; mix well. Shape pork mixture into about 30 (1-inch) meatballs. In large skillet brown meatballs in hot oil. Drain well.

In small saucepan combine tomato sauce, apple jelly and curry powder; simmer until jelly is melted, stirring occasionally. Pour sauce over meatballs. Cover and simmer 15 to 20 minutes, stirring often.
       Makes 4 servings

Prep Time: 20 minutes
Cook Time: 15 minutes

*Favorite recipe from **National Pork Producers Council***

Mexicali Appetizer Meatballs

19 FESTIVE COCKTAIL MEATBALLS

1½ pounds ground beef
1 cup uncooked MINUTE® Original Rice
1 can (8 ounces) crushed pineapple in juice, undrained
½ cup finely shredded carrot
⅓ cup chopped onion
1 egg, slightly beaten
1 teaspoon ground ginger
1 bottle (8 ounces) prepared French dressing
2 tablespoons soy sauce

Mix ground beef, rice, pineapple with juice, carrot, onion, egg and ginger in medium bowl. Form into 1-inch meatballs. Place on greased baking sheets. Bake at 400°F for 15 minutes or until browned.

Meanwhile, mix together dressing and soy sauce. Serve meatballs with dressing mixture.   *Makes 50 to 60 meatballs*

20 MINI COCKTAIL MEATBALLS

1 envelope LIPTON® Recipe Secrets® Onion, Onion-Mushroom, Beefy Mushroom or Beefy Onion Soup Mix
1 pound ground beef
½ cup plain dry bread crumbs
¼ cup dry red wine or water
2 eggs, slightly beaten

Preheat oven to 375°F.

In medium bowl, combine all ingredients; shape into 1-inch meatballs.

In shallow baking pan, arrange meatballs and bake 18 minutes or until done. Serve, if desired, with assorted mustards or tomato sauce.   *Makes about 4 dozen meatballs*

21 SWEET AND SOUR PORK MEATBALLS

1 pound lean ground pork
¼ cup finely chopped water chestnuts
¼ cup chopped onion
1 egg, slightly beaten
4 tablespoons soy sauce, divided
⅛ teaspoon ground ginger
1 teaspoon vegetable oil
1 can (8 ounces) pineapple chunks
1 tablespoon vinegar
1 tablespoon cornstarch
1 tablespoon sugar

In large bowl combine pork, water chestnuts, onion, egg, 2 tablespoons soy sauce and ginger; shape into 1-inch balls. In nonstick skillet cook meatballs in hot oil until browned. Remove meatballs and drain on paper towels, reserving drippings in skillet.

Drain pineapple, reserving juice. In 1-cup measure combine pineapple juice, remaining 2 tablespoons soy sauce and vinegar. Add water to equal 1 cup liquid. In mixing bowl combine cornstarch and sugar. Gradually stir in pineapple juice mixture; mix well. Add juice mixture to pan drippings. Cook over medium heat until thickened and bubbly, stirring constantly. Stir in meatballs and reserved pineapple. Cook 4 to 5 minutes or until heated through.

Makes 24 servings

Prep Time: 25 minutes

Favorite recipe from **National Pork Producers Council**

Festive Cocktail Meatballs

CASUAL SNACKS & PARTY TIDBITS

22 ELEGANT PORK TERRINE

2 tablespoons butter or margarine
1 cup chopped onion
2 cloves garlic, minced
1 pound sweet Italian sausage
1 pound ground pork
2 eggs, slightly beaten
¼ cup light cream
2 tablespoons brandy
⅛ teaspoon ground allspice
⅛ teaspoon ground cloves
⅛ teaspoon pepper
½ pound sliced Canadian bacon, cut into julienne strips
8 to 10 fresh asparagus spears

In large skillet melt butter. Add onion and garlic; cook and stir until tender. Remove from skillet and set aside.

Remove sausage from casing and crumble into skillet. Add ground pork and cook 4 minutes or until partially cooked. Drain pan drippings. Let pork mixture stand about 10 minutes to cool. Stir in onion mixture, eggs, light cream, brandy, allspice, cloves and pepper; mix well.

Spread ⅓ of meat mixture in lightly greased 8×4×2-inch loaf pan. Evenly layer Canadian bacon on top. Top with ⅓ of meat mixture. Remove tough ends of asparagus. Peel lower stalks to remove scales. Place asparagus over meat mixture. Top with remaining ⅓ of meat mixture.

Wrap entire loaf pan with heavy-duty foil, sealing edges. Fill large roasting pan about half full of water. Place loaf pan in roasting pan. Bake at 350°F 1 to 1½ hours or until done. Remove loaf pan from roasting pan; let stand about 15 minutes. Place another loaf pan filled with dried beans on top of terrine. Let stand 2 hours. Remove weight and refrigerate terrine overnight.

To serve, remove foil and loosen edges of terrine with knife. Turn out onto serving platter. Garnish as desired. Serve with assorted crackers.   *Makes 16 servings*

Prep Time: 30 minutes
Cook Time: 90 minutes

Favorite recipe from **National Pork Producers Council**

23 PORK–APPLE BITES

1 pound ground pork
1 teaspoon salt
¼ teaspoon ground cinnamon
⅛ teaspoon pepper
½ cup shredded pared apple
¼ cup soft rye bread crumbs
¼ cup chopped walnuts
½ cup water
½ cup apple jelly

Sprinkle salt, cinnamon and pepper over pork; add apple, bread crumbs and walnuts. Mix lightly but thoroughly. Shape mixture into 40 meatballs (1 scant tablespoon each). Brown meatballs, in batches, in large skillet. Pour off drippings. Return meatballs to skillet. Add water, cover tightly and cook over low heat 15 minutes. Transfer meatballs to warm chafing dish using slotted spoon. Stir apple jelly into cooking liquid in skillet and cook until melted. Pour sauce over meatballs.   *Makes 40 appetizers*

Prep Time: 10 minutes
Cook Time: 15 minutes

Favorite recipe from **National Pork Producers Council**

Elegant Pork Terrine

CASUAL SNACKS & PARTY TIDBITS

24 MEXI–BEEF BITES

1 pound ground beef
1 cup (4 ounces) shredded Cheddar
   cheese
1 cup (4 ounces) shredded Monterey Jack
   cheese
1 can (4 ounces) chopped green chilies,
   drained
½ cup bottled green taco or enchilada
   sauce
2 large eggs, beaten
   Tortilla chips (optional)

Cook and stir beef in large skillet over medium-high heat until beef loses pink color. Pour off drippings. Stir in cheeses, chilies, taco sauce and eggs. Transfer mixture to 8×8-inch baking pan. Bake at 350°F 35 to 40 minutes or until knife inserted in center comes out clean and top is golden brown. Cool in pan 15 minutes. Cut into 36 squares. Serve with tortilla chips.

Makes 36 appetizers

Favorite recipe from **National Cattlemen's Beef Association**

25 ORANGE MAPLE SAUSAGE BALLS

1 pound BOB EVANS FARMS® Original
   Recipe Roll Sausage
1 small onion, finely chopped
1 small red or yellow bell pepper, finely
   chopped
1 egg
2 tablespoons uncooked cream of wheat
   cereal
½ cup maple syrup or maple-flavored
   syrup
3 to 5 tablespoons frozen orange juice
   concentrate, slightly thawed, to taste

Combine first 5 ingredients in large bowl until well blended. Shape into ¾-inch balls. Cook in large skillet over medium-high heat until browned on all sides and no longer pink in centers. Drain off drippings. Add syrup and orange juice concentrate to sausage mixture. Cook and stir over medium heat 2 to 3 minutes or until thick bubbly syrup forms. Serve hot. Refrigerate leftovers.

Makes about 24 appetizers

SERVING SUGGESTIONS: Serve on party picks with sautéed mushrooms and water chestnuts. These meatballs would also make an excellent breakfast item; serve with small pancakes.

26 HAWAIIAN COCKTAIL MEATBALLS

1 can (20 ounces) pineapple chunks in
   juice
1 package (14 ounces) ground chicken
1 cup cooked wild rice
¼ cup finely chopped green bell pepper
¼ cup fine cracker crumbs
1 egg
1 teaspoon onion salt
¼ teaspoon ground ginger
1 tablespoon vegetable oil
1 cup sweet and sour sauce

Drain pineapple, reserving juice. In large bowl, combine chicken, wild rice, green bell pepper, cracker crumbs, 2 tablespoons of the pineapple juice, egg, onion salt and ginger; mix well. Form mixture into 1-inch meatballs. In large skillet, heat oil over medium heat. Brown meatballs; drain. Add remaining pineapple and juice; cover and cook over medium heat 10 to 15 minutes or until meatballs are no longer pink in center. Stir sweet and sour sauce into meatballs and pineapple; cook 4 to 5 minutes until mixture is heated through. Serve on toothpicks with pineapple chunks.

Makes 35 to 40 appetizers

NOTE: For main dish, serve meatballs over cooked rice or noodles. Makes 5 main-dish servings.

*Favorite recipe from **Minnesota Cultivated Wild Rice Council***

27 SWEET 'N' SOUR MEATBALLS

1 pound lean ground beef
1 cup soft bread crumbs
1 egg, slightly beaten
2 tablespoons minced onion
2 tablespoons milk
1 clove garlic, minced
½ teaspoon salt
⅛ teaspoon pepper
1 tablespoon vegetable oil
⅔ cup HEINZ® Chili Sauce
⅔ cup red currant or grape jelly

Combine beef, crumbs, egg, onion, milk, garlic, salt and pepper; form into 40 bite-size meatballs, using 1 teaspoon meat mixture for each. In large skillet, brown meatballs lightly in hot oil. Cover; cook over low heat 5 minutes. Drain excess fat. Combine chili sauce and jelly; pour over meatballs. Heat, stirring occasionally, until jelly is melted. Simmer mixture 10 to 12 minutes until sauce has thickened, basting meatballs occasionally.

Makes 40 appetizers (¾ cup sauce)

28 PORK BALLS ORIENTAL

1 pound ground pork
3 tablespoons cracker crumbs
¼ cup finely chopped onion
1 egg
1 teaspoon salt, divided
   Dash black pepper
2 cups sliced celery
2 cups sliced fresh mushrooms
2 tablespoons Worcestershire sauce
1 can (8 ounces) bamboo shoots, drained
1 can (8 ounces) water chestnuts, drained and chopped
1 package (6 ounces) frozen pea pods, blanched and drained

Combine ground pork, cracker crumbs, onion, egg, ½ teaspoon salt and pepper; mix well. Shape mixture into 24 balls (about 1 tablespoon each). Cook pork balls in large skillet until browned. Remove and keep warm. Drain drippings. Add celery and cook over medium heat 3 to 4 minutes, stirring occasionally. Add mushrooms and Worcestershire sauce and continue cooking 1 minute, stirring constantly. Add bamboo shoots, water chestnuts and pea pods. Reduce heat to low; cover and cook 3 to 4 minutes. Sprinkle vegetables with remaining ½ teaspoon salt, stirring to combine. Return pork balls to pan and cook until mixture is heated through, stirring gently.

Makes 4 servings

Prep Time: 20 minutes
Cook Time: 25 minutes

*Favorite recipe from **National Pork Producers Council***

29 STUFFED GRAPE LEAVES

½ pound ground beef
1 medium onion, chopped
   Greek Salad Dressing (recipe follows)
¾ cup uncooked MINUTE® Original Rice
¼ cup chopped parsley
¼ teaspoon salt
20 canned grape leaves

Brown beef with onion in medium skillet. Stir in ¼ cup dressing, rice, parsley and salt. With shiny surface of leaf down, place 1 tablespoon of the meat mixture in the center of each leaf. Fold edges of leaf toward center and roll up. Place in large skillet. Pour remaining ¾ cup dressing over stuffed leaves and simmer over low heat until liquid is absorbed, about 5 minutes. Cover and chill. *Makes 20 servings*

GREEK SALAD DRESSING
3 tablespoons lemon juice
3 tablespoons water
1 envelope GOOD SEASONS® Lemon and Herbs or Italian Salad Dressing Mix
⅔ cup olive oil
3 tablespoons feta cheese, crumbled (optional)
½ teaspoon dried oregano leaves

Combine lemon juice, water and salad dressing mix in cruet or jar. Shake well. Add olive oil, feta cheese and oregano. Shake well. *Makes 1 cup*

30 THAI LAMB & COUSCOUS ROLLS

16 large napa or Chinese cabbage leaves, stems trimmed
2 tablespoons minced fresh ginger
1 teaspoon crushed red pepper
⅔ cup uncooked quick-cooking couscous
½ pound ground lean lamb
½ cup chopped green onions
3 cloves garlic, minced
¼ cup plus 2 tablespoons minced fresh cilantro or mint, divided
2 tablespoons reduced-sodium soy sauce
1 tablespoon lime juice
1 teaspoon Oriental sesame oil
1 cup plain nonfat yogurt

Place 4 cups water in medium saucepan; bring to a boil over high heat. Drop cabbage leaves into water; cook 30 seconds. Drain. Rinse under cold water until cool; pat dry with paper towels.

Place 1 cup water, ginger and red pepper in medium saucepan; bring to a boil over high heat. Stir in couscous; cover. Remove saucepan from heat; let stand 5 minutes.

Spray large saucepan with nonstick cooking spray; add lamb, onions and garlic. Cook and stir over medium-high heat 5 minutes or until lamb is no longer pink. Remove lamb from skillet; drain in colander. Combine couscous, lamb, ¼ cup cilantro, soy sauce, lime juice and oil in medium bowl. Spoon evenly down centers of cabbage leaves. Fold ends of cabbage leaves over filling; roll up. Combine yogurt and remaining 2 tablespoons cilantro in small bowl; spoon evenly over rolls. Serve warm. Garnish as desired. *Makes 16 appetizers*

Thai Lamb & Couscous Rolls

31 ■ MEAT–FILLED ORIENTAL PANCAKES

6 Oriental Pancakes (recipe follows)
1 tablespoon cornstarch
3 tablespoons KIKKOMAN® Soy Sauce
1 tablespoon dry sherry
¾ pound ground beef
½ pound ground pork
⅔ cup chopped green onions and tops
1 teaspoon minced fresh ginger root
1 clove garlic, pressed

Prepare Oriental Pancakes. Combine cornstarch, soy sauce and sherry in large bowl. Add beef, pork, green onions, ginger and garlic; mix until thoroughly combined. Spread ½ cup meat mixture evenly over each pancake, leaving about a ½-inch border on 1 side. Starting with opposite side, roll up pancake jelly-roll fashion. Place rolls, seam side down, in single layer on heatproof plate; place plate on steamer rack. Set rack in large pot or wok of boiling water. Cover and steam 15 minutes. (For best results, steam all rolls at the same time.) Just before serving, cut rolls diagonally into quarters. Arrange on serving platter and serve hot.

Makes 2 dozen appetizers

ORIENTAL PANCAKES: Beat *4 eggs* in large bowl with wire whisk. Combine *½ cup water*, *3 tablespoons cornstarch*, *2 teaspoons KIKKOMAN® Soy Sauce* and *½ teaspoon sugar*; pour into eggs and beat well. Heat an 8-inch omelet or crêpe pan over medium heat. Brush bottom of pan with *½ teaspoon vegetable oil*; reduce heat to low. Beat egg mixture; pour ¼ cup into skillet, lifting and tipping pan from side to side to form a thin round pancake. Cook 1 to 1½ minutes, or until firm. Carefully lift with spatula and transfer to sheet of waxed paper. Continue procedure, adding *½ teaspoon oil* to pan for each pancake. Makes 6 pancakes.

32 ■ PARTY BEEF ROLL–UPS

1 pound lean ground beef
1 cup cooked wild rice
½ cup chopped onion
½ cup fine dry bread crumbs
2 eggs, slightly beaten
1 clove garlic, minced
2 cups barbecue sauce, divided
8 (8-inch) flour tortillas
¾ cup chopped green onions
½ cup fresh cilantro leaves

Preheat oven to 450°F. In medium bowl, combine beef, wild rice, chopped onion, crumbs, eggs, garlic and 2 tablespoons sauce. Shape into 8 (8-inch) logs; place on baking sheets. Bake about 14 minutes or until no longer pink and juices run clear; set aside. Microwave each tortilla at HIGH 5 seconds; spread with about 2 teaspoons sauce. Top with green onions and cilantro. Place 1 log at edge of each tortilla. Roll up and secure with toothpicks; cut each roll into 6 to 8 pieces. Serve with remaining sauce for dipping.

Makes 48 to 64 appetizers

NOTE: Serve whole for 4 main-dish servings.

*Favorite recipe from **Minnesota Cultivated Wild Rice Council***

Meat-Filled Oriental Pancakes

33 MEAT–FILLED SAMOSAS

1 cup all-purpose flour
1 cup whole wheat flour
1¼ teaspoons salt, divided
2 tablespoons plus 2 teaspoons vegetable oil, divided
⅓ to ½ cup water
1 small onion, finely chopped
2 cloves garlic, minced
1 teaspoon finely chopped fresh ginger
¾ pound lean ground lamb or ground round
2 teaspoons Garam Masala* (page 29)
¾ cup frozen peas
1 small tomato, peeled, seeded and chopped
2 teaspoons finely chopped cilantro
1 green jalapeño pepper,** seeded and chopped
Additional vegetable oil for frying
Cilantro Chutney (page 29) (optional)

Also available at specialty stores and Indian markets

**Jalapeño and hot green chili peppers can sting and irritate the skin; wear rubber gloves when handling peppers and do not touch eyes. Wash hands after handling.*

Combine flours and ½ teaspoon salt in large bowl. Stir in 2 tablespoons oil with fork; mix until mixture resembles fine crumbs. Gradually stir in enough water, about ⅓ cup, until dough forms a ball and is no longer sticky. Place dough on lightly floured surface; flatten slightly. Knead dough 5 minutes or until smooth and elastic. Divide dough in half and form 2 ropes, each about 9 inches long and 1 inch thick. Wrap in plastic wrap; let stand 1 hour.

Meanwhile, heat remaining 2 teaspoons oil in large skillet over medium heat. Add onion, garlic and ginger; cook and stir 5 minutes or until onion is softened. Crumble meat into skillet; cook 6 to 8 minutes or until browned, stirring to separate meat. Spoon off and discard fat. Stir in Garam Masala and remaining ¾ teaspoon salt. Add peas, tomato, cilantro and jalapeño to skillet; mix well. Cover and cook 5 minutes or until peas are heated through. Cool to room temperature before filling samosas.

To form samosas, divide each rope of dough into 9 equal portions. Roll each piece on lightly floured surface into 4- to 5-inch round. Keep remaining dough pieces wrapped in plastic wrap to prevent drying. Cut each round of dough in half, forming 2 semi-circles. Moisten straight edge of 1 semi-circle with water and fold in half; press moistened edges together to seal. Spread dough apart to form cone; fill with 2 teaspoons meat filling. Press meat mixture into cone, leaving ½ inch of dough above meat mixture. Moisten edges of dough and press firmly together. Place samosas on work surface and seal edges with fork.

Heat 3 to 4 inches oil in large heavy skillet over medium-high heat to 375°F on deep-fat thermometer. Cook 4 to 6 samosas at a time 3 to 4 minutes or until crisp and golden. Drain on paper towels. Serve with Cilantro Chutney.   *Makes 36 samosas*

CASUAL SNACKS & PARTY TIDBITS

GARAM MASALA

- 2 teaspoons cumin seeds
- 2 teaspoons whole black peppercorns
- 1½ teaspoons coriander seeds
- 1 teaspoon fennel seeds
- ¾ teaspoon whole cloves
- ½ teaspoon whole cardamom seeds, pods removed
- 1 cinnamon stick, broken

Preheat oven to 250°F. Combine spices in baking pan; bake 30 minutes, stirring occasionally. Transfer spices to clean coffee or spice grinder or use mortar and pestle to pulverize. Store in covered glass jar.

CILANTRO CHUTNEY

- ½ cup green onions, cut into ½-inch lengths
- 1 to 2 hot green chili peppers,** seeded and coarsely chopped
- 2 tablespoons chopped fresh ginger
- 2 cloves garlic, peeled
- 1 cup packed cilantro leaves
- 2 tablespoons vegetable oil
- 2 tablespoons lime juice
- 1 teaspoon salt
- 1 teaspoon sugar
- ¼ teaspoon ground cumin

Drop green onions, chilies, ginger and garlic through feed tube of food processor with motor running. Stop machine and add cilantro, oil, lime juice, salt, sugar and cumin; process until cilantro is finely chopped.

Meat-Filled Samosas

CASUAL SNACKS & PARTY TIDBITS

34 SAVORY SAUSAGE MUSHROOM TURNOVERS

1 (12-ounce) package frozen bulk pork sausage, thawed
1 cup chopped mushrooms
1/3 cup chopped onion
1/2 cup shredded Swiss cheese (2 ounces)
1/3 cup GREY POUPON® COUNTRY DIJON® Mustard
2 tablespoons diced red bell pepper
1/2 teaspoon dried thyme leaves
2 (8-ounce) packages refrigerated crescent dinner roll dough
1 egg, beaten
Sesame or poppy seed

In large skillet, over medium heat, cook sausage, mushrooms and onion until sausage is cooked, stirring occasionally to break up sausage. Remove from heat. Stir in cheese, mustard, bell pepper and thyme.

Separate each package of dough into 4 rectangles; press perforations together to seal. On floured surface, roll each rectangle into 6-inch square. Cut each square into quarters, making 32 squares total. Place 1 scant tablespoon sausage mixture on each square; fold dough over filling on the diagonal to form triangle. Press edges with fork to seal. Place on greased baking sheets.

Brush triangles with beaten egg and sprinkle with sesame or poppy seed. Bake at 375°F for 10 to 12 minutes or until golden brown. Serve warm.   *Makes 32 appetizers*

35 EMPANDILLAS

1/2 pound ground beef
1 cup chopped ripe olives
3/4 cup chopped fresh mushrooms
1/4 cup water
1 package (1.0 ounce) LAWRY'S® Taco Spices & Seasonings
1 package (17¼ ounces) frozen puff pastry sheets, thawed
1 egg white, beaten

In medium bowl, combine ground beef, olives, mushrooms, water and Taco Spices & Seasonings; blend well. Roll each pastry sheet into a 12-inch square. Cut each sheet into 9 squares. Place approximately 2 teaspoons meat mixture in center of each square; moisten edges with water. Fold one corner over to form triangle and pinch edges together to seal. Brush with egg white. Place on ungreased baking sheet. Bake in 375°F oven 15 to 20 minutes or until golden brown.   *Makes 18 appetizers*

PRESENTATION: Serve with guacamole and sour cream.

HINTS: Two cans (8 ounces each) refrigerated crescent roll dough can be used in place of puff pastry sheets. Roll out dough into 12-inch squares. Follow directions above. Stir 3 tablespoons shredded cheese into filling for extra flavor.

Savory Sausage Mushroom Turnovers

36 MINI SAUSAGE QUICHES

½ cup butter or margarine, softened
3 ounces cream cheese, softened
1 cup all-purpose flour
½ pound BOB EVANS FARMS® Italian Roll Sausage
1 cup (4 ounces) shredded Swiss cheese
1 tablespoon snipped fresh chives
2 eggs
1 cup half-and-half
¼ teaspoon salt
Dash cayenne pepper

Beat butter and cream cheese in medium bowl until creamy. Blend in flour; refrigerate 1 hour. Roll into 24 (1-inch) balls; press each into ungreased mini-muffin cup to form pastry shell. Preheat oven to 375°F. To prepare filling, crumble sausage into small skillet. Cook over medium heat until browned, stirring occasionally. Drain off any drippings. Sprinkle evenly into pastry shells in muffin cups; sprinkle with Swiss cheese and chives. Whisk eggs, half-and-half, salt and cayenne until blended; pour into pastry shells. Bake 20 to 30 minutes or until set. Remove from pans. Serve hot. Refrigerate leftovers. *Makes 24 appetizers*

SERVING SUGGESTION: Use 12 standard 2½-inch muffin cups to make larger individual quiches. Serve for breakfast.

37 SOMBRERO TACO CUPS

1 pound ground beef or pork
1 package (1.0 ounce) LAWRY'S® Taco Spices & Seasonings
¾ cup water
¼ cup salsa
2 packages (7.5 ounces each) refrigerated biscuits
½ cup (2 ounces) shredded Cheddar cheese

In medium skillet, brown ground beef until crumbly; drain fat. Add Taco Spices & Seasonings and water; blend well. Bring to a boil; reduce heat and simmer, uncovered, 10 minutes. Stir in salsa. Separate biscuits and press each biscuit into an ungreased muffin cup. Spoon equal amounts of meat mixture into each muffin cup; sprinkle each with cheese. Bake, uncovered, in 350°F oven 12 minutes or until biscuit cups are browned and cheese is melted. *Makes 12 cups*

PRESENTATION: Serve as a main dish or as a snack.

HINT: For an extra treat, flatten any leftover biscuit dough into disks; sprinkle with cinnamon-sugar mixture and bake in 350°F oven 5 to 7 minutes or until golden.

Mini Sausage Quiches

CASUAL SNACKS & PARTY TIDBITS

38 STEAMED PORK AND SHRIMP DUMPLINGS

1 package (5 ounces) frozen cooked tiny shrimp, thawed and rinsed
1 pound lean ground pork
½ cup finely chopped water chestnuts
2 green onions with tops, finely chopped
1 tablespoon soy sauce
1 tablespoon dry sherry
2 teaspoons cornstarch
1 teaspoon minced fresh ginger
½ teaspoon sesame oil
¼ teaspoon sugar
1 egg, separated
1 tablespoon water
36 round wonton wrappers (3 inches in diameter)*
36 fresh green peas (5 or 6 pods)
    Additional soy sauce (optional)
    Chili oil (optional)

If round wrappers are unavailable, trim square wrappers into 3-inch circles with tip of paring knife, using round cookie cutter as a guide.

Drain shrimp on paper towels. Set aside 36 shrimp. Place remaining shrimp in large bowl. Add pork, water chestnuts, green onions, 1 tablespoon soy sauce, sherry, cornstarch, ginger, sesame oil and sugar; mix well. Stir in egg white until well blended; set aside. Place egg yolk in cup. Whisk water into egg yolk; set aside.

To fill wontons, work with 4 wrappers at a time, keeping remaining wrappers covered with plastic wrap to prevent drying. Lightly brush each wonton wrapper with egg yolk mixture. Spoon 1½ tablespoons pork mixture onto center of each wrapper. Bring edge of wrapper up around filling in small pleats, leaving top of filling exposed. Press wrapper around filling.

To steam dumplings, place 12-inch bamboo steamer in wok. Add water to ½ inch *below* steamer. (Water should not touch steamer.) Remove steamer. Cover wok; bring water to a boil over high heat. Oil inside of bamboo steamer (bottom only). Arrange ½ of dumplings about ½ inch apart in steamer. Brush tops lightly with egg yolk mixture; press 1 pea and 1 reserved shrimp into top of each dumpling. Place steamer in wok over boiling water; reduce heat to medium. Cover and steam dumplings about 12 minutes or until pork is firm to the touch. Remove wok from heat. Transfer dumplings to serving plate. Repeat with remaining dumplings. Serve immediately with soy sauce and chili oil for dipping. Garnish as desired.

Makes 3 dozen dumplings

Steamed Pork and Shrimp Dumplings

CASUAL SNACKS & PARTY TIDBITS

39 CALZONE ITALIANO

Pizza dough for one 14-inch pizza
1¾ cups (15-ounce can) CONTADINA®
** Pizza Sauce, *divided***
3 ounces sliced pepperoni *or* ½ pound
** crumbled Italian sausage, cooked,**
** drained**
2 tablespoons chopped green bell pepper
1 cup (4 ounces) shredded mozzarella
** cheese**
1 cup (8 ounces) ricotta cheese

Divide dough into 4 equal portions. Place on lightly floured, large, rimless cookie sheet. Press or roll out dough to 7-inch circles. Spread *2 tablespoons* pizza sauce onto half of each circle to within ½ inch of edge; top with ¼ each: pepperoni, bell pepper and mozzarella cheese. Spoon ¼ cup ricotta cheese onto remaining half of each circle; fold dough over. Press edges together tightly to seal. Cut slits into top of dough to allow steam to escape. Bake in preheated 350°F. oven for 20 to 25 minutes or until crusts are golden brown. Meanwhile, heat *remaining* pizza sauce; serve over calzones.

Makes 4 servings

NOTE: If desired, 1 large calzone may be made instead of 4 individual calzones. To prepare, shape dough into 1 (13-inch) circle. Spread *½ cup* pizza sauce onto half of dough; proceed as above. Bake for 25 minutes.

40 SAUSAGE FILLED WONTONS

1 pound BOB EVANS FARMS® Original
** Recipe Roll Sausage**
¼ cup chopped onion
½ cup (2 ounces) shredded American
** cheese**
3 ounces cream cheese
½ teaspoon dried marjoram leaves
¼ teaspoon dried tarragon leaves
30 wonton wrappers
** Vegetable oil**
** Dipping sauce, such as plum sauce or**
** sweet and sour sauce (optional)**

To prepare filling, crumble sausage into large skillet. Add onion. Cook over medium heat until sausage is browned, stirring occasionally. Remove from heat; drain off any drippings. Stir in next 4 ingredients. Mix until cheeses melt. Lightly dampen 1 wonton wrapper by dipping your finger in water and wiping all the edges, making ¼-inch border around square. (To keep wrappers from drying, cover remaining wrappers with damp kitchen towel while working.) Place rounded teaspoonful sausage mixture in the middle of wrapper. Fold wrapper over filling to form triangle, sealing edges and removing any air bubbles. Repeat with remaining wrappers and filling.

Heat 4 inches oil in deep fryer or heavy large saucepan to 350°F; fry wontons, a few at a time, until golden brown. Remove with slotted spoon; drain on paper towels. Reheat oil between batches. Serve hot with dipping sauce, if desired. Refrigerate leftovers.

Makes 30 appetizers

Calzone Italiano

41 TACO BASEBALL CAPS

CAPS
- 2 cups Corn CHEX® brand cereal, crushed to ¾ cup
- 2 cups all-purpose flour
- 1 package (1.25 ounces) taco seasoning, divided
- 1 tablespoon grated American cheese food powder
- ¼ teaspoon baking powder
- ¼ teaspoon garlic powder
- ½ cup vegetable shortening
- ½ cup warm water

FILLING
- ½ pound lean ground beef
- ¾ cup shredded lettuce
- ½ cup chopped tomato
- ¾ cup shredded Cheddar cheese

1. Preheat oven to 375°F. Combine cereal, flour, 1 tablespoon taco seasoning, cheese powder, baking powder and garlic powder. Cut in shortening until mixture resembles coarse crumbs. Gradually stir in water, mixing well to form soft dough. (If dough is too dry, add more water, 1 tablespoon at a time.) Divide dough into 2 equal portions; keep covered with damp towel until ready to roll.

2. Roll out dough, one portion at a time, on lightly floured surface to ¹⁄₁₆-inch thickness. Cut into six 4-inch circles. Using every other cup of a 12-cup (2¾-inch) muffin pan, place dough even with rim of muffin cup on one side. On opposite side, extend dough over rim and press firmly to form "bill" of cap. Press dough firmly and evenly onto bottom and side of cup. Bake 15 to 20 minutes or until golden brown. Remove from muffin cups and cool. Repeat with remaining dough.

3. Using remaining taco seasoning, prepare ground beef according to taco seasoning package directions. Fill each cap with equal amounts of lettuce, tomato, seasoned ground beef and shredded cheese.

Makes 12 snacks

42 SAUSAGE PINWHEELS

- 2 cups biscuit mix
- ½ cup milk
- ¼ cup butter or margarine, melted
- 1 pound BOB EVANS FARMS® Original Recipe Roll Sausage

Combine biscuit mix, milk and butter in large bowl until blended. Refrigerate 30 minutes. Divide dough into two portions. Roll out one portion on floured surface to ⅛-inch-thick rectangle, about 10×7 inches. Spread with half the sausage. Roll lengthwise into long roll. Repeat with remaining dough and sausage. Place rolls in freezer until hard enough to cut easily. Preheat oven to 400°F. Cut rolls into thin slices. Place on baking sheets. Bake 15 minutes or until golden brown. Serve hot. Refrigerate leftovers.

Makes 48 appetizers

NOTE: This recipe may be doubled. Refreeze after slicing. When ready to serve, thaw slices in refrigerator and bake.

Sausage Pinwheels

The Best in
Burgers

43 DIJON BACON CHEESEBURGERS

**1 cup shredded Cheddar cheese
(4 ounces)**
**5 tablespoons GREY POUPON® Dijon
Mustard,* divided**
2 teaspoons dried minced onion
1 teaspoon prepared horseradish*
1 pound lean ground beef
4 onion sandwich rolls, split and toasted
1 cup shredded lettuce
4 slices tomato
4 slices bacon, cooked and halved

5 tablespoons Grey Poupon® Horseradish Mustard may be substituted for Dijon mustard; omit horseradish.

In small bowl, combine cheese, 3 tablespoons mustard, onion and horseradish; set aside.

In medium bowl, combine ground beef and remaining 2 tablespoons mustard; shape mixture into 4 patties. Grill or broil burgers over medium heat for 5 minutes on each side or until desired doneness; top with cheese mixture and cook until cheese melts, about 2 minutes. Top each roll bottom with ¼ cup shredded lettuce, 1 tomato slice, burger, 2 bacon pieces and roll top. Serve immediately. *Makes 4 burgers*

44 BACON BURGERS

1 pound lean ground beef
4 crisply cooked bacon slices, crumbled
**1½ teaspoons chopped fresh thyme *or*
½ teaspoon dried thyme leaves**
**½ teaspoon salt
Dash freshly ground pepper**
4 slices Swiss cheese

Preheat grill.

Combine ground beef, bacon and seasonings in medium bowl; mix lightly. Shape into four patties.

Grill 4 minutes; turn. Top with cheese. Continue grilling 2 minutes or to desired doneness. *Makes 4 servings*

Dijon Bacon Cheeseburger

THE BEST IN BURGERS

45 ALL–AMERICAN ONION BURGER

1 pound ground beef
2 tablespoons FRENCH'S® Worcestershire Sauce
1¹⁄₃ cups (2.8-ounce can) FRENCH'S® French Fried Onions, divided
¹⁄₂ teaspoon garlic salt
¹⁄₄ teaspoon ground black pepper
4 hamburger rolls

Combine beef, Worcestershire, *²⁄₃ cup* French Fried Onions, garlic salt and pepper. Form into 4 patties. Place patties on grid. Grill over hot coals about 10 minutes or until meat thermometer inserted into beef reaches 160°F, turning once. Top with remaining *²⁄₃ cup* onions. Serve on rolls.

Makes 4 servings

Prep Time: 10 minutes
Cook Time: 10 minutes

LUSCIOUS ONIONY CHEESEBURGER: Place 1 slice cheese on each burger before topping with French Fried Onions.

TANGY WESTERN BURGER: Top each burger with 1 tablespoon prepared barbecue sauce and 1 strip crisp bacon before topping with French Fried Onions.

CALIFORNIA BURGER: Combine 2 tablespoons *each* French's® Dijon Mustard, mayonnaise and sour cream in small bowl; spoon on top of burgers before topping with French Fried Onions. Top each burger with avocado slices, sprouts and French Fried Onions.

PIZZA BURGER: Top each burger with prepared pizza sauce and mozzarella cheese before topping with French Fried Onions.

SALISBURY STEAK BURGER: Prepare 1 package brown gravy mix according to package directions; stir in 1 can (4 ounces) drained sliced mushrooms. Spoon over burgers before topping with French Fried Onions.

46 STUFFED CHEESE BURGERS

1¹⁄₂ cups shredded Monterey Jack cheese (about 6 ounces)
1 can (2¹⁄₄ ounces) chopped black olives, drained
¹⁄₈ teaspoon hot pepper sauce
1³⁄₄ pounds ground beef
¹⁄₄ cup finely chopped onion
1 teaspoon salt
¹⁄₂ teaspoon black pepper
6 whole wheat hamburger buns
Butter or margarine, melted

Combine cheese, olives and hot pepper sauce; mix well. Divide mixture evenly and shape into 6 balls. Mix ground beef with onion, salt and pepper; shape into 12 thin patties. Place a cheese ball in center of 6 patties and top each with a second patty. Seal edges of each patty to enclose cheese ball. Lightly oil grid. Grill patties, on covered grill, over medium-hot KINGSFORD® Briquets 5 to 6 minutes on each side or until done.

Split buns, brush with butter and place, cut sides down, on grill to heat through. Serve cheeseburgers on buns.

Makes 6 servings

California Burger

47 AMERICA'S FAVORITE CHEDDAR BEEF BURGERS

1 pound ground beef
⅓ cup A.1.® Steak Sauce, divided
1 medium onion, cut into strips
1 medium green or red bell pepper, cut into strips
1 tablespoon margarine
4 ounces Cheddar cheese, sliced
4 hamburger rolls
4 tomato slices

In medium bowl, combine ground beef and 3 tablespoons steak sauce; shape mixture into 4 patties. Set aside.

In medium skillet, over medium heat, cook onion and pepper in margarine until tender, stirring occasionally. Stir in remaining steak sauce; keep warm.

Grill burgers over medium heat for 4 minutes on each side or until done. When almost done, top with cheese; grill until cheese melts. Spoon 2 tablespoons onion mixture onto each roll bottom; top each with burger, tomato slice, some of remaining onion mixture and roll top. Serve immediately.
Makes 4 servings

48 BURGERS DELUXE

6 slices bacon
1 tablespoon browning sauce
1 tablespoon water
1 pound ground beef
4 slices American cheese
8 slices dill pickle
4 sesame seed buns, split
    Green onions (optional)

1. Arrange bacon in single layer on roasting rack or on rack placed in baking dish. Microwave, covered with paper towels, at HIGH until slightly underdone, 4½ to 6 minutes (45 to 60 seconds per slice). Bacon fat will be bubbly and still slightly translucent. Let stand, covered, 5 minutes to complete cooking.

2. Mix browning sauce with water in a cup. Shape beef into 4 even patties, each ½ inch thick; arrange evenly spaced on roasting rack. Brush tops and sides with sauce mixture. Microwave, covered with waxed paper, at HIGH 2 minutes. Turn patties over; brush with sauce mixture. Microwave, covered, at HIGH until done slightly less than desired, 1½ to 2½ minutes for medium-done burgers. (For well-done burgers, increase cooking time by about ½ minute.)

3. Top each burger with 1½ slices bacon and 1 slice cheese. Let stand, loosely covered, 1 to 2 minutes. (Cheese should melt slightly during standing time. If necessary, microwave, uncovered, at HIGH 15 to 45 seconds or until cheese begins to melt.) Top burgers with pickle slices. Place in buns and serve, garnished with green onions if desired. *Makes 4 servings*

America's Favorite Cheddar Beef Burger

THE BEST IN BURGERS

49 SOUTHWEST PESTO BURGERS

CILANTRO PESTO
1 large clove garlic
4 ounces fresh cilantro, stems removed
1½ teaspoons bottled minced jalapeño pepper *or* 1 tablespoon bottled sliced jalapeño pepper
¼ teaspoon salt
¼ cup vegetable oil

BURGERS
1¼ pounds ground beef
¼ cup plus 1 tablespoon Cilantro Pesto, divided
½ teaspoon salt
4 slices Pepper Jack cheese
2 tablespoons light or regular mayonnaise
4 Kaiser rolls, split
Lettuce leaves
1 ripe avocado, peeled and sliced
Salsa

1. For pesto, with motor running, drop garlic through feed tube of food processor; process until minced. Add cilantro, jalapeño pepper and salt; process until cilantro is chopped.

2. With motor running, slowly pour oil through feed tube; process until thick paste forms.

3. Prepare barbecue grill for direct cooking.

4. Combine beef, ¼ cup pesto and salt in large bowl; mix well. Form into 4 patties. Place patties on grid over medium-hot coals. Grill, uncovered, 4 to 5 minutes per side or until meat is no longer pink in center. Add cheese to patties during last 1 minute of grilling. While patties are cooking, combine mayonnaise and remaining 1 tablespoon pesto in small bowl; mix well. Spread on bottom halves of rolls. Top with lettuce, patties, avocado, salsa and top halves of rolls. *Makes 4 servings*

50 SPICY TACO BURGERS

1½ pounds lean ground beef
1 package (1.0 ounce) LAWRY'S® Taco Spices & Seasonings
3 tablespoons chili sauce or ketchup
1 cup (4 ounces) shredded Monterey Jack cheese
3 tablespoons diced green chiles
6 Cheddar cheese slices
6 tomato slices
6 flour tortillas, warmed

In medium bowl, combine ground beef, Taco Spices & Seasonings and chili sauce; blend well. Form into 12 patties. Sprinkle 6 of the patties with Monterey Jack cheese and green chiles. Top with remaining 6 patties, sealing around edges so cheese does not leak out. Grill or broil burgers 5 to 7 minutes on each side. Top with Cheddar cheese. Place 1 patty and 1 tomato slice near upper edge of each tortilla. Fold in sides and fold bottom half of tortilla up over burger. Secure with toothpicks. *Makes 6 servings*

PRESENTATION: Serve with guacamole, dairy sour cream and fresh salsa.

Southwest Pesto Burger

51 MEXICALI BURGERS

Guacamole (recipe follows)
1 pound ground beef
1/3 cup prepared salsa or picante sauce
1/3 cup crushed tortilla chips
3 tablespoons finely chopped cilantro
2 tablespoons finely chopped onion
1 teaspoon ground cumin
4 slices Monterey Jack or Cheddar cheese
4 Kaiser rolls or hamburger buns, split
Lettuce leaves (optional)
Sliced tomatoes (optional)

To prevent sticking, spray grill with nonstick cooking spray. Prepare coals for grilling. Meanwhile, prepare Guacamole.

Combine beef, salsa, tortilla chips, cilantro, onion and cumin in medium bowl until well blended. Shape mixture into 4 burgers. Place burgers on grill, 6 inches from medium coals. Grill, covered, 8 to 10 minutes for medium or until desired doneness is reached, turning once. Place 1 slice cheese on each burger during last 1 to 2 minutes of grilling. If desired, place rolls, cut sides down, on grill to toast lightly during last 1 to 2 minutes of grilling. Place burgers between rolls; top burgers with Guacamole. Serve with lettuce and tomatoes. Garnish as desired.

Makes 4 servings

GUACAMOLE

1 ripe avocado, seeded
1 tablespoon salsa or picante sauce
1 teaspoon lime or lemon juice
1/4 teaspoon garlic salt

Place avocado in medium bowl; mash with fork until avocado is slightly chunky. Add salsa, lime juice and garlic salt; blend well.

Makes about 1/2 cup

52 PITA BURGERS WITH CUCUMBER–YOGURT SAUCE

1 pound lean ground beef
1/2 cup plain low-fat yogurt
1/3 cup chopped cucumber
2 teaspoons Pepper-Herb Mix, divided (recipe follows)
1/4 teaspoon salt
2 pita pocket breads, halved and warmed
1 medium tomato, cut into 8 thin slices

Combine yogurt, cucumber, 1/2 teaspoon Pepper-Herb Mix and salt in small bowl; reserve. Shape ground beef into four 1/2-inch-thick patties. Sprinkle remaining 1 1/2 teaspoons Pepper-Herb Mix over both sides of patties. Meanwhile heat large nonstick skillet over medium heat 5 minutes. Place patties in skillet and cook 6 to 8 minutes, turning once. Season with salt, if desired. To serve, place a burger in each pita half; add 2 tomato slices and yogurt sauce as desired.

Makes 4 servings

PEPPER–HERB MIX

2 tablespoons dried basil leaves
1 tablespoon lemon pepper
1 tablespoon onion powder
1 1/2 teaspoons rubbed sage

Combine all ingredients. Store, covered, in airtight container. Shake before using to blend.

Makes about 1/3 cup

*Favorite recipe from **National Cattlemen's Beef Association***

Mexicali Burger

THE BEST IN BURGERS

53 TASTY TACO BURGERS

1 pound ground beef
1 package (1¼ ounces) taco seasoning mix
8 KRAFT® American Singles Pasteurized
**   Process Cheese Food**
4 Kaiser rolls, split
**   Lettuce leaves**
**   Salsa**
**   BREAKSTONE'S® or KNUDSEN® Sour**
**   Cream (optional)**

MIX ground beef and taco seasoning mix. Shape into 4 patties.

GRILL patties over hot coals 6 to 8 minutes on each side or to desired doneness. Top each patty with 2 process cheese food slices. Continue grilling until process cheese food is melted.

FILL rolls with lettuce and cheeseburgers. Top with salsa and sour cream, if desired.

Makes 4 servings

54 LIPTON® ONION BURGERS

2 pounds ground beef
1 envelope LIPTON® Recipe Secrets®
**   Onion Soup Mix***
½ cup water

• In large bowl, combine all ingredients; shape into 8 patties.

• Grill or broil to desired doneness.

Makes about 8 servings

Also terrific with Lipton® Recipe Secrets® Beefy Onion, Onion-Mushroom, Beefy Mushroom or Savory Herb with Garlic Soup Mix.

55 FIERY BOURSIN BURGERS

1 pound lean ground beef
1 egg, beaten
1 tablespoon Worcestershire Sauce
¾ teaspoon TABASCO® pepper sauce
1 package (5 ounces) boursin or herbed
**   chèvre cheese**

• Preheat broiler.

• In medium bowl, combine beef, egg, Worcestershire and TABASCO® sauce until well mixed. Divide into five portions.

• Form three-quarters of each portion into a patty, reserving the remainder. Make indentation in center of each patty and fill with 2 tablespoons of the cheese. Cover cheese with reserved meat and form a finished patty.

• Broil patties 3 to 5 minutes on each side or to desired doneness. Serve immediately.

Makes 5 servings

Tasty Taco Burger

56 BARBECUED CHEESE BURGERS

BARBECUE SPREAD
¼ **cup reduced calorie mayonnaise**
¼ **cup bottled barbecue sauce**
¼ **cup red or green pepper hamburger relish**

BURGERS
1½ **pounds ground lean turkey or ground beef round**
⅓ **cup bottled barbecue sauce**
⅓ **cup minced red onion**
1 **teaspoon hot red pepper sauce**
½ **teaspoon garlic salt**
6 **sesame seed hamburger buns, split**
6 **slices (1 ounce each) ALPINE LACE® Fat Free Pasteurized Process Skim Milk Cheese Product—For Cheddar Lovers**

1. To make the Barbecue Spread: In a small bowl, stir all of the spread ingredients together until well blended. Cover and refrigerate.

2. To make the Burgers: In a medium-size bowl, mix the turkey, barbecue sauce, onion, hot pepper sauce and garlic salt. Form into 6 patties (5 inches each), about 1¼ inches thick. Cover with plastic wrap and refrigerate for at least 30 minutes or overnight.

3. To cook the Burgers: Preheat the grill (or broiler). Grill over medium-hot coals (or broil) 4 inches from the heat for 4 minutes on each side for medium or until cooked the way you like them. Place the buns alongside the burgers for the last 5 minutes to heat, if you wish. Top each burger with a slice of cheese.

4. To serve, spread the insides of the buns with the Barbecue Spread and stuff each bun with a burger. *Makes 6 burgers*

57 MISSISSIPPI BARBECUE BURGERS

1 **cup FRANK'S or SnowFloss Kraut, drained**
⅓ **cup cranberry sauce**
¼ **cup MISSISSIPPI Barbecue Sauce**
2 **tablespoons brown sugar**
1 **egg, slightly beaten**
1 **envelope dried onion soup mix**
¼ **cup water**
1 **pound ground beef**
4 **onion or sesame seed hamburger rolls, split, lightly toasted**

1. Mix kraut, cranberry sauce, barbecue sauce and brown sugar in small saucepan; bring to a boil. Reduce heat and simmer about 15 minutes, stirring occasionally.

2. Meanwhile, in medium bowl combine egg, soup mix and water. Let stand 5 minutes. Add ground beef; mix thoroughly. Form into 4 patties.

3. Barbecue patties over mesquite or charcoal to desired doneness. Serve on toasted rolls topped with kraut mixture.
Makes 4 servings

Prep Time: 30 minutes
Grill Time: 10 to 15 minutes

Barbecued Cheese Burger

58 BBQ CHEESEBURGERS

1 pound lean ground beef
¼ cup finely chopped onion
   Prepared barbecue sauce
4 slices (1 ounce each) Cheddar or
   mozzarella cheese
4 crusty rolls, split
   Romaine lettuce
   Sliced tomato

1. In medium bowl, combine ground beef and onion, mixing lightly but thoroughly. Shape into four ½-inch-thick patties.

2. Place patties on grid over medium ash-covered coals. Grill uncovered 14 to 16 minutes or until centers are no longer pink, turning once. Approximately 1 minute before burgers are done, brush with barbecue sauce; top with cheese.

3. Line bottom half of each roll with lettuce and tomato; top with burger. Close sandwiches.   *Makes 4 servings*

Prep and Cook Time: 30 minutes

*Favorite recipe from **National Cattlemen's Beef Association***

59 BASIC BEEFY BURGERS

1 pound lean ground beef
1 cup Corn CHEX® brand cereal, crushed
   to ⅓ cup
1 egg, slightly beaten
2 tablespoons ketchup
½ teaspoon onion powder
⅛ teaspoon garlic powder

1. Combine beef, cereal, egg, ketchup, onion powder and garlic powder. Shape mixture into five patties.

2. Grill 10 to 12 minutes or until no longer pink in center, turning once. Serve on buns with cheese slices, tomato slices, lettuce, pickles, ketchup and mustard, if desired.
                    Makes 5 servings

CHEESY PIZZA BURGERS: Substitute 3 tablespoons pizza sauce for ketchup. Add ⅔ cup shredded mozzarella cheese and ¼ teaspoon dried oregano leaves to beef mixture. Serve on toasted English muffin halves topped with additional pizza sauce, if desired.

TASTY TACO BURGERS: Substitute 3 tablespoons taco sauce or salsa for ketchup. Add ½ teaspoon chili powder and 2 to 3 dashes ground cumin, if desired, to beef mixture. Serve on buns with sliced Monterey Jack or Cheddar cheese, shredded lettuce, chopped tomato and additional taco sauce, if desired.

INSIDE–OUT BACON CHEESEBURGERS: Add 6 to 8 slices bacon, cooked and coarsely crumbled, to beef mixture. Shape into ten thin patties. Place 1 rounded tablespoon shredded Cheddar cheese in center of five patties; top with remaining patties. Press edges firmly together to seal. After grilling cheeseburgers, let cool 5 minutes before serving (cheese filling will be very hot after grilling). Serve on buns with lettuce, tomato, pickle and barbecue sauce, if desired.

BBQ Cheeseburger

THE BEST IN BURGERS

60 MEDITERRANEAN BURGERS

½ cup crumbled feta cheese (3 ounces)
5 tablespoons GREY POUPON®
    COUNTRY DIJON® Mustard, divided
2 tablespoons mayonnaise*
2 tablespoons sliced ripe olives
2 tablespoons diced pimientos
1 pound lean ground beef
4 sesame seed sandwich rolls, split and
    toasted
4 Bibb lettuce leaves
4 thin slices red onion

Lowfat mayonnaise may be substituted for regular mayonnaise.

In small bowl, combine cheese, 3 tablespoons mustard, mayonnaise, olives and pimientos; set aside.

In medium bowl, combine ground beef and remaining 2 tablespoons mustard; shape mixture into 4 patties. Grill or broil burgers over medium heat for 5 minutes on each side or until desired doneness. Top each roll bottom with 1 lettuce leaf, 1 tablespoon cheese mixture, burger, 1 onion slice, 1 tablespoon cheese mixture and roll top. Serve immediately.   *Makes 4 burgers*

61 BROILED STUFFED BURGERS

1½ pounds lean ground beef
    Salt, pepper and garlic powder to taste
½ cup shredded Monterey Jack or Swiss
    cheese
¼ cup finely grated onion
¼ cup BLUE DIAMOND® Chopped Natural
    Almonds
2 tablespoons minced fresh parsley

Season ground beef with salt, pepper and garlic powder; shape into 8 or 10 thin patties. Combine cheese, onion, almonds and parsley, mixing well. Divide cheese mixture evenly among half of the patties, placing mixture in center of meat. Top with remaining patties; pinch edges to seal tightly. Broil, about 4 inches from heat, 4 to 6 minutes on each side, or until desired doneness.   *Makes 4 to 5 burgers*

62 SWISS BURGERS

1½ pounds ground beef
¾ cup shredded Swiss cheese (about
    3 ounces)
1 can (8 ounces) sauerkraut, heated and
    drained
½ cup WISHBONE® Thousand Island or
    Lite Thousand Island Dressing

Shape ground beef into 6 patties. Grill or broil until desired doneness. Top evenly with cheese, sauerkraut and Thousand Island dressing. Serve, if desired, with rye or pita bread.   *Makes 6 servings*

63 DEVILED BURGERS

2 slices bread, finely chopped
¼ cup finely chopped onion
¼ cup tomato ketchup
1 tablespoon Worcestershire sauce
2 teaspoons prepared mustard
2 teaspoons creamy horseradish
½ teaspoon garlic powder
½ teaspoon chili powder
1 pound extra-lean ground beef
6 hamburger buns

1. Preheat broiler. Combine bread, onion, ketchup, Worcestershire sauce, mustard, horseradish, garlic powder and chili powder in large bowl until well blended. Gently blend ground beef into mixture. *(Do not overwork.)*

2. Shape mixture into 6 (3-inch) burgers. Place burgers on ungreased jelly-roll pan.

3. Broil burgers 4 inches from heat source 4 minutes per side or until desired doneness. Serve on hamburger buns. Garnish, if desired.   *Makes 6 servings*

Deviled Burgers

THE BEST IN BURGERS

64 BIG D RANCH BURGERS

1 cup sliced onions
1/3 cup green bell pepper strips
1/3 cup red bell pepper strips
1 tablespoon margarine
3 tablespoons A.1.® Steak Sauce
2 teaspoons prepared horseradish
1 pound ground beef
4 onion rolls, split

In medium skillet, over medium heat, cook onions, green pepper and red pepper in margarine until tender-crisp. Stir in steak sauce and horseradish; keep warm.

Shape ground beef into 4 patties. Grill burgers over medium heat for 5 minutes on each side or until desired doneness. Place burgers on roll bottoms; top each with 1/4 cup pepper mixture and roll top. Serve immediately.   *Makes 4 servings*

65 NUTTY BURGERS

1 1/2 pounds ground beef
1 medium onion, finely chopped
1 cup dry bread crumbs
2/3 cup pine nuts
1/3 cup grated Parmesan cheese
1/3 cup chopped fresh parsley
2 eggs
1 1/2 teaspoons salt
1 teaspoon pepper
1 clove garlic, finely chopped

Combine all ingredients; blend well. Shape into 6 thick patties. Grill patties, on covered grill, over medium-hot KINGSFORD® Briquets 5 minutes on each side or until desired doneness.   *Makes 6 servings*

Big D Ranch Burger

66 BEACH BLANKET BURGERS

1/2 cup MIRACLE WHIP® Salad Dressing
1/2 teaspoon *each* garlic powder and onion powder
1 pound ground beef
2 tablespoons dry bread crumbs
3/4 teaspoon salt
1/4 teaspoon coarse grind black pepper
4 KRAFT® Deluxe Pasteurized Process American Cheese Slices
4 whole wheat hamburger buns, split, toasted
Lettuce and tomato slices

MIX salad dressing, garlic powder and onion powder; reserve 1/4 cup. Mix meat, remaining salad dressing mixture, bread crumbs, salt and pepper. Shape into 4 (1/2-inch-thick) patties.

PLACE on greased grill over hot coals or on greased rack of broiler pan 5 to 7 inches from heat. Grill or broil 3 to 4 minutes on each side or to desired doneness. Top each patty with 1 process cheese slice; continue grilling or broiling just until process cheese melts.

SPREAD buns with reserved salad dressing mixture; fill with lettuce, patties and tomato slices.   *Makes 4 servings*

Prep Time: 5 minutes
Grill Time: 10 minutes

67 PIZZA BURGERS

1 pound lean ground beef
1 cup (4 ounces) shredded mozzarella
    cheese
1 tablespoon minced onion
1½ teaspoons chopped fresh oregano *or*
    ½ teaspoon dried oregano leaves
1 tablespoon chopped fresh basil *or*
    1 teaspoon dried basil leaves
½ teaspoon salt
    Dash freshly ground pepper
    Prepared pizza sauce, heated
    English muffins, split

Preheat grill.

Combine ground beef, cheese, onion and
seasonings in medium bowl; mix lightly.
Shape into four patties.

Grill 8 minutes or to desired doneness,
turning once. Top with pizza sauce. Serve on
English muffins.   *Makes 4 servings*

68 BACKYARD BURGERS

1½ pounds ground beef
    ⅓ cup barbecue sauce, divided
    2 tablespoons finely chopped onion
    ½ teaspoon dried oregano leaves, crushed
    6 onion hamburger buns, split and toasted

1. In large bowl, combine ground beef,
2 tablespoons barbecue sauce, onion and
oregano. Shape into six 1-inch-thick patties.

2. Place patties on grill rack directly above
medium coals. Grill, uncovered, until desired
doneness, turning and brushing often with
remaining barbecue sauce. To serve, place
patties on buns.   *Makes 6 servings*

69 HOMETOWN BURGERS

1 pound ground beef
¾ cup thinly sliced mushrooms
¼ cup finely chopped onion
¼ teaspoon salt
    Generous dash pepper
⅓ cup barbecue sauce
4 hamburger buns, split, toasted and
    buttered
    Lettuce leaves
    Tomato slices
    Sliced onion

In large bowl, combine beef, mushrooms,
chopped onion, salt and pepper. Shape into
four 1-inch-thick patties.

Place patties on grill rack directly above
medium coals. Grill, uncovered, until desired
doneness, turning and brushing often with
barbecue sauce. Place patties on buns with
lettuce, tomato and sliced onion.
                          Makes 4 servings

70 SESAME–SOY BURGERS

2 pounds ground beef
¼ cup finely chopped celery
¼ cup KIKKOMAN® Soy Sauce
2 tablespoons sesame seed, toasted
½ teaspoon garlic powder

Thoroughly combine beef, celery, soy sauce,
sesame seed and garlic powder; shape into
6 patties. Place on grill 4 to 5 inches from
hot coals. Cook 10 minutes (for medium),
or to desired doneness, turning over after
5 minutes. (Or, broil patties 5 minutes on
each side [for medium], or to desired
doneness.)   *Makes 6 servings*

Pizza Burger

THE BEST IN BURGERS

71 BLUE CHEESE BURGERS

1¼ pounds lean ground beef
1 tablespoon finely chopped onion
1½ teaspoons chopped fresh thyme *or*
    ½ teaspoon dried thyme leaves
¾ teaspoon salt
    Dash ground pepper
4 ounces blue cheese, crumbled

Preheat grill.

Combine ground beef, onion and seasonings in medium bowl; mix lightly. Shape into eight patties.

Place cheese in center of four patties to within ½ inch of outer edge; top with remaining burgers. Press edges together to seal.

Grill 8 minutes or to desired doneness, turning once. Serve with lettuce, tomatoes and Dijon mustard on whole wheat buns, if desired.   *Makes 4 servings*

72 GRILLED KIKKO–BURGERS

1 pound ground beef
2 tablespoons instant minced onion
¼ teaspoon pepper
¼ teaspoon ground ginger
2 tablespoons KIKKOMAN® Soy Sauce

Thoroughly combine beef, onion, pepper, ginger and soy sauce; shape into 4 patties. Place 4 to 5 inches from hot coals; cook 10 minutes (for medium), or to desired doneness, turning over after 5 minutes. (Or, place patties on rack of broiler pan; broil 5 minutes on each side [for medium], or to desired doneness.)   *Makes 4 servings*

73 GARDEN BURGERS

1½ pounds ground beef or turkey
1 envelope LIPTON® Recipe Secrets®
    Onion Soup Mix*
2 small carrots, finely shredded
1 small zucchini, shredded
1 egg, slightly beaten
¼ cup plain dry bread crumbs

Preheat oven to 375°F.

In large bowl, combine all ingredients; shape into 6 patties. In 13×9-inch baking pan, arrange patties. Bake, uncovered, 45 minutes or until done. Serve on hamburger buns or whole wheat rolls, if desired.
Makes 6 servings

Also terrific with Lipton® Recipe Secrets® Savory Herb with Garlic, Golden Herb with Lemon or Onion-Mushroom Soup Mix.

74 CURRIED BEEF BURGERS

1 pound lean ground beef
¼ cup mango chutney, chopped
¼ cup grated apple
1½ teaspoons curry powder
½ teaspoon salt
    Dash freshly ground pepper
1 large red onion, sliced ¼ inch thick

Preheat grill.

Combine ground beef, chutney, apple, curry powder, salt and pepper in medium bowl; mix lightly. Shape into four patties.

Grill 8 minutes or to desired doneness, turning once. Grill onion 5 minutes or until lightly charred, turning once. Serve with burgers.   *Makes 4 servings*

Blue Cheese Burger

75 GREEK BURGERS

Yogurt Sauce (recipe follows)
1 pound ground beef
2 tablespoons red wine
1 tablespoon chopped fresh oregano *or*
　　1 teaspoon dried oregano leaves
2 teaspoons ground cumin
½ teaspoon salt
　Dash ground red pepper
　Dash black pepper
2 pita breads, cut in half
　Lettuce
　Chopped tomatoes

Prepare Yogurt Sauce.

Soak 4 bamboo skewers in water. Combine ground beef, wine and seasonings in medium bowl; mix lightly. Divide mixture into eight equal portions; form each portion into an oval, each about 4 inches long. Cover; chill 30 minutes.

Preheat grill. Insert skewers lengthwise through centers of ovals, placing 2 on each skewer. Grill about 8 minutes or to desired doneness, turning once. Fill pita bread with lettuce, meat and chopped tomatoes. Serve with Yogurt Sauce.　　*Makes 4 servings*

YOGURT SAUCE
2 cups plain yogurt
1 cup chopped red onion
1 cup chopped cucumber
¼ cup chopped fresh mint *or* 1 tablespoon
　　plus 1½ teaspoons dried mint leaves
1 tablespoon chopped fresh marjoram *or*
　　1 teaspoon dried marjoram leaves

Combine ingredients in small bowl. Cover; chill up to 4 hours before serving.

76 SCANDINAVIAN BURGERS

1 pound lean ground beef
¾ cup shredded zucchini
⅓ cup shredded carrot
2 tablespoons finely minced onion
1 tablespoon fresh chopped dill *or*
　　1 teaspoon dried dill weed
½ teaspoon salt
　Dash freshly ground pepper
1 egg, beaten
¼ cup beer

Preheat grill. Combine ground beef, zucchini, carrot, onion and seasonings in medium bowl; mix lightly. Stir in egg and beer. Shape into four patties.

Grill 8 minutes or to desired doneness, turning once. Serve on whole wheat buns or rye rolls, if desired.　　*Makes 4 servings*

Greek Burgers

THE BEST IN BURGERS

77 LAHAINA BURGERS

1¼ pounds lean ground beef
¼ cup plus 1 tablespoon KIKKOMAN® Lite
    Teriyaki Marinade & Sauce, divided
4 green onions and tops, chopped
1 teaspoon minced fresh ginger root
1 large clove garlic, minced
1 egg, slightly beaten
1 slice bread, torn into small pieces
1 can (8 ounces) sliced pineapple, drained

Thoroughly combine beef, ¼ cup lite teriyaki sauce, green onions, ginger, garlic, egg and bread; shape into 4 patties. Place on grill 4 to 5 inches from hot coals. Cook 5 minutes; turn over. Cook 5 minutes longer (for medium), or to desired doneness. During last 2 minutes of cooking time, place pineapple slices on grill. Cook 1 minute. Turn over and brush with remaining 1 tablespoon lite teriyaki sauce. Cook 1 minute longer. (Or, place patties on rack of broiler pan. Broil 5 minutes; turn over. Broil 5 minutes longer [for medium], or to desired doneness. During last 2 minutes of cooking time, place pineapple slices on broiler pan. Broil 1 minute. Turn over and brush with remaining 1 tablespoon lite teriyaki sauce. Broil 1 minute longer.) Top patties with pineapple just before serving.

Makes 4 servings

78 HAWAIIAN–STYLE BURGERS

1½ pounds ground beef
⅓ cup chopped green onions
2 tablespoons Worcestershire sauce
⅛ teaspoon pepper
⅓ cup pineapple preserves
⅓ cup barbecue sauce
6 pineapple slices
6 hamburger buns, split and toasted

1. In large bowl, combine beef, onions, Worcestershire and pepper. Shape into six 1-inch-thick patties.

2. In small saucepan, combine preserves and barbecue sauce. Over medium heat, bring to a boil, stirring often.

3. On grill rack, place patties directly above medium coals. Grill, uncovered, until desired doneness, turning and brushing often with sauce. Place pineapple on grill; grill 1 minute or until browned, turning once.

4. To serve, place patties on buns with pineapple.   *Makes 6 servings*

BROILING DIRECTIONS: Arrange patties on rack in broiler pan. Broil 4 inches from heat until desired doneness, turning and brushing often with sauce. Broil pineapple 1 minute, turning once.

Hawaiian-Style Burger

THE BEST IN BURGERS

79 TWO–WAY BURGERS

GRILLED BURGERS*
  1 pound ground beef
  ¼ cup minced onion
  ¼ teaspoon ground pepper

Combine ground beef, onion and ground pepper, mixing lightly but thoroughly. Divide beef mixture into 4 equal portions and form into patties 4 inches in diameter. Broil patties on grid over medium coals, turning once. Broil 11 to 13 minutes for medium. Prepare recipe for California Burgers or English Burgers as desired and assemble as directed.   *Makes 4 beef patties*

Prep Time: 10 minutes
Cook Time: 11 to 13 minutes

CALIFORNIA BURGERS
  1 recipe Grilled Burgers*
  ¼ cup plain yogurt
  1 teaspoon Dijon-style mustard
  4 whole wheat hamburger buns, split
 12 large spinach leaves, stems removed
  4 thin slices red onion
  4 large mushrooms, sliced
  1 small avocado, peeled, seeded and cut
      into 12 wedges

Combine yogurt and mustard. On bottom half of each bun, layer an equal amount of spinach leaves, onions and mushrooms; top each with a Grilled Burger. Arrange 3 avocado wedges on each patty; top with an equal amount of yogurt mixture. Close each sandwich with bun top.
          Makes 4 servings

Prep Time: 15 minutes

ENGLISH BURGERS
  1 recipe Grilled Burgers*
  ¼ cup *each* horseradish sauce and
      chopped tomato
  2 tablespoons crumbled crisply cooked
      bacon
  4 English muffins, split, lightly toasted

Combine horseradish sauce, tomato and bacon. Place a Grilled Burger on each muffin half. Spoon an equal amount of horseradish sauce mixture over each patty. Cover with remaining muffin half.   *Makes 4 servings*

Prep Time: 15 minutes

*Favorite recipe from **National Cattlemen's Beef Association***

80 BLACK GOLD BURGERS

  ¾ cup finely chopped onion
  6 large cloves garlic, minced (about
      3 tablespoons)
  2 tablespoons margarine
  1 tablespoon sugar
  ¾ cup A.1.® Steak Sauce
 1½ pounds ground beef
  6 hamburger rolls, split

In medium skillet, over medium heat, cook and stir onion and garlic in margarine until tender but not brown; stir in sugar. Reduce heat to low; cook for 10 minutes. Stir in steak sauce; keep warm. Shape ground beef into 6 patties. Grill burgers over medium heat for 5 minutes on each side or until done. Place burgers on roll bottoms; top each with 3 tablespoons sauce and roll top. Serve immediately; garnish as desired.
          Makes 6 servings

English Burger

THE BEST IN BURGERS

81 WISCONSIN CHEESE STUFFED BURGERS

3 pounds ground beef
½ cup dry bread crumbs
2 eggs
1¼ cups (5 ounces) of your favorite shredded Wisconsin cheese, shredded pepper Havarti cheese, crumbled blue cheese or crumbled basil & tomato feta cheese

In large mixing bowl, combine beef, bread crumbs and eggs; mix well, but lightly. Divide mixture into 24 balls; flatten each on waxed paper to 4 inches across. Place 1 tablespoon cheese on each of 12 patties. Top with remaining patties, carefully pressing edges to seal. Grill patties 4 inches from coals, turning only once, 6 to 9 minutes on each side or until no longer pink. To keep cheese between patties as it melts, do not flatten burgers with spatula while grilling. Serve in buns with lettuce and tomato, if desired.   *Makes 12 servings*

CAUTION: Cheese filling may be very hot if eaten immediately after cooking.

Favorite recipe from **Wisconsin Milk Marketing Board**

Wisconsin Cheese Stuffed Burger

THE BEST IN BURGERS

82 PITA DE CARNE

1 pound ground beef
3 tablespoons milk, divided
2 tablespoons cornmeal
2 tablespoons finely chopped onion
1 clove garlic, minced
1 teaspoon dried oregano leaves, crushed
$\frac{1}{2}$ teaspoon lemon pepper
$\frac{1}{2}$ teaspoon salt
$\frac{1}{3}$ cup shredded mozzarella cheese
$\frac{1}{4}$ teaspoon ground cumin
$\frac{1}{4}$ teaspoon ground red pepper
2 large pita bread rounds, cut in half
2 cups shredded lettuce
   Tomato slices and black olives for
     garnish

1. In bowl combine 2 tablespoons of the milk, cornmeal, onion, garlic, oregano, lemon pepper and salt. Add ground beef and mix well. Shape into eight $\frac{1}{4}$-inch-thick patties. Combine mozzarella cheese with remaining 1 tablespoon milk. Place 1 tablespoon of mozzarella mixture in center of 4 patties. Top each with a remaining patty and press edges together to seal. Combine cumin and red pepper; sprinkle on patties.

2. Heat large nonstick skillet over medium heat 5 minutes. Place patties in skillet and cook 7 minutes. Turn and cook 6 to 8 minutes more or until ground beef is cooked through with no visible pink color remaining.

3. Serve in pitas with shredded lettuce. Garnish with tomato slices and black olives.
                                      Makes 4 servings

*Favorite recipe from **North Dakota Beef Commission***

83 GLAZED BURGERS

$\frac{1}{4}$ cup KIKKOMAN® Teriyaki Baste & Glaze
3 tablespoons instant minced onion
2 slices day-old bread
1 egg
2 pounds ground beef
   Additional KIKKOMAN® Teriyaki Baste &
   Glaze

Combine $\frac{1}{4}$ cup teriyaki baste & glaze with onion in large bowl; let stand 5 minutes. Cover bread slices with enough water to thoroughly soak; squeeze out excess liquid. Finely tear bread. Add to combined onion mixture, egg and beef; mix well. Shape into 6 patties. Place on grill 4 inches from hot coals; cook 5 minutes on each side (for medium), or to desired doneness, brushing occasionally with additional teriyaki baste & glaze. (Or, place patties on rack of broiler pan; brush with additional teriyaki baste & glaze. Broil 5 minutes; turn over. Brush with additional teriyaki baste & glaze. Broil 5 minutes longer [for medium], or to desired doneness.)   *Makes 6 servings*

84 GREEK LAMB BURGERS

¼ **cup pine nuts**
1 **pound lean ground lamb**
¼ **cup finely chopped onion**
3 **cloves garlic, minced, divided**
¾ **teaspoon salt**
¼ **teaspoon freshly ground black pepper**
¼ **cup plain yogurt**
¼ **teaspoon sugar**
4 **slices red onion (¼ inch thick)**
1 **tablespoon olive oil**
8 **pumpernickel bread slices**
12 **thin cucumber slices**
4 **tomato slices**

Prepare grill for direct cooking. Meanwhile, heat small skillet over medium heat until hot. Add pine nuts; cook 30 to 45 seconds until light brown, shaking pan occasionally.

Combine lamb, pine nuts, chopped onion, 2 cloves garlic, salt and pepper in large bowl; mix well. Shape mixture into 4 patties, about ½ inch thick and 4 inches in diameter. Combine yogurt, sugar and remaining garlic in small bowl; set aside.

Brush 1 side of each patty and onion slice with oil; place on grid, oil sides down. Brush other sides with oil. Grill, on covered grill, over medium-hot coals 8 to 10 minutes for medium or to desired doneness, turning halfway through grilling time. Place bread on grid to toast during last few minutes of grilling time; grill 1 to 2 minutes per side.

Top 4 bread slices with patties and onion slices; top each with 3 cucumber slices and 1 tomato slice. Dollop evenly with yogurt mixture. Close sandwiches with remaining 4 bread slices. Serve immediately.

Makes 4 servings

85 SUPER PORK BURGERS

1 **(8-ounce) can crushed pineapple**
¾ **pound fully cooked boneless smoked ham**
¾ **pound ground pork**
½ **cup finely chopped green pepper**
2 **tablespoons all-purpose flour**
¼ **teaspoon ground allspice**

Drain pineapple, reserving juice.

Coarsely chop ham. Place ham in food processor bowl; process about 30 seconds or until coarsely ground.

In mixing bowl combine pineapple, ground ham, ground pork, green pepper, flour and allspice; mix well. Shape into six ½-inch-thick patties. Place patties on unheated rack in broiler pan. Broil 6 inches from heat about 8 minutes.

Meanwhile, in small saucepan cook pineapple juice over medium heat until reduced by half. Brush patties with half of pineapple juice; turn and broil 6 minutes longer. Brush patties with remaining pineapple juice. *Makes 6 servings*

Prep Time: 15 minutes
Cook Time: 15 minutes

Favorite recipe from **National Pork Producers Council**

Greek Lamb Burger

THE BEST IN BURGERS

86 MUSHROOM–STUFFED PORK BURGERS

¾ **cup thinly sliced fresh mushrooms**
¼ **cup thinly sliced green onion**
1 **clove garlic, minced**
2 **teaspoons butter or margarine**
1½ **pounds lean ground pork**
1 **teaspoon Dijon-style mustard**
1 **teaspoon Worcestershire sauce**
¼ **teaspoon salt**
⅛ **teaspoon freshly ground pepper**

In skillet, sauté mushrooms, onion and garlic in butter until tender, about 2 minutes; set aside.

Combine ground pork, mustard, Worcestershire sauce, salt and pepper; mix well. Shape into 12 patties, about 4 inches in diameter. Spoon mushroom mixture onto center of 6 patties. Spread to within ½ inch of edges. Top with remaining 6 patties; seal edges.

Place patties on grill about 6 inches over medium coals. Grill 10 to 15 minutes or until cooked through, turning once. Serve on buns, if desired.   *Makes 6 servings*

Prep Time: 15 minutes
Cook Time: 15 minutes

*Favorite recipe from **National Pork Producers Council***

87 SOPHISTICATED BLUEBURGERS

1 **pound lean ground pork**
4 **tablespoons crumbled blue cheese**
   Dash garlic salt
   Dash black pepper
¼ **cup dry red wine**
2 **tablespoons water**
1 **teaspoon Worcestershire sauce**

Divide ground pork into eight portions. Place 4 portions between layers of waxed paper. With a rolling pin, roll thin patties to 4-inch diameters. Sprinkle each with 1 tablespoon blue cheese. Roll remaining patties between layers of waxed paper.

Place over blue cheese; seal edges of patties. In large skillet, brown burgers quickly on both sides; pour off any accumulated drippings. Reduce heat, sprinkle lightly with garlic salt and pepper. Add wine, water and Worcestershire sauce. Cover and simmer 5 minutes.   Makes 4 servings

Prep Time: 15 minutes
Cook Time: 20 minutes

*Favorite recipe from **National Pork Producers Council***

Mushroom-Stuffed Pork Burger

THE BEST IN BURGERS

88 THE OTHER BURGER

1 pound ground pork, about 80% lean
1 teaspoon ground black pepper
¼ teaspoon salt

Gently mix together ground pork and seasonings. Shape into 4 burgers, each about ¾ inch thick. Place over moderately hot coals in kettle-style grill. Cover and grill for 5 minutes; turn and finish grilling 4 to 5 minutes more or until no longer pink in center. Serve immediately, on sandwich buns if desired. *Makes 4 servings*

EASTERN BURGER: To Other Burger basic mix, add 2 tablespoons dry sherry, 1 tablespoon grated ginger root and 2 teaspoons soy sauce.

VEGGIE BURGER: To Other Burger basic mix, add 1 grated carrot, 3 tablespoons chopped fresh parsley and 3 drops hot pepper sauce.

SOUTH–OF–THE–BORDER BURGER: To Other Burger basic mix, add ¼ teaspoon *each* ground cumin, oregano, seasoned salt and crushed red chiles.

ITALIAN BURGER: To Other Burger basic mix, add 1 crushed garlic clove, 2 teaspoons *each* red wine and olive oil and 1 teaspoon crushed fennel seed.

Prep Time: 10 minutes
Cook Time: 10 minutes

*Favorite recipe from **National Pork Producers Council***

89 PORK PATTIES SUPREME

1 teaspoon salt
⅛ teaspoon pepper
2 pounds ground pork
2 tablespoons chopped fresh parsley
3 tablespoons Worcestershire sauce, divided
¼ cup mayonnaise
1 teaspoon prepared mustard
8 hamburger buns, split and toasted

Sprinkle salt and pepper over pork; add parsley and 1 tablespoon Worcestershire sauce. Mix lightly but thoroughly. Shape mixture into eight ½-inch-thick patties. Place on rack in broiler pan so top of meat is 3 inches from heat. Broil 5 minutes, turn and broil second side 4 minutes. Combine mayonnaise, remaining 2 tablespoons Worcestershire sauce and mustard. Serve broiled patties with mayonnaise sauce on toasted buns. *Makes 8 servings*

*Favorite recipe from **National Pork Producers Council***

THE BEST IN BURGERS

90 ALL–AMERICAN STUFFED TURKEY BURGER

   1 pound ground turkey
¼ cup uncooked quick rolled oats
   1 egg
½ teaspoon garlic powder
   Dash pepper
½ cup chopped onion
¼ cup dill pickle relish, drained
   2 tablespoons ketchup
   2 teaspoons prepared mustard
   2 slices (1 ounce each) reduced-calorie
      low-sodium process American cheese,
      cut into 4 equal strips
   Lettuce leaves (optional)
   Tomato slices (optional)

1. Preheat charcoal grill for direct-heat cooking.

2. In medium bowl combine turkey, oats, egg, garlic powder and pepper. Divide turkey mixture in half. On 2 (11×10-inch) pieces wax paper, shape each half of turkey mixture into burgers 6 inches in diameter.

3. Sprinkle onion and relish over one burger, leaving ½-inch border around outside edge; top with ketchup and mustard. Arrange cheese strips, spoke-fashion, over ketchup and mustard. Carefully invert second burger over cheese. Remove top piece wax paper. Press edges of burgers together to seal.

4. Lightly grease cold grill rack and position over hot coals. Invert turkey burger onto grill rack; remove wax paper. Grill burger 8 minutes per side or until internal temperature of 165°F is reached on meat thermometer. To turn burger, slide flat cookie sheet under burger and invert onto second flat cookie sheet, then carefully slide burger back onto grill rack.*

5. To serve, cut burger into quarters. Serve with lettuce and tomato, if desired.

Makes 4 servings

Can use greased wire grill basket, if desired.

*Favorite recipe from **National Turkey Federation***

91 BASIC TURKEY BURGERS

   1 pound ground turkey
½ cup seasoned dry bread crumbs
⅓ cup finely chopped onion
   1 egg, beaten
   1 teaspoon soy sauce
   1 teaspoon Worcestershire sauce
½ teaspoon garlic powder
¼ teaspoon dry mustard

1. In large bowl combine turkey, bread crumbs, onion, egg, soy sauce, Worcestershire sauce, garlic powder and mustard.

2. Shape meat mixture into 4 patties, each ½ inch thick. On lightly greased broiling pan, about 6 inches from heat, broil burgers 3 to 4 minutes per side, or until no longer pink in center. *Makes 4 servings*

*Favorite recipe from **National Turkey Federation***

92 BURGERS AL GRECO

Basic Turkey Burgers (page 77)
4 pita breads
6 tablespoons crumbled feta cheese
1 medium tomato, chopped (about 1 cup)
½ medium cucumber, peeled and thinly
**   sliced (about ½ cup)**
1 medium onion, thinly sliced (about
**   ½ cup)**

Prepare Basic Turkey Burgers. Slice top
¼ off pita breads. Place burgers with
remaining ingredients in pita breads.

Makes 4 servings

*Favorite recipe from **National Turkey Federation***

93 MEXICAN STUFFED TURKEY BURGER

1 pound ground turkey
½ cup quick rolled oats
1 egg
1 tablespoon dried minced onion
1 teaspoon chili powder
½ teaspoon garlic powder
½ teaspoon ground cumin
½ teaspoon salt
¼ teaspoon cayenne pepper
1 can (4 ounces) whole green chili
**   peppers, drained and seeded**
2 ounces Monterey Jack cheese, cut into
**   ¼-inch-thick slices**

1. Remove grill rack from charcoal grill and
set aside. Preheat grill for direct heat
cooking method according to manufacturer's
directions.

2. In medium bowl combine turkey, oats,
egg, onion, chili powder, garlic powder,
cumin, salt and cayenne pepper. Divide
turkey mixture in half. On 2 (11×10-inch)
pieces wax paper, shape each half of turkey
mixture into burgers 6 inches in diameter.

3. Arrange half of chili peppers, cutting to
fit, over one burger leaving ½-inch border
around outside edge. Top with cheese slices
and remaining chili peppers. Carefully invert
second burger over chili peppers. Remove
top piece wax paper. Press edges together to
seal.

4. Lightly grease cold grill rack and position
over hot coals. Invert giant turkey burger
onto grill rack; remove wax paper. Grill
8 minutes per side or until an internal
temperature of 165°F is reached on meat
thermometer. To turn giant burger, slide flat
cookie sheet under burger and invert onto
another flat cookie sheet, then carefully
slide burger back onto grill rack.*

5. To serve, cut burger into fourths.

Makes 4 servings

*Can use greased wire grill basket, if desired.

*Favorite recipe from **National Turkey Federation***

Burger Al Greco

THE BEST IN BURGERS

94 TURKEY BURGERS

¼ cup Cowpoke Barbecue Sauce (recipe
    follows)*
1 pound ground turkey breast
1 cup whole wheat bread crumbs
1 egg white
½ teaspoon dried sage leaves
½ teaspoon dried marjoram leaves
¼ teaspoon salt
¼ teaspoon ground black pepper
1 teaspoon vegetable oil
4 whole grain sandwich rolls, split in half

Or substitute prepared barbecue sauce.

1. Prepare Cowpoke Barbecue Sauce.
Combine turkey, bread crumbs, egg white,
sage, marjoram, salt and pepper in large
bowl until well blended. Shape into 4 patties.

2. Heat oil in large nonstick skillet over
medium-high heat until hot. Add patties.
Cook 10 minutes or until patties are no
longer pink in center, turning once.

3. Place one burger on bottom half of each
roll. Spoon 1 tablespoon Cowpoke Barbecue
Sauce over top of each burger. Place tops of
rolls over burgers. Serve with lettuce and
tomato and garnish with carrot slices, if
desired. *Makes 4 burgers*

COWPOKE BARBECUE SAUCE

1 teaspoon vegetable oil
¾ cup chopped green onions
3 cloves garlic, finely chopped
1 can (14½ ounces) crushed tomatoes
½ cup ketchup
¼ cup water
¼ cup orange juice
2 tablespoons cider vinegar
2 teaspoons chili sauce
    Dash Worcestershire sauce

Heat oil in large nonstick saucepan over
medium heat until hot. Add onions and
garlic. Cook and stir 5 minutes or until
onions are tender. Stir in remaining
ingredients. Reduce heat to medium-low.
Cook 15 minutes, stirring occasionally.

Makes 2 cups

95 ROMANIAN BURGERS

1 pound raw ground turkey
1 to 2 cloves garlic, crushed
½ teaspoon dried thyme leaves
½ teaspoon salt
¼ teaspoon ground allspice
¼ teaspoon ground cloves
¼ teaspoon pepper

Combine all ingredients; shape into burgers
about ½ inch thick. Broil on lightly greased
rack in broiling pan about 6 inches from
heat, 3 to 4 minutes per side. (Or, heat about
1 tablespoon oil or margarine in large skillet
and pan fry about 2 to 3 minutes per side.)
Cook only until centers are no longer pink.

Makes 4 burgers

*Favorite recipe from **National Turkey Federation***

Turkey Burger

THE BEST IN BURGERS

96 SAVORY STUFFED TURKEY BURGERS

1 pound ground turkey
¼ cup A.1.® Steak Sauce, divided
¼ cup chopped onion
½ teaspoon dried thyme leaves
¼ teaspoon ground black pepper
½ cup prepared herb bread stuffing
½ cup whole berry cranberry sauce
4 slices whole wheat bread, toasted
4 lettuce leaves

In medium bowl, combine turkey, 2 tablespoons steak sauce, onion, thyme and pepper; shape into 8 thin patties. Place 2 tablespoons prepared stuffing in center of each of 4 patties. Top with remaining patties. Seal edges to form 4 patties; set aside.

In small bowl, combine remaining 2 tablespoons steak sauce and cranberry sauce; set aside.

Grill burgers over medium heat for 10 minutes on each side or until done. Top each bread slice with lettuce leaf and burger. Serve immediately topped with prepared cranberry sauce mixture.

Makes 4 servings

97 TURKEY TERIYAKI BURGERS

1 pound ground turkey
½ cup finely chopped water chestnuts
2 tablespoons teriyaki sauce
1 tablespoon sesame seeds, toasted and divided
1 teaspoon Chinese five-spice powder, divided
½ teaspoon onion salt
¼ teaspoon pepper
¼ cup plum preserves
4 hamburger buns, split

1. Prepare charcoal grill for direct-heat cooking.

2. In medium bowl, combine turkey, water chestnuts, teriyaki sauce, 2 teaspoons sesame seeds, ½ teaspoon Chinese five-spice powder, onion salt and pepper. Shape mixture into 4 burgers, approximately 4½ inches in diameter.

3. Grill 4 to 5 minutes per side or until meat thermometer registers 160 to 165°F and meat is no longer pink in center.

4. In small saucepan over low heat, combine preserves, remaining 1 teaspoon sesame seeds and remaining ½ teaspoon Chinese five-spice powder. Heat 4 to 5 minutes or until preserves are melted.

5. To serve, place a burger on bottom half of each bun, drizzle preserves mixture over each burger and top with other half of bun.

Makes 4 servings

*Favorite recipe from **National Turkey Federation***

Savory Stuffed Turkey Burger

THE BEST IN BURGERS

98 BURRITO TURKEY BURGERS

Vegetable cooking spray
2 pounds ground turkey
1 cup chopped onion
1 can (4 ounces) chopped green chilies, drained
1 package (1¼ ounces) taco seasoning mix
8 flour tortillas (8 inches)
1 can (16 ounces) nonfat refried beans
Shredded lettuce
½ cup shredded nonfat Cheddar cheese, divided
Salsa (optional)

1. Spray cold grill rack with vegetable cooking spray. Preheat charcoal grill for direct-heat cooking.

2. In medium bowl combine turkey, onion, chilies and seasoning mix. Shape turkey mixture into 8 (9×2-inch) rectangular-shaped burgers. Grill burgers 3 to 4 minutes; turn and continue cooking 2 to 3 minutes or until 160°F is reached on meat thermometer and meat is no longer pink in center. Remove and keep warm.

3. Heat tortillas according to package directions. Spread each tortilla with ¼ cup refried beans and sprinkle with lettuce. Place 1 burger in center of each tortilla and sprinkle with 1 tablespoon cheese. Fold sides of tortillas over burgers to create burritos. Serve with salsa, if desired.

Makes 8 servings

Favorite recipe from **National Turkey Federation**

Burrito Turkey Burger

THE BEST IN BURGERS

99 MEDITERRANEAN STUFFED TURKEY BURGER

1 pound ground turkey
1/4 cup quick rolled oats
1 egg
1/2 teaspoon salt
1/4 teaspoon dried mint leaves, crumbled
1/4 teaspoon garlic powder
1/8 teaspoon ground cinnamon
1/2 cup low-fat cottage cheese, drained
1/4 cup crumbled feta cheese
2 tablespoons sliced pitted black olives
1/2 teaspoon dried oregano leaves
Chopped cucumber, chopped tomato and sliced onion (optional)

1. Remove grill rack from charcoal grill and set aside. Preheat grill for direct-heat cooking method according to manufacturer's directions.

2. In medium bowl combine turkey, oats, egg, salt, mint, garlic powder and cinnamon. Divide turkey mixture in half. On 2 (11×10-inch) pieces wax paper, shape each half of turkey mixture into burgers 6 inches in diameter.

3. In small bowl combine cottage cheese, feta cheese, olives and oregano. Spoon cheese mixture over one burger, leaving 1/2-inch border around outside edge. Carefully invert second burger over cheese mixture. Remove top piece wax paper. Press edges together to seal.

4. Lightly grease cold grill rack and position over hot coals. Invert giant turkey burger onto grill rack; remove wax paper. Grill burger 8 minutes per side or until internal temperature of 165°F is reached on meat thermometer. To turn giant burger, slide flat

cookie sheet under burger and invert onto another flat cookie sheet, then carefully slide burger back onto grill rack.*

5. To serve, cut burger into fourths. Serve with cucumber, tomato and onion, if desired.

Makes 4 servings

*Can use greased wire grill basket, if desired.

*Favorite recipe from **National Turkey Federation***

100 GREEK TURKEY BURGERS

1 pound ground turkey
4 pimiento-stuffed green olives, chopped
1 tablespoon dried parsley flakes
1 teaspoon minced garlic
1/2 teaspoon salt
1/4 teaspoon pepper
1/4 teaspoon ground cinnamon
1/8 teaspoon ground nutmeg
1/4 cup nonfat sour cream
4 hamburger buns, split
1 small cucumber, diced
1/4 cup crumbled feta cheese

1. Prepare charcoal grill for direct-heat cooking.

2. In medium bowl combine turkey, olives, parsley, garlic, salt, pepper, cinnamon and nutmeg. Shape mixture into 4 burgers approximately 4 1/2 inches in diameter.

3. Grill burgers 2 to 3 minutes per side until meat thermometer registers 160 to 165°F and meat is no longer pink in center.

4. To serve, spread 1 tablespoon sour cream on bottom half of each bun. Top with cooked burger, cucumber, 1 tablespoon feta cheese and top half of bun. *Makes 4 servings*

*Favorite recipe from **National Turkey Federation***

THE BEST IN BURGERS

101 TURKEY BURGERS WITH CILANTRO PESTO

1 pound ground turkey
½ cup chopped onion
¼ cup chunky salsa
1 jalapeño pepper, seeded and minced
1 teaspoon chopped garlic
½ teaspoon *each* dried oregano leaves and salt
4 rolls, split and toasted
Cilantro Pesto (recipe follows)

1. Prepare charcoal grill for direct-heat cooking.

2. In medium bowl combine turkey, onion, salsa, jalapeño, garlic, oregano and salt. Shape mixture into four burgers, approximately 4½ inches in diameter.

3. Grill 5 to 6 minutes per side until meat thermometer registers 160 to 165°F and meat is no longer pink in center.

4. To serve, place cooked burgers on bottom halves of rolls; top each burger with 2 tablespoons Cilantro Pesto and top halves of rolls.   *Makes 4 servings*

CILANTRO PESTO
1 large clove garlic
1 cup packed cilantro leaves
¼ cup *each* chopped walnuts and grated Parmesan cheese
¼ teaspoon salt
¼ cup olive oil

1. In food processor, fitted with metal blade with motor running, drop garlic through feed tube to finely chop. Add cilantro, walnuts, cheese and salt. Process 45 to 47 seconds or until smooth. Scrape sides of bowl.

2. With motor running, slowly add olive oil and process until well blended. Cover and refrigerate several hours.   *Makes ⅔ cup*

Favorite recipe from **National Turkey Federation**

102 ITALIAN SAUSAGE TURKEY BURGERS

1 pound ground turkey
1 pound Italian turkey sausage
8 hamburger buns
½ cup bottled marinara sauce
8 slices low-fat mozzarella cheese

1. Preheat charcoal grill for direct-heat cooking.

2. In large bowl combine ground turkey and Italian sausage. Shape mixture into 8 burgers approximately 3½ inches in diameter. Grill burgers 5 to 6 minutes per side or until 160°F is reached on meat thermometer and meat is no longer pink in center.

3. To serve, place burgers on bottom halves of buns. Top each burger with 1 tablespoon marinara sauce, 1 slice mozzarella cheese and other half of bun.   *Makes 8 servings*

Favorite recipe from **National Turkey Federation**

Turkey Burger with Cilantro Pesto

THE BEST IN BURGERS

103 GOURMET OLÉ BURGERS

1½ pounds ground beef
1 package (1.0 ounce) LAWRY'S® Taco
    Spices & Seasonings
¼ cup ketchup
    Monterey Jack cheese slices
    Salsa

In medium bowl, combine ground beef, Taco Spices & Seasonings and ketchup; blend well. Shape into patties. Grill or broil burgers 5 to 7 minutes on each side or to desired doneness. Top each burger with a slice of cheese. Return to grill or broiler until cheese melts. Top with a dollop of salsa. *Makes 6 to 8 servings*

PRESENTATION: Serve on lettuce-lined hamburger buns. Garnish with avocado slices, if desired.

NOTE: Cut cheese with cookie cutters for interesting shapes.

104 TURKEY BURGERS WITH ZESTY SALSA

1 pound ground turkey
½ cup seasoned bread crumbs
⅓ cup finely chopped onion
1 egg, beaten
¼ cup FRENCH'S® Deli Brown or Classic
    Yellow® Mustard
½ teaspoon garlic powder
    Zesty Salsa (recipe follows)

Mix together turkey, bread crumbs, onion, egg, mustard and garlic powder in large bowl. Shape into 4 patties, pressing firmly.

Place patties on oiled grid. Grill over hot coals 15 minutes or until no longer pink in center, turning once. Serve with Zesty Salsa. *Makes 4 servings*

ZESTY SALSA
1 pound ripe plum tomatoes, seeded and
    chopped
1 can (4 ounces) diced green chilies,
    drained
2 to 3 tablespoons FRANK'S® Original
    REDHOT® Cayenne Pepper Sauce or
    to taste
2 tablespoons finely chopped green onion
2 tablespoons minced fresh cilantro leaves
1 clove garlic, minced

Combine ingredients in small bowl; mix well. *Makes 2 cups*

Prep Time: 25 minutes
Cook Time: 15 minutes

Gourmet Olé Burger

Sandwiches
& Salads

105 SPINACH AND BEEF PITA SANDWICHES

1 pound lean ground beef
1 package (10 ounces) frozen chopped
   spinach, thawed
1 bunch green onions, chopped
1 can (2¼ ounces) sliced ripe olives,
   drained
2 teaspoons LAWRY'S® Lemon Pepper,
   divided
1 large tomato, diced
1 cup plain nonfat yogurt or dairy sour
   cream
½ cup reduced-calorie mayonnaise
6 (6-inch) pita breads, warmed
   Lettuce leaves
1 cup (4 ounces) crumbled feta cheese

In large skillet, brown ground beef, stirring until cooked through; drain fat. Place spinach in strainer; press with back of spoon to remove as much moisture as possible. Add spinach, green onions, olives and 1 teaspoon Lemon Pepper to beef; cook 2 minutes. Stir in tomato. In small bowl, combine yogurt, mayonnaise and remaining 1 teaspoon Lemon Pepper. Split open pita breads. Line insides with lettuce. Stir cheese into beef mixture and divide among pita pockets. Serve with yogurt sauce.

Makes 6 servings

PRESENTATION: Pass the remaining yogurt sauce separately.

HINT: Use scissors to cut open pita breads.

Spinach and Beef Pita Sandwich

106 AMIGO PITA POCKET SANDWICHES

1 pound ground turkey
1 package (1.0 ounce) LAWRY'S® Taco
   Spices & Seasonings
1 can (6 ounces) tomato paste
½ cup water
½ cup chopped green bell pepper
1 can (7 ounces) whole kernel corn,
   drained
8 pita breads
   Curly lettuce leaves
   Shredded Cheddar cheese

In large skillet, brown turkey; drain fat. Add remaining ingredients except pita bread, lettuce and cheese; blend well. Bring to a boil; reduce heat and simmer, uncovered, 15 minutes. Cut off top ¼ of pita breads. Open pita breads to form pockets. Line each with lettuce leaves. Spoon ½ cup filling into each pita bread and top with cheese.

Makes 8 servings

PRESENTATION: Serve with vegetable sticks and fresh fruit.

Amigo Pita Pocket Sandwiches

107 STUFFED FRENCH BREAD

1 pound ground beef
1 package (1¼ ounces) taco seasoning mix
1 loaf (1 pound) French or Italian bread, cut in half lengthwise
⅔ cup chopped lettuce
⅔ cup chopped pitted ripe olives
⅔ cup chopped green pepper
⅔ cup chopped tomato
⅔ cup tortilla chips, crushed
⅔ cup taco flavored cheese
    Taco sauce (optional)
    Sour cream (optional)

Brown ground beef and drain. Add taco seasoning and cook meat according to package directions. Hollow out French bread halves to form shells. Layer ground beef mixture, lettuce, olives, green pepper and tomato in bottom half of loaf. Top with tortilla chips, cheese and top half of loaf. Wrap loaf in paper towels. Heat stuffed loaf in microwave oven just until cheese melts. Cut into quarters and serve with taco sauce and sour cream, if desired.

Makes 4 servings

Favorite recipe from **North Dakota Beef Commission**

108 SUN–DRIED TOMATO AND SAUSAGE STUFFED FRENCH BREAD

1 large loaf French bread
¼ pound bulk Italian sausage
¼ pound lean ground beef
½ medium yellow onion, chopped
½ cup CHRISTOPHER RANCH™ Sun-Dried Tomatoes, sliced
¼ cup sliced mushrooms
1 egg, lightly beaten
1 tablespoon CHRISTOPHER RANCH™ Pesto Sauce
1 tablespoon chopped fresh parsley
    Salt and pepper to taste
¾ cup shredded mozzarella or Monterey Jack cheese

Preheat oven to 400°F. Cut French bread in half lengthwise and hollow out centers. Chop bread centers in food processor or by hand to make coarse crumbs. Brown sausage, beef and onion in large skillet over medium heat. Combine bread crumbs, meat mixture, sun-dried tomatoes, mushrooms, egg, pesto sauce, parsley, salt and pepper in large bowl. Spoon half of mixture into each bread shell. Top each with cheese. Place on cookie sheet and bake until cheese is lightly browned and bubbly. Slice to serve.

Makes 4 servings

SANDWICHES & SALADS

109 ITALIAN MEATBALL SUBS

  Nonstick cooking spray
½ **cup chopped onion**
 3 **teaspoons finely chopped garlic, divided**
 1 **can (14½ ounces) Italian-style crushed tomatoes, undrained**
 2 **bay leaves**
2½ **teaspoons dried basil leaves, divided**
 2 **teaspoons dried oregano leaves, divided**
¾ **teaspoon ground black pepper, divided**
¼ **teaspoon crushed red pepper**
½ **pound lean ground beef**
⅓ **cup chopped green onions**
⅓ **cup dry bread crumbs**
¼ **cup chopped fresh parsley**
 1 **egg white**
½ **teaspoon dried marjoram leaves**
½ **teaspoon ground mustard**
 4 **French bread rolls, warmed, halved**

1. Spray large nonstick saucepan with cooking spray. Heat over medium heat until hot. Add onion and 2 teaspoons garlic. Cook and stir 5 minutes or until onion is tender. Add tomatoes with liquid, bay leaves, 2 teaspoons basil, 1 teaspoon oregano, ½ teaspoon black pepper and red pepper; cover. Simmer 30 minutes, stirring occasionally. Remove and discard bay leaves.

2. Combine meat, green onions, bread crumbs, parsley, egg white, 2 tablespoons water, remaining 1 teaspoon garlic, ½ teaspoon basil, 1 teaspoon oregano, ¼ teaspoon black pepper, marjoram and mustard in medium bowl until well blended. Shape into 16 small meatballs.

3. Spray large nonstick skillet with cooking spray. Heat over medium heat until hot. Add meatballs. Cook 5 minutes or until meatballs are no longer pink in centers, turning occasionally.

4. Add meatballs to tomato sauce. Cook 5 minutes, stirring occasionally.

5. Place 4 meatballs in each roll. Spoon additional sauce over meatballs. Serve immediately.   *Makes 4 servings*

110 SPECIAL SAN FRANCISCO PITA POCKETS

 1 **package (10 ounces) frozen chopped spinach**
¾ **pound lean ground beef**
½ **pound fresh mushrooms, sliced**
½ **cup chopped onion**
 3 **tablespoons butter or margarine**
¾ **teaspoon dill weed**
½ **teaspoon LAWRY'S® Seasoned Salt**
½ **teaspoon LAWRY'S® Garlic Powder with Parsley**
½ **teaspoon LAWRY'S® Seasoned Pepper**
 2 **cups (8 ounces) shredded cheese (½ Cheddar and ½ Monterey Jack)**
 4 **pita breads, cut in half**

Make slit in spinach package; place, slit side up, on paper towel. Microwave on HIGH (100%) 5 minutes. Squeeze liquid from spinach. In microwave-safe dish, microwave ground beef on HIGH 6 to 7 minutes, stirring once or twice. Drain fat. In 13×9×2-inch microwave-safe baking dish, microwave mushrooms, onion and butter on HIGH 8 to 10 minutes. Stir in seasonings. Microwave on HIGH 3 minutes, stirring once. Stir spinach and cooked ground beef into mushroom mixture. Fold in cheese. Cover with waxed paper and microwave on HIGH 3 minutes. Wrap pita breads loosely in plastic wrap; microwave on HIGH 30 seconds to warm. Open pita breads and fill with meat mixture. Serve immediately.   *Makes 8 servings*

111 SAVORY GRAPE PICNIC BUNS

½ **pound ground turkey**
1 **cup chopped green cabbage**
¼ **cup chopped onion**
1½ **cups California seedless grapes**
1 **teaspoon chopped fresh thyme** *or*
    ¼ **teaspoon dried thyme leaves**
½ **teaspoon cornstarch**
½ **teaspoon salt**
    Dash ground black pepper
1 **package (16 ounces) hot roll mix**
2 **tablespoons honey**

Preheat oven to 350°F. Combine turkey, cabbage and onion in large nonstick skillet. Cook and stir over medium heat 5 minutes or until turkey is no longer pink. Add grapes, thyme, cornstarch, salt and pepper; stir to combine. Remove skillet from heat; cool. Prepare dough according to package directions. Divide dough into 12 portions; flatten into circles. Place 2 heaping tablespoonfuls filling in center of each circle. Fold edges of circles over fillings; seal buns. Place buns, sealed side down, on baking sheet. Bake 12 to 15 minutes or until golden brown. Glaze with honey before serving.   *Makes 1 dozen*

Favorite recipe from **California Table Grape Commission**

112 CHILI DOGS

1 **pound ground beef**
2 **cups chopped red onions**
2 **teaspoons finely chopped garlic**
2 **cups water**
1 **package LIPTON® Rice & Sauce—
    Spanish**
½ **cup ketchup**
1 **tablespoon prepared mustard**
1 **tablespoon chili powder**
¼ **teaspoon dried oregano leaves**
¼ **teaspoon ground cumin (optional)**
    Ground black pepper to taste
8 **frankfurters, cooked**
8 **frankfurter rolls**

In 12-inch skillet, cook ground beef, onions and garlic over medium-high heat, stirring frequently, 5 minutes or until beef is browned; drain fat. Stir in water, rice & sauce—Spanish, ketchup, mustard, chili powder, oregano and cumin. Bring to a boil over high heat. Reduce heat to low and simmer, stirring occasionally, 10 minutes or until rice is tender; add pepper. Serve over frankfurters in rolls and top, if desired, with additional chopped onion and shredded Cheddar cheese.

Makes about 4 servings

MICROWAVE DIRECTIONS: In 2-quart microwave-safe round casserole, microwave beef, onions and garlic, uncovered, at HIGH (100% power) 4 minutes, stirring once; drain fat. Stir in water, rice & sauce—Spanish, ketchup, mustard, chili powder, oregano and cumin. Microwave 14 minutes or until rice is tender; stir in pepper. Let stand covered 5 minutes. Serve as above.

SANDWICHES & SALADS

113 MEATY CHILI DOGS

1 pound ground beef
¼ pound Italian sausage, casings removed
1 large onion, chopped
2 medium ribs celery, diced
2 fresh jalapeño peppers*, seeded, chopped
2 cloves garlic, minced
1 teaspoon sugar
1 teaspoon chili powder
½ teaspoon salt
½ teaspoon ground cumin
½ teaspoon dried thyme leaves
⅛ teaspoon ground black pepper
1 can (28 ounces) tomatoes, chopped, undrained
1 can (15 ounces) pinto beans, rinsed and drained
1 can (12 ounces) tomato juice
1 cup water
¼ cup ketchup
8 frankfurters
8 frankfurter buns, split and toasted

*Jalapeños can sting and irritate the skin; wear rubber gloves when handling peppers and do not touch eyes. Wash hands after handling.

Cook beef, sausage, onion, celery, jalapeño peppers and garlic in 5-quart Dutch oven over medium heat until meat is no longer pink and onion is tender; drain.

Stir in sugar, chili powder, salt, cumin, thyme and black pepper. Add tomatoes, beans, tomato juice, water and ketchup. Bring to a boil over high heat. Reduce heat to low; simmer, uncovered, 30 minutes, stirring occasionally.

Arrange frankfurters on grill rack directly above medium-hot coals. Grill, uncovered, 5 to 8 minutes or until heated through, turning often. Place frankfurters in buns. Spoon about ¼ cup chili over each.

Makes 8 servings

Meaty Chili Dogs

114 JUNIOR JOES

1 pound ground beef
1 can (10¾ ounces) condensed tomato
   soup
¼ cup water
1 tablespoon parsley flakes
1 teaspoon instant minced onion
½ teaspoon salt
¼ teaspoon TABASCO® pepper sauce
   Processed American cheese slices
6 hamburger buns, split and toasted

Break up ground beef with fork in large
skillet. Cook over medium heat, stirring
frequently until meat loses pink color; drain.
Add undiluted tomato soup, water, parsley,
onion, salt and TABASCO® sauce. Cook over
low heat, stirring occasionally, 15 to 20
minutes. Cut letters from cheese slices to
make names or initials. Spoon hamburger
mixture over bottom halves of toasted buns.
Top with cheese names or initials. Serve
with top halves of buns.

Makes 6 servings

115 SLOPPY JOES

8 ounces lean ground beef or turkey
½ cup finely chopped onion
½ cup CONTADINA® Pizza Sauce
2 sandwich-size English muffins, split,
   toasted
½ cup (2 ounces) shredded cheddar cheese

In medium skillet, brown ground beef with
onion; drain. Stir in pizza sauce; simmer,
uncovered, for 5 to 8 minutes or until heated
through, stirring occasionally. Spoon
mixture evenly onto muffin halves; sprinkle
with cheese. Broil 6 to 8 inches from heat for
1 to 2 minutes or until cheese is melted.

Makes 4 servings

116 SLOPPY JOES

1 pound BOB EVANS FARMS® Italian Roll
   Sausage
1 medium onion, chopped
½ green bell pepper, chopped
½ cup ketchup
2 tablespoons Dijon mustard
2 tablespoons cider vinegar
1 tablespoon sugar
1 teaspoon minced garlic
8 sandwich buns, split and toasted

Crumble sausage into medium skillet. Add
onion and pepper. Cook over medium heat
until sausage is browned, stirring
occasionally. Drain off any drippings. Stir in
all remaining ingredients except buns. Bring
to a boil. Reduce heat to low; simmer
30 minutes. Serve hot on buns. Refrigerate
leftovers.

Makes 8 servings

117 TURKEY JOES

1 pound ground raw turkey
½ cup chopped onion
½ cup chopped green bell pepper
1 cup HEINZ® Tomato Ketchup
2 tablespoons brown sugar
2 tablespoons HEINZ® Vinegar
1½ teaspoons prepared mustard
1 teaspoon HEINZ® Worcestershire Sauce
6 sandwich buns

In large nonstick skillet, cook turkey, onion
and pepper until turkey is no longer pink,
stirring to break up pieces. Add ketchup and
remaining ingredients except buns. Cover;
simmer 10 minutes, stirring occasionally.
Serve on buns. *Makes 6 servings*
(about 3¼ cups meat mixture)

118 DOUBLE DUTY TACOS

MEXICALI CHILI RUB
- ¼ cup chili powder
- 3 tablespoons garlic salt
- 2 tablespoons ground cumin
- 2 tablespoons dried oregano leaves
- ½ teaspoon ground red pepper

TACOS
- 2 pounds lean ground beef
- 1 large onion, chopped
- 3 tablespoons Mexicali Chili Rub
- 2 tablespoons tomato paste
- 16 packaged crispy taco shells
- 2 cups (8 ounces) shredded Monterey Jack cheese
- 2 cups shredded lettuce
- 1 cup chopped fresh tomatoes
- 1 cup diced ripe avocado
- ½ cup light or regular sour cream
  Salsa

1. For rub, combine chili powder, garlic salt, cumin, oregano and ground red pepper in small bowl; mix well. Transfer to container with tight-fitting lid. Store in cool dry place up to 2 months.

2. For tacos, cook beef and onion in large deep skillet over medium-high heat until no longer pink; pour off drippings. Sprinkle chili rub over beef mixture; cook 1 minute. Reduce heat to medium.

3. Add ¾ cup water and tomato paste. Cover; simmer 5 minutes.

4. Spoon beef mixture into taco shells; top with cheese. Arrange lettuce, tomatoes, avocado, sour cream and salsa in bowls. Serve tacos with toppings as desired.

Makes 8 servings

SERVING SUGGESTION: Serve tacos with refried beans and Spanish rice.

119 REALLY MADE RIGHTS

- 1 pound lean ground pork
  Water
- ½ cup beer
- 1 tablespoon sugar
- 1 teaspoon dry mustard
- ¾ teaspoon ground white pepper
  Salt to taste
- 6 soft sandwich buns

In large skillet, cover pork with water; simmer until cooked through, breaking apart pork as it cooks. (Pork will be completely white.) Drain well; add beer, sugar, dry mustard and pepper; simmer 10 minutes. Season to taste with salt. Place on sandwich buns. Serve with dill pickles, chopped onion and prepared mustard, if desired.

Makes 6 servings

Prep Time: 15 minutes

Favorite recipe from **National Pork Producers Council**

Double Duty Tacos

SANDWICHES & SALADS

120 TACOS SUAVE DE CARNE CON SALSA ROJA

¾ cup vegetable oil, divided
1 tablespoon pure ground chile pepper*
1 pound ground beef
2 teaspoons ground cumin
1 tablespoon CHEF PAUL PRUDHOMME'S® Seafood Magic®
1 tablespoon CHEF PAUL PRUDHOMME'S® Meat Magic®
1 cup chopped onion
½ cup chopped green bell pepper
3 tablespoons corn flour or all-purpose flour
1½ cups beef stock or water
12 (6-inch) corn tortillas
   Shredded lettuce
   Chopped fresh tomatoes
   Shredded Cheddar cheese

You can find pure ground chile pepper (ground dried chiles) in a Mexican or Latin grocery store. However, if you cannot find it, substitute an equal amount of chili powder.

Heat ¼ cup of the oil in a heavy 10-inch skillet over high heat 1 minute. Stir in chile pepper and cook 1½ minutes, stirring frequently. Add ground beef and cumin. Cook, stirring frequently, to break up meat chunks, about 2 minutes. Add Seafood Magic® and Meat Magic® and stir to mix well. Cook 1 minute more. Add onion and bell pepper. Cook 6 minutes, stirring occasionally, or until meat is well browned. Stir in flour. Cook, without stirring, about 2 minutes or until a brown crust forms on bottom of pan. Stir in stock to deglaze pan, stirring and scraping pan bottom well to get up all browned bits. Cook about 3 minutes or until sauce is boiling. Reduce heat to low and simmer about 8 minutes or until sauce has reduced somewhat and flavors have blended. Turn heat off.

In an 8-inch skillet, heat the remaining ½ cup oil over high heat about 3 minutes or until it reaches 300°F. Slide 1 tortilla into hot oil and, using tongs, immediately turn tortilla over and then immediately pull it out of pan. Tortilla should be very soft and pliable. Drain on paper towels. Repeat with the remaining tortillas. Blot any of the remaining oil with fresh paper towels.

To assemble, lay tortillas on serving plates, allowing 2 per person. Spoon ¼ cup meat mixture over half of each tortilla. Top with lettuce, tomatoes and cheese. Fold each half over filling. Serve immediately.

Makes 6 servings

121 TURKEY TACOS

1 pound ground raw turkey
1 package (1¼ ounces) taco seasoning mix
½ cup water
½ cup HEINZ® Tomato Ketchup
10 taco shells
   Shredded lettuce
   Chopped tomatoes
   Shredded Cheddar cheese

In large nonstick skillet, cook turkey until no longer pink. Stir in taco seasoning and water. Simmer 2 minutes or until slightly thickened. Stir in ketchup; heat. Spoon mixture into taco shells. Top with lettuce, tomatoes and cheese as desired.

Makes 5 servings (2 tacos each)

Tacos Suave De Carne Con Salsa Roja

122 TACOS PICADILLOS

¾ **pound ground pork**
1 **medium onion, chopped**
½ **teaspoon ground cinnamon**
½ **teaspoon ground cumin**
1 **can (14½ ounces) DEL MONTE®**
  Mexican Recipe Stewed Tomatoes
⅓ **cup DEL MONTE® Seedless Raisins**
⅓ **cup toasted chopped almonds**
6 **flour tortillas**
  Lettuce, cilantro and sour cream
  (optional)

In large skillet, brown meat with onion and spices over medium-high heat. Season to taste with salt and pepper, if desired. Stir in tomatoes and raisins. Cover and cook 10 minutes. Remove cover; cook over medium-high heat 5 minutes or until thickened, stirring occasionally. Just before serving, stir in almonds. Fill tortillas with meat mixture; roll to enclose. Garnish with lettuce, cilantro and sour cream, if desired. Serve immediately.   *Makes 6 servings*

Prep Time: 5 minutes
Cook Time: 25 minutes

HELPFUL HINT: If ground pork is not available, boneless pork may be purchased and ground in food processor. Cut pork into 1-inch cubes before processing.

123 EASY CHICKEN RICE TACOS

1 **tablespoon margarine or butter**
½ **pound ground chicken or turkey**
1 **small onion, chopped**
1 **package (1¼ ounces) taco seasoning mix**
1¼ **cups water**
1 **can (8 ounces) tomato sauce**
1½ **cups MINUTE® Original Rice, uncooked**
1 **can (16 ounces) kidney beans, drained**
  (optional)
16 **taco shells, heated**
  Suggested Toppings: shredded cheddar
  cheese, shredded lettuce, chopped
  tomatoes, sour cream

MELT margarine in large skillet on medium-high heat. Add chicken, onion and seasoning mix; cook and stir until chicken is no longer pink.

STIR in water and tomato sauce. Bring to boil. Reduce heat to low; cover and simmer 5 minutes.

STIR in rice and beans; cover. Remove from heat. Let stand 5 minutes. Fill each taco shell with chicken mixture. Serve with Suggested Toppings.   *Makes 16 tacos or 8 servings*

Prep Time: 5 minutes
Cook Time: 15 minutes

Taco Picadillo

SANDWICHES & SALADS

124 QUICK 'N EASY TACOS

1 pound ground beef
1 can (14½ ounces) whole peeled
    tomatoes, undrained and coarsely
    chopped
1 medium green pepper, finely chopped
1 envelope LIPTON® Recipe Secrets®
    Onion Soup Mix*
1 tablespoon chili powder
3 drops hot pepper sauce
8 taco shells
    Taco Toppings**

In 10-inch skillet, brown ground beef over medium-high heat; drain. Stir in tomatoes, green pepper, onion soup mix, chili powder and hot pepper sauce. Bring to a boil, then simmer 15 minutes or until slightly thickened. Serve in taco shells with assorted Taco Toppings. *Makes 4 servings*

Also terrific with Lipton® Recipe Secrets® Onion-Mushroom or Beefy Mushroom Soup Mix.

**TACO TOPPINGS: Use shredded cheddar or Monterey Jack cheese, shredded lettuce, chopped tomatoes, sliced pitted ripe olives, sour cream or taco sauce.*

125 TACOS CON PUERCO

1 pound ground pork
1 can (8 ounces) whole tomatoes,
    undrained, cut up
¼ cup chopped onion
1 tablespoon chili powder
¼ teaspoon garlic powder
    Salt and pepper
8 taco shells
2 fresh tomatoes, cut into wedges
2 cups shredded iceberg lettuce

In heavy skillet, brown ground pork; drain any excess drippings. Stir in undrained canned tomatoes, onion, chili powder and

garlic powder. Bring to a boil; reduce heat and simmer, uncovered, until most liquid evaporates, about 15 minutes, stirring occasionally. Season to taste with salt and pepper. Heat taco shells according to package directions. Portion filling into shells; top with fresh tomatoes and lettuce.
Makes 4 servings

Prep Time: 10 minutes
Cook Time: 15 minutes

Favorite recipe from ***National Pork Producers Council***

126 SPICY BURRITO BONANZA

½ pound ground beef
½ pound spicy pork sausage
1 medium tomato, chopped
¼ cup thinly sliced green onions
1½ teaspoons chili powder
½ teaspoon LAWRY'S® Garlic Powder with
    Parsley
1 can (8¼ ounces) refried beans
6 large flour tortillas, warmed
1½ cups (6 ounces) shredded Monterey Jack
    cheese
    Shredded lettuce

In large skillet, brown ground beef and sausage; drain fat. Add tomato, green onions, chili powder and Garlic Powder with Parsley; blend well. Bring to a boil; reduce heat and simmer, uncovered, 10 minutes. Add refried beans; heat 5 minutes. Spread ½ cup meat mixture on each warm tortilla. Top with a sprinkling of cheese and lettuce. Fold in sides and roll to enclose filling.
Makes 6 servings

PRESENTATION: Serve topped with sour cream and avocado slices.

Soft Turkey Tacos

127 SOFT TURKEY TACOS

     8 (6-inch) corn tortillas*
1½ teaspoons vegetable oil
     1 pound ground turkey
     1 small onion, chopped
     1 teaspoon dried oregano leaves
        Salt and pepper
        Chopped tomatoes
        Shredded lettuce
        Salsa
        Refried beans (optional)

*Substitute 8 (10-inch) flour tortillas for corn
tortillas, if desired.*

1. Wrap tortillas in foil. Place in cold oven;
set temperature to 350°F.

2. Heat oil in large skillet over medium heat.
Add turkey and onion; cook until turkey is
no longer pink, stirring occasionally. Stir in
oregano. Season with salt and pepper to
taste. Keep warm.

3. For each taco, fill warm tortilla with
turkey mixture; top with tomatoes, lettuce
and salsa. Serve with refried beans, if
desired.   *Makes 4 servings*

NOTE: To warm tortillas in microwave oven,
wrap loosely in damp paper towel.
Microwave at HIGH (100% Power) 2 minutes
or until hot.

128 SPEEDY BEEF & BEAN BURRITOS

8 (7-inch) flour tortillas
1 pound ground beef
1 cup chopped onion
1 teaspoon bottled minced garlic
1 can (15 ounces) black beans, drained and rinsed
1 cup spicy thick and chunky salsa
2 teaspoons ground cumin
1 bunch cilantro
2 cups (8 ounces) shredded cojack or Monterey Jack cheese

1. Wrap tortillas in aluminum foil; place in oven. Turn temperature to 350°F; heat tortillas 15 minutes.

2. While tortillas are warming, prepare burrito filling. Combine meat, onion and garlic in large skillet; cook over medium-high heat until meat is no longer pink, breaking meat apart with wooden spoon. Pour off drippings.

3. Stir beans, salsa and cumin into meat mixture; reduce heat to medium. Cover and simmer 10 minutes, stirring once.

4. While filling is simmering, chop enough cilantro to measure ¼ cup. Stir into filling. Spoon filling down centers of warm tortillas; top with cheese. Roll up and serve immediately.   *Makes 4 servings*

Prep and Cook Time: 20 minutes

129 THAI PORK BURRITOS

1 pound lean ground pork
2 tablespoons grated fresh ginger root
1 clove garlic, peeled and crushed
2 cups coleslaw mix with carrots
1 small onion, thinly sliced
3 tablespoons soy sauce
2 tablespoons lime juice
1 tablespoon honey
2 teaspoons ground coriander
1 teaspoon sesame oil
½ teaspoon crushed red pepper
4 large (10-inch) flour tortillas, warmed
Fresh cilantro, chopped (optional)

Heat large nonstick skillet over high heat. Add pork; cook and stir until pork is no longer pink, 3 to 4 minutes. Drain any excess drippings. Stir in ginger and garlic. Add coleslaw mix and onion and stir-fry with pork for 2 minutes, until vegetables are wilted. Combine all remaining ingredients except tortillas and cilantro in small bowl and add to skillet. Stir constantly to blend all ingredients well, about 1 minute. Spoon equal portions of mixture onto warm flour tortillas and garnish with cilantro, if desired. Roll up to encase filling and serve.

Makes 4 servings

Prep Time: 15 minutes

Favorite recipe from **National Pork Producers Council**

Speedy Beef & Bean Burritos

130 ON–THE–RUN BURRITOS

1 pound lean ground beef
½ cup chopped green onions
1 (15-ounce) can HUNT'S® Ready Tomato Sauces Chunky Mexican
1 (8¾-ounce) can whole kernel corn, drained
1 (4-ounce) can diced green chiles, drained
1 (2¼-ounce) can sliced ripe olives, drained
8 burrito-size (10-inch) flour tortillas, warmed
1 cup shredded Cheddar cheese

In large skillet, brown beef with green onions; drain. Stir in *remaining* ingredients *except* tortillas and cheese; heat through. Spoon *½ cup* beef mixture down center of *one* tortilla and top with *2 tablespoons* cheese. Fold bottom end up about 2 inches, then roll up burrito from long side to enclose filling. Repeat with *remaining* ingredients.

Makes 8 burritos

131 ZESTY TACO SALAD

2 tablespoons vegetable oil
1 clove garlic, finely chopped
¾ pound ground turkey
1¾ teaspoons chili powder
¼ teaspoon ground cumin
3 cups washed, torn lettuce leaves
1 can (14½ ounces) Mexican-style diced tomatoes, drained
1 cup rinsed, drained canned garbanzo beans (chick-peas) or pinto beans
⅔ cup chopped peeled cucumber
⅓ cup frozen whole kernel corn, thawed
¼ cup chopped red onion
1 to 2 jalapeño peppers, seeded, finely chopped* (optional)
1 tablespoon red wine vinegar
12 nonfat tortilla chips
Fresh greens (optional)

*Jalapeño peppers can sting and irritate the skin; wear rubber gloves when handling peppers and do not touch eyes. Wash hands after handling.

1. Combine oil and garlic in small bowl; let stand 1 hour at room temperature.

2. Combine turkey, chili powder and cumin in large nonstick skillet. Cook over medium heat 5 minutes or until turkey is no longer pink, stirring to crumble.

3. Combine turkey, lettuce, tomatoes, beans, cucumber, corn, onion and jalapeño in large bowl. Remove garlic from oil; discard garlic. Combine oil and vinegar in small bowl. Drizzle over salad; toss to coat. Serve on tortilla chips and fresh greens, if desired. Serve with additional tortilla chips and garnish with cilantro, if desired.

Makes 4 servings

Zesty Taco Salad

SANDWICHES & SALADS

132 AZTEC CHILI SALAD

1 pound ground beef
1 package (1.48 ounces) LAWRY'S® Spices & Seasonings for Chili
½ cup water
1 can (15½ ounces) kidney beans, undrained
1 can (14½ ounces) whole peeled tomatoes, undrained and cut up
½ cup dairy sour cream
3 tablespoons mayonnaise
1 fresh medium tomato, diced
¼ cup chopped fresh cilantro
½ teaspoon LAWRY'S® Seasoned Pepper
1 head leaf lettuce
1 red bell pepper, sliced
¼ cup sliced green onions
1½ cups (6 ounces) shredded Cheddar cheese
¼ cup sliced ripe olives

In large skillet, brown ground beef until crumbly; drain fat. Stir in Spices & Seasonings for Chili, water, beans and canned tomatoes; blend well. Bring to a boil; reduce heat and simmer, uncovered, 10 minutes. For dressing, in blender or food processor, blend sour cream, mayonnaise, fresh tomato, cilantro and Seasoned Pepper. Refrigerate until chilled. On 6 individual plates, layer lettuce, chili meat, bell pepper, green onions, cheese and olives. Drizzle with chilled dressing. *Makes 6 servings*

PRESENTATION: Serve with jicama wedges arranged around salad plates.

HINT: Ground turkey or shredded chicken can be used in place of ground beef in chili mixture.

133 TOSTADA SALAD

1 pound ground beef
1 package (1.0 ounce) LAWRY'S® Taco Spices & Seasonings
¾ cup water
1 can (15½ ounces) kidney beans, drained
4 medium tomatoes, cut into wedges
1 avocado, thinly sliced
8 ounces tortilla chips
1 head iceberg lettuce, torn into bite-size pieces
1 cup (4 ounces) shredded Cheddar cheese
1 cup chopped onion

In large skillet, brown ground beef until crumbly; drain fat. Add Taco Spices & Seasonings, water and beans; blend well. Bring to a boil; reduce heat, cover and simmer 10 minutes. Reserve some tomato wedges, avocado slices and tortilla chips for garnish. In large salad bowl, combine all remaining ingredients; add ground beef mixture and toss lightly.
Makes 6 to 8 servings

PRESENTATION: Garnish with reserved tomatoes, avocado and tortilla chips. Serve with sour cream and salsa or Thousand Island dressing.

HINT: Omit tortilla chips and layer remaining ingredients on heated Lawry's® Tostada Shells.

Aztec Chili Salad

SANDWICHES & SALADS

134 TACO SALAD

1 pound extra-lean (90% lean) ground
    beef
1 small onion, finely chopped
1 clove garlic, minced
2 teaspoons chili powder
1 teaspoon ground cumin
½ teaspoon salt
    Dash freshly ground black pepper
1 large head iceberg lettuce, torn into
    bite-size pieces (about 10 cups)
2 large tomatoes
1 medium avocado, peeled, sliced
2 cups salsa

Brown ground beef in medium skillet. Drain.
Add onion and garlic; cook until tender. Stir
in seasonings.

Combine lettuce, tomatoes and avocado in
large serving bowl; toss lightly. Top with
ground beef mixture. Serve with salsa.

Makes 4 servings

135 GREEK PASTA SALAD

½ pound extra-lean (90% lean) ground
    beef
⅓ cup chopped fresh mint *or*
    2 tablespoons dried mint leaves
1 clove garlic, minced
1¾ cups (about 6 ounces) small shell
    macaroni, cooked
10 cherry tomatoes, quartered
2 ounces feta cheese, crumbled
½ red bell pepper, chopped
½ red onion, cut into rings
¼ cup reduced-calorie Italian dressing
2 tablespoons lemon juice
    Salt and freshly ground black pepper
    Lettuce leaves

Brown ground beef in medium skillet. Drain.
Add mint and garlic; cook 2 minutes, stirring
constantly.

Spoon ground beef mixture into large bowl.
Stir in pasta, tomatoes, cheese, red bell
pepper and onion. Add dressing and lemon
juice; toss lightly. Season with salt and black
pepper to taste. Serve on lettuce-covered
salad plates. *Makes 4 servings*

NOTE: Salad can be made up to 4 hours in
advance.

136 THAI BEEF SALAD WITH CUCUMBER DRESSING

    Cucumber Dressing (page 113)
1 pound extra-lean (90% lean) ground
    beef
½ red bell pepper, cut into thin strips
6 mushrooms, quartered
2 green onions, diagonally cut into 1-inch
    pieces
1 clove garlic, minced
1 tablespoon seasoned rice vinegar
1 teaspoon soy sauce
    Salt and freshly ground black pepper
    Lettuce leaves
3 ounces ramen noodles, cooked
12 cherry tomatoes, halved
    Mint sprigs

Prepare Cucumber Dressing; set aside. Brown beef in medium skillet. Drain. Add red bell pepper, mushrooms, onions and garlic; cook until tender. Stir in vinegar and soy sauce; season with salt and black pepper to taste.

Arrange lettuce on four plates. Top with noodles and beef mixture. Garnish with tomatoes and mint. Serve with dressing.

Makes 4 servings

CUCUMBER DRESSING
   1 medium cucumber, coarsely chopped
   ¹/₂ cup coarsely chopped onion
   ¹/₂ cup loosely packed cilantro leaves
   1 clove garlic, minced
   1 tablespoon diced jalapeño or green chili pepper*
   ¹/₂ cup seasoned rice vinegar

*Jalapeño and chili peppers can sting and irritate the skin; wear rubber gloves when handling peppers and do not touch eyes. Wash hands after handling.

Place cucumber, onion, cilantro, garlic and jalapeño pepper in food processor container; process 1 minute. Spoon mixture into small bowl; stir in vinegar.

TIP: Cool cooked ramen noodles in bowl of iced water; drain well just before serving.

Thai Beef Salad with Cucumber Dressing

Hearty Soups &
Spicy Chilies

137 ALBÓNDIGAS

1 pound lean ground beef
½ small onion, finely chopped
1 egg
¼ cup dry bread crumbs
1 tablespoon chili powder
1 teaspoon ground cumin
½ teaspoon salt
3 cans (about 14 ounces each) chicken broth
1 medium carrot, thinly sliced
1 package (10 ounces) frozen corn or thawed frozen leaf spinach
¼ cup dry sherry

1. Mix ground beef, onion, egg, bread crumbs, chili powder, cumin and salt in medium bowl until well blended. Place mixture on lightly oiled cutting board; pat evenly into 1-inch-thick square. Cut into 36 squares with sharp knife; shape each square into a ball.

2. Place meatballs slightly apart in single layer in microwavable container. Cover and cook on HIGH 3 minutes or until meatballs are no longer pink (or just barely pink) in center.

3. While meatballs are cooking, bring broth and carrot to a boil in covered Dutch oven over high heat. Stir in corn and sherry. Transfer meatballs to broth with slotted spoon. Reduce heat to medium and simmer 3 to 4 minutes or until meatballs are cooked through. (Stir in spinach, if using, and simmer until heated through.)

Makes 6 servings

Prep and Cook Time: 30 minutes

NOTE: For a special touch, sprinkle soup with chopped fresh cilantro.

Albóndigas

138 ALL–IN–ONE BURGER STEW

1 pound lean ground beef
2 cups frozen Italian vegetables
1 can (14½ ounces) chopped tomatoes
  with basil and garlic
1 can (about 14 ounces) beef broth
2½ cups uncooked medium egg noodles

1. Cook meat in Dutch oven or large skillet over medium-high heat until no longer pink, breaking meat apart with wooden spoon. Drain drippings.

2. Add vegetables, tomatoes and broth; bring to a boil over high heat.

3. Add noodles; reduce heat to medium. Cover and cook 12 to 15 minutes or until noodles have absorbed liquid and vegetables are tender. Add salt and pepper to taste.

Makes 6 servings

Prep and Cook Time: 25 minutes

NOTE: For a special touch, sprinkle with chopped parsley before serving.

139 BEEFY BROCCOLI & CHEESE SOUP

2 cups chicken broth
1 package (10 ounces) frozen chopped
  broccoli, thawed
¼ cup chopped onion
¼ pound ground beef
1 cup milk
2 tablespoons all-purpose flour
4 ounces (1 cup) shredded sharp Cheddar
  cheese
1½ teaspoons chopped fresh oregano *or*
  ½ teaspoon dried oregano leaves
Salt and freshly ground pepper
Hot pepper sauce

Bring broth to a boil in medium saucepan. Add broccoli and onion; cook 5 minutes or until broccoli is tender.

Meanwhile, brown ground beef in small skillet; drain. Gradually add milk to flour, mixing until well blended. Add with ground beef to broth mixture; cook, stirring constantly, until mixture is thickened and bubbly.

Add cheese and oregano; stir until cheese is melted. Season with salt, pepper and hot pepper sauce to taste.

Makes 4 to 5 servings

All-in-One Burger Stew

140 ALBÓNDIGAS SOUP

1 pound ground beef
¼ cup long-grain rice
1 egg
1 tablespoon chopped fresh cilantro
1 teaspoon LAWRY'S® Seasoned Salt
¼ cup ice water
2 cans (14½ ounces each) chicken broth
1 can (14½ ounces) whole peeled
　　tomatoes, undrained and cut up
¼ cup chopped onion
1 stalk celery, diced
1 large carrot, diced
1 medium potato, diced
¼ teaspoon LAWRY'S® Garlic Powder with
　　Parsley

In medium bowl, combine ground beef, rice, egg, cilantro, Seasoned Salt and ice water; form into small meatballs. In large saucepan, combine broth, vegetables and Garlic Powder with Parsley. Bring to a boil; add meatballs. Reduce heat; cover and simmer 30 to 40 minutes, stirring occasionally.

Makes 6 to 8 servings

PRESENTATION: Serve with lemon wedges and warm tortillas.

HINT: For a lower salt version, use homemade chicken broth or low-sodium chicken broth.

141 SUPER BEEF AND BARLEY SOUP

1 pound ground beef
3 tablespoons vegetable oil (optional)
3 cups tomato vegetable juice
2 cups water
1 can (10¾ ounces) condensed cream of
　　celery soup
1 cup cooked pearled barley
1 cup shredded carrots
½ cup sliced celery
¼ cup sliced onion
½ teaspoon salt
¼ teaspoon pepper

In large saucepan, brown meat in oil (if desired); drain off fat. Add remaining ingredients. Bring to a boil; reduce heat to low. Simmer until carrots are tender, about 20 minutes.　　*Makes 4 servings*

Prep Time: 65 minutes

*Favorite recipe from **North Dakota Barley Council***

Albóndigas Soup

HEARTY SOUPS & SPICY CHILIES

142 TURKEY MEATBALL SOUP

1 pound ground turkey
2/3 cup matzo meal
1/4 cup EGG BEATERS® Healthy Real Egg Product
2 tablespoons FLEISCHMANN'S® Sweet Unsalted Spread
2 cloves garlic, minced
6 cups water
4 cups low-sodium tomato juice
1 1/2 cups uncooked tri-color pasta twists
2 large carrots, peeled and thinly sliced
2 large tomatoes, chopped
1 large onion, chopped
1 tablespoon Italian seasoning
1/2 teaspoon ground black pepper
1 (10-ounce) package frozen chopped spinach, thawed

In small bowl, thoroughly mix turkey, matzo meal and egg product. Shape into 24 (1-inch) meatballs. In large saucepan over medium-high heat, brown meatballs, in batches, in spread. Remove meatballs. In same saucepan, cook and stir garlic for 3 minutes or until lightly browned. Add water, tomato juice, meatballs, pasta, carrots, tomatoes, onion, Italian seasoning and pepper. Heat to a boil. Cover; reduce heat. Simmer 15 minutes. Add spinach; cook an additional 5 minutes or until pasta is tender.

Makes 10 (1½-cup) servings

143 ITALIAN TOMATO SOUP

1/2 pound lean ground beef
1/2 cup chopped onion
1 clove garlic, minced
1 can (28 ounces) tomatoes, undrained, cut into pieces
1 can (15 ounces) white kidney beans, drained, rinsed
3/4 cup HEINZ® Tomato Ketchup
1/2 cup thinly sliced carrots
1 teaspoon dried basil leaves
1/4 teaspoon salt

In medium saucepan, brown beef, onion and garlic; drain excess fat. Add tomatoes and remaining ingredients. Cover; simmer 15 minutes.

Makes 4 to 6 servings (about 6 cups)

HEARTY SOUPS & SPICY CHILIES

144 QUICK ITALIAN BEEF & VEGETABLE SOUP

1 pound lean ground beef
1 large clove garlic, crushed
½ teaspoon pepper
¼ teaspoon salt
2 cans (13¾ to 14½ ounces each) ready-to-serve beef broth
1 can (14½ ounces) Italian-style stewed tomatoes, undrained, broken up
1 cup sliced (¼-inch-thick) carrots
1 can (15 to 19 ounces) cannellini (white kidney) or Great Northern beans, rinsed, drained
1 medium zucchini, cut lengthwise in half and crosswise into ¼-inch-thick slices
2 cups torn spinach leaves, lightly packed

1. Heat Dutch oven or large saucepan over medium heat until hot. Add ground beef and garlic; brown 4 to 5 minutes, breaking beef up into ¾-inch crumbles. Pour off drippings. Season beef with pepper and salt.

2. Stir broth, tomatoes and carrots into beef. Bring to a boil; reduce heat to low. Simmer, uncovered, 10 minutes. Stir in beans and zucchini; continue to cook 4 to 5 minutes or until zucchini is crisp-tender. Remove from heat; stir in spinach. Garnish as desired.
Makes 4 servings (serving size: 2 cups)

Total Prep and Cook Time: 30 minutes

*Favorite recipe from **National Cattlemen's Beef Association***

Quick Italian Beef & Vegetable Soup

145 QUICK BEEF SOUP

1½ pounds lean ground beef
1 cup chopped onion
2 cloves garlic, finely chopped
1 can (28 ounces) tomatoes, undrained
6 cups water
6 beef bouillon cubes
¼ teaspoon pepper
½ cup uncooked orzo
1½ cups frozen peas, carrots and corn
      vegetable blend
      French bread (optional)

Cook beef, onion and garlic in large saucepan over medium-high heat until beef is brown, stirring to separate meat; drain fat.

Purée tomatoes with juice in covered blender or food processor. Add tomatoes, water, bouillon cubes and pepper to meat mixture. Bring to a boil; reduce heat to low. Simmer, uncovered, 20 minutes. Add orzo and vegetables. Simmer 15 minutes more. Serve with French bread.

Makes 6 servings

Favorite recipe from **North Dakota Beef Commission**

146 WILD RICE SOUP

½ cup uncooked wild rice
1 pound lean ground beef
1 can (14½ ounces) chicken broth
1 can (10¾ ounces) condensed cream of
      mushroom soup
2 cups milk
1 cup (4 ounces) shredded Cheddar
      cheese
⅓ cup shredded carrot
1 package (.4 ounce) HIDDEN VALLEY
      RANCH® Buttermilk Recipe Original
      Ranch® salad dressing mix
      Chopped green onions with tops

Cook rice according to package directions to make about 1½ cups cooked rice. In Dutch oven or large saucepan, brown beef; drain off excess fat. Stir in rice, chicken broth, cream of mushroom soup, milk, cheese, carrot and dry salad dressing mix. Heat to a simmer over low heat, stirring occasionally, about 15 minutes. Serve in warmed soup bowls; top with green onions. Garnish with additional green onions, if desired.

Makes 6 to 8 servings

Quick Beef Soup

HEARTY SOUPS & SPICY CHILIES

147 HANOI BEEF AND RICE SOUP

1½ **pounds ground beef chuck**
2 **tablespoons cold water**
2 **tablespoons soy sauce**
2 **teaspoons sugar**
2 **teaspoons cornstarch**
2 **teaspoons lime juice**
½ **teaspoon ground black pepper**
2 **cloves garlic, minced**
2 **teaspoons fennel seeds**
1 **teaspoon anise seeds**
1 **cinnamon stick (3 inches long)**
2 **bay leaves**
6 **whole cloves**
1 **tablespoon vegetable oil**
1 **cup uncooked long-grain white rice**
1 **tablespoon minced fresh ginger**
1 **medium yellow onion, peeled, sliced and separated into rings**
4 **cans (13¾ ounces each) beef broth**
2 **cups water**
½ **pound fresh snow peas (Chinese pea pods), stemmed and cut diagonally in half**

Combine beef, 2 tablespoons water, soy sauce, sugar, cornstarch, lime juice, black pepper and garlic in large bowl; mix well. Place meat mixture on lightly oiled cutting board; pat evenly into 1-inch-thick square. Cut meat into 36 squares; shape each square into a ball.

Bring 4 inches water to a boil in wok over high heat. Add meatballs and return water to boiling. Cook meatballs 3 to 4 minutes until firm, stirring occasionally. Transfer meatballs to bowl with slotted spoon. Discard water.

Place fennel seeds, anise seeds, cinnamon, bay leaves and cloves on 12-inch double-thick square of dampened cheesecloth. Tie with string into spice bag; set aside.

Heat wok over medium heat 1 minute or until hot. Drizzle oil into wok and heat 30 seconds. Add rice; cook and stir 3 to 4 minutes or until lightly browned. Add ginger and onion. Stir-fry 1 minute. Add broth, 2 cups water and spice bag. Cover and bring to a boil. Reduce heat to low; simmer 25 minutes. Remove spice bag and discard. Add meatballs and snow peas to soup in wok. Cook and stir until heated through. Ladle soup into tureen or individual serving bowls. Garnish as desired.

Makes 6 main-dish servings

Hanoi Beef and Rice Soup

HEARTY SOUPS & SPICY CHILIES

148 KANSAS CITY STEAK SOUP

½ pound ground sirloin or ground round beef
1 cup chopped onion
3 cups frozen mixed vegetables
2 cups water
1 can (14½ ounces) stewed tomatoes, undrained
1 cup sliced celery
1 beef bouillon cube
½ to 1 teaspoon ground black pepper
1 can (10½ ounces) defatted beef broth
½ cup all-purpose flour

1. Spray Dutch oven with nonstick cooking spray. Heat over medium-high heat until hot. Add beef and onion. Cook and stir 5 minutes or until beef is browned.

2. Add mixed vegetables, water, tomatoes, celery, bouillon cube and pepper. Bring to a boil. Whisk beef broth into flour until smooth; add to beef mixture, stirring constantly. Return mixture to a boil. Reduce heat to low. Cover and simmer 15 minutes, stirring frequently.   *Makes 6 servings*

NOTE: If time permits, allow the soup to simmer an additional 30 minutes—the flavors just get better and better.

149 SPICY TORTILLA SOUP

½ pound lean ground pork
½ cup chopped onion
4 cups canned crushed tomatoes
2 cups chicken broth
1 (8-ounce) jar salsa, medium or hot
1 teaspoon ground cumin
1 teaspoon chili powder
½ teaspoon salt
½ teaspoon garlic powder
½ teaspoon ground black pepper
4 corn tortillas, cut into thin strips

Brown pork and onion over medium-high heat in large saucepan, stirring occasionally. Drain any excess drippings. Add remaining ingredients except tortilla strips. Cover and simmer 20 minutes. Stir tortilla strips into soup and simmer 5 to 10 minutes more, until tortilla strips are softened. Serve hot.

Makes 6 servings

Prep Time: 10 minutes
Cook Time: 20 minutes

*Favorite recipe from **National Pork Producers Council***

Kansas City Steak Soup

HEARTY SOUPS & SPICY CHILIES

150 TACO SOUP

Nonstick cooking spray
½ pound ground sirloin or ground round beef
1 cup chopped onion
1 can (16 ounces) pinto beans in Mexican-style sauce
1 can (about 14 ounces) no-salt-added stewed tomatoes
1 can (10 ounces) diced tomatoes and green chilies
2 teaspoons chili powder
5 (8-inch) corn tortillas
5 cups shredded iceberg lettuce
½ cup shredded low-sodium, reduced-fat sharp Cheddar cheese
¼ cup chopped cilantro (optional)

1. Preheat oven to 350°F. Spray large saucepan with cooking spray. Heat over medium-high heat until hot. Add beef and onion. Cook and stir 6 minutes or until beef is browned. Add beans, stewed tomatoes, diced tomatoes and green chilies and chili powder. Bring to a boil. Reduce heat to low. Cover and simmer 10 minutes.

2. Place tortillas on a baking sheet. Spray tortillas lightly on both sides with cooking spray. Using pizza cutter, cut each tortilla into 6 wedges. Bake 5 minutes.

3. Divide lettuce equally among soup bowls. Ladle beef mixture over lettuce. Top with cheese and cilantro. Serve with tortilla wedges. *Makes 5 servings*

Prep and Cook Time: 25 minutes

151 MEXICAN PORK AND BEAN SOUP

½ pound lean ground pork
1 small onion, diced
1 clove garlic, minced
1 (15-ounce) can pinto beans, drained
1 (14½-ounce) can chicken broth
1 (14½-ounce) can Mexican-style chopped tomatoes
1 teaspoon chili powder
1 teaspoon ground cumin
½ teaspoon dried oregano leaves
½ teaspoon salt
¼ teaspoon cayenne pepper

In large heavy saucepan brown and crumble ground pork. Stir in onion and garlic; cook and stir until onion is soft, about 3 minutes. Drain any excess drippings. Stir in all remaining ingredients. Bring to a boil, lower heat and simmer about 10 minutes.
Makes six 1-cup servings

Prep Time: 15 minutes

*Favorite recipe from **National Pork Producers Council***

Taco Soup

152 FARMER'S STEW ARGENTINA

3 cups water
1 pound lean ground beef
2 tablespoons vegetable oil
1 medium onion, chopped
1 green bell pepper, cut into ½-inch
    pieces
1 red bell pepper, cut into ½-inch pieces
1 small sweet potato, peeled and cut into
    ½-inch pieces
1 large clove garlic, minced
1 tablespoon chopped fresh parsley
1 teaspoon salt
½ teaspoon granulated sugar
⅛ teaspoon ground cumin
3 cups beef broth, heated
½ pound zucchini, cut into ½-inch pieces
1 cup whole kernel corn
2 tablespoons raisins
½ teaspoon TABASCO® pepper sauce
1 small pear, firm but ripe, cut into 1-inch
    pieces
6 cups cooked white rice

In large saucepan bring water to a boil. Remove saucepan from heat. Add ground beef, stirring to break meat into little pieces. Let stand 5 minutes, stirring once or twice, until most of the pink disappears from meat. Drain meat well, discarding water.

In large deep skillet or Dutch oven, heat oil over medium-high heat. Add onion and cook 4 to 5 minutes, stirring constantly, until limp and slightly brown. Add beef. Continue cooking, stirring constantly, until all liquid has evaporated from pan and meat is lightly browned, about 10 minutes.

Reduce heat to medium. Add bell peppers, sweet potato and garlic. Continue cooking and stirring 5 minutes, or until peppers and potatoes are slightly tender. Add parsley, salt, sugar and cumin. Stir and cook 1 minute to blend flavors. Pour beef broth into skillet. Add zucchini, corn, raisins and Tabasco® sauce. Simmer gently 10 minutes, being careful not to boil. Add pear and simmer 10 additional minutes, or until all fruits and vegetables are tender. Ladle over rice in individual serving bowls.

Makes 6 servings

153 RAVIOLI SOUP

¾ pound hot Italian sausage, crumbled and
    cooked
1 can (14½ ounces) DEL MONTE® Italian
    Recipe Stewed Tomatoes
1 can (14 ounces) beef broth
1 package (9 ounces) fresh or frozen
    cheese ravioli or tortellini, cooked
    and drained
1 can (14½ ounces) DEL MONTE®
    FreshCut™ Cut Green Italian Beans,
    drained
2 green onions, sliced

1. In 5-quart pot, combine sausage, tomatoes, broth and 1¾ cups water; bring to a boil over high heat.

2. Reduce heat to low; stir in ravioli, green beans and onions. Gently cook until ravioli are heated through. Season with pepper and sprinkle with grated Parmesan cheese, if desired.

Makes 4 servings (about 2½ cups each)

Prep & Cook Time: 15 minutes

Ravioli Soup

HEARTY SOUPS & SPICY CHILIES

154 MEXICAN BEEF SOUP IN TORTILLA BOWLS

1½ pounds lean ground beef
1 large onion, cut lengthwise in half and
  cut crosswise into thin slices
1 tablespoon ground cumin
¼ teaspoon pepper
2 cans (10½ ounces each) condensed beef
  consommé
1 can (15¼ ounces) whole kernel corn,
  drained
1 can (10 ounces) diced tomatoes with
  green chilies, undrained
1 cup water
6 medium (8 inches) flour tortillas
2 tablespoons chopped fresh cilantro

1. Heat Dutch oven or large saucepan over medium heat until hot. Add ground beef and onion; brown 4 to 5 minutes, breaking beef up into ¾-inch crumbles. Pour off drippings. Season beef with cumin and pepper.

2. Stir consommé, corn, tomatoes and water into beef. Bring to a boil; reduce heat to low. Simmer, uncovered, 10 minutes.

3. Meanwhile gently press tortillas into 6 individual microwave-safe (2-cup) soup bowls. Microwave, 3 bowls at a time, on HIGH 5 to 6 minutes or until tortillas are slightly crisp, rotating and rearranging cups halfway.

4. Stir cilantro into soup; spoon soup into tortilla bowls. Garnish as desired; serve immediately.
  Makes 6 servings (serving size: 1⅓ cups)

Total Prep and Cook Time: 25 minutes

COOK'S TIP: Tortilla chips may be substituted for tortilla bowls. Spoon soup into 4 individual soup bowls; serve with tortilla chips.

*Favorite recipe from **National Cattlemen's Beef Association***

Mexican Beef Soup in Tortilla Bowls

HEARTY SOUPS & SPICY CHILIES

155 6–WAY CHILI

1 pound lean ground beef
1 medium onion, chopped
2 cloves garlic, minced
1 can (14½ ounces) Italian-style tomatoes, drained, coarsely chopped
1 can (14½ ounces) beef broth
1 to 2 tablespoons chili powder
½ teaspoon ground turmeric
½ teaspoon ground cumin
½ teaspoon ground allspice
½ teaspoon black pepper
8 ounces uncooked spaghetti
½ ounce unsweetened chocolate, finely chopped
1 can (15½ ounces) red kidney beans, drained
2 cans (4 ounces each) sliced mushrooms, drained
4 green onions, chopped
1 cup (4 ounces) shredded Cheddar cheese

Brown beef in medium saucepan over medium-high heat; drain fat. Add onion and garlic; cook over medium heat 5 minutes or until onion is tender. Stir in tomatoes, broth, chili powder, turmeric, cumin, allspice and black pepper. Bring to a boil; reduce heat and simmer, covered, 20 minutes.

Prepare spaghetti according to package directions. Keep warm. Uncover chili; simmer 10 minutes or until thickened. Remove from heat; add chocolate, stirring until melted.

Arrange spaghetti, beans, mushrooms, green onions and cheese in separate bowls. Serve chili over spaghetti; top with beans, mushrooms, green onions and cheese, if desired. *Makes 4 to 6 servings*

Favorite recipe from Canned Food Information Council

156 FIX–IT–FAST CHILI

½ pound ground beef
¾ cup chopped onion
½ teaspoon finely chopped garlic
1 can (14½ ounces) whole peeled tomatoes, undrained and chopped
1 cup water
1 package LIPTON® Rice & Sauce— Spanish
2 teaspoons chili powder
½ teaspoon ground cumin (optional)
1 cup red kidney beans, rinsed and drained

In 12-inch skillet, cook ground beef, onion and garlic over medium-high heat, stirring occasionally, 5 minutes or until browned; drain. Stir in tomatoes, water, rice & sauce— Spanish, chili powder and cumin and bring to a boil. Reduce heat and simmer, stirring occasionally, 10 minutes or until rice is tender. Stir in beans and heat through. Top, if desired, with shredded cheddar cheese and crumbled corn muffins.

Makes about 4 servings

MICROWAVE DIRECTIONS: In 1½-quart microwave-safe casserole, microwave ground beef, onion and garlic, uncovered, at HIGH (100% power) 5 minutes or until ground beef is browned, stirring once; drain. Stir in tomatoes, water, rice & sauce— Spanish, chili powder and cumin. Microwave at HIGH 10 minutes or until rice is tender. Stir in beans. Let stand covered 5 minutes. Top as above.

HEARTY SOUPS & SPICY CHILIES

157 NELL'S CHILI CON CARNE

2 tablespoons vegetable oil
2 cups diced onions
1 green bell pepper, seeded and chopped
3 cloves garlic, minced
2 pounds lean, coarsely ground beef
2 cups dried kidney beans, soaked overnight
1 jar (32 ounces) NEWMAN'S OWN® Spaghetti Sauce
2 to 3 cups water
2 to 3 tablespoons chili powder
1 teaspoon ground cumin
Salt and black pepper
1 cup chopped celery
1 can (8¾ ounces) whole kernel corn, drained
Sour cream and lime wedges (optional)

Heat oil in Dutch oven over medium-high heat. Add onions, bell pepper and garlic; cook and stir until vegetables are tender. Add beef; cook until browned. Add kidney beans, Newman's Own® Spaghetti Sauce, water, chili powder, cumin, salt and black pepper to taste. Simmer, uncovered, 1 hour, stirring frequently. Add celery and corn and simmer 1 hour. Garnish with sour cream and lime wedges, if desired.

Makes 8 servings

NOTE: Three cups of cooked rice can be substituted for meat to make vegetarian chili.

158 CAMPFIRE 7-SPICE CHILI & JOHNNY CAKE

1 package (8.5 ounces) corn muffin mix
¼ cup chopped pimiento (optional)
¼ cup shredded Cheddar or Monterey Jack cheese (optional)
1 jar (16 ounces) Original or Spicy TABASCO® 7-Spice Chili Recipe
1 pound ground beef
¾ cup water, tomato juice or beer

Grease large cast iron skillet. Prepare corn muffin mix according to package directions, adding pimiento and cheese, if desired.

Pour mixture into skillet; cover with aluminum foil and place directly in campfire embers. Cook 15 minutes (checking often) or until golden brown.

Remove from heat. Let stand 5 minutes before removing from skillet. Wrap in aluminum foil while preparing chili.

In same skillet, prepare chili with ground beef and water according to directions on jar.

Slice corn bread into 4 to 6 servings and serve with chili.   *Makes 4 to 6 servings*

HEARTY SOUPS & SPICY CHILIES

159 RIVERBOAT CHILI

2 pounds lean ground beef
2 large onions, chopped
1 large green pepper, chopped
2 cans (14.5 ounces each) FRANK'S or SnowFloss Original Style Diced Tomatoes, undrained
1 can (14.5 ounces) FRANK'S or SnowFloss Stewed Tomatoes, undrained
1/3 cup MISSISSIPPI Barbecue Sauce
2 bay leaves
3 whole cloves
2 teaspoons chili powder
1/2 teaspoon cayenne pepper
1/2 teaspoon paprika
4 cans (15.5 ounces each) dark red kidney beans

1. Brown ground beef in large stock pot. Drain grease.

2. Add onions, green pepper, diced tomatoes, stewed tomatoes, barbecue sauce, bay leaves, cloves, chili powder, cayenne pepper and paprika. Stir well.

3. Add kidney beans and stir well.

4. Cover and simmer 2 hours, stirring occasionally.   *Makes 4 to 6 servings*

MICROWAVE DIRECTIONS: 1. Crumble beef into large casserole dish. Cook uncovered about 6 minutes stirring at least twice to break up meat. Drain grease.

2. Add onions, green pepper, diced tomatoes, stewed tomatoes, barbecue sauce, bay leaves, cloves, chili powder, cayenne pepper and paprika. Cook 1 minute. Stir well.

3. Add kidney beans and stir well.

4. Cover and cook 15 to 20 minutes, stirring occasionally.

5. Cover and let stand 5 minutes.

Prep Time: 30 minutes
Cook Time: 2 hours

160 ALL–AMERICAN CHILI

1 pound ground beef
1/3 cup chopped onion
1/3 cup chopped green pepper
2 cans (15 ounces each) chili beans in sauce
1 can (14 1/2 ounces) stewed tomatoes
1 clove garlic, minced
1 can (15 ounces) VEG-ALL® Mixed Vegetables, undrained

1. In 3-quart saucepan, cook ground beef, onion and green pepper. Drain.

2. Add chili beans, stewed tomatoes and garlic. Bring to a boil; cover, reduce heat and simmer 30 minutes.

3. Stir in Veg-All® Mixed Vegetables and cook 10 minutes longer.

Makes 6 servings

161 QUICK CHUNKY CHILI

1 pound lean ground beef
1 medium onion, chopped
1 tablespoon chili powder
1½ teaspoons ground cumin
2 cans (14½ ounces each) diced tomatoes, undrained
1 can (15 ounces) pinto beans, drained
½ cup prepared salsa
½ cup (2 ounces) shredded Cheddar cheese
3 tablespoons sour cream
4 teaspoons sliced black olives

Combine meat and onion in 3-quart saucepan; cook over high heat until meat is no longer pink, breaking meat apart with wooden spoon. Add chili powder and cumin; stir 1 minute or until fragrant. Add tomatoes, beans and salsa. Bring to a boil; stir constantly. Reduce heat to low; simmer, covered, 10 minutes. Ladle into bowls. Top with cheese, sour cream and olives.

Makes 4 (1½-cup) servings

Prep and Cook Time: 25 minutes

162 TEXAS–STYLE CHILI

1½ pounds ground beef or cubed round steak
1 tablespoon vegetable oil
1 green bell pepper, diced
1 onion, diced
1 can (2.25 ounces) diced green chilies, drained
1 package (1.48 ounces) LAWRY'S® Spices & Seasonings for Chili
1½ tablespoons cornmeal
1 tablespoon chili powder
1 teaspoon sugar
¼ teaspoon cayenne pepper
1 can (14½ ounces) diced tomatoes, undrained
¾ cup water
Sour cream (optional)
Shredded Cheddar cheese (optional)

In Dutch oven or large saucepan, brown beef in oil until crumbly. Drain beef, reserving fat; set beef aside. Add bell pepper and onion to Dutch oven; sauté 5 minutes or until vegetables are crisp-tender. Return beef to Dutch oven. Add chilies, Spices & Seasonings for Chili, cornmeal, chili powder, sugar and cayenne pepper; blend well. Stir in tomatoes and water. Bring to a boil. Reduce heat to low; cover. Simmer 30 minutes, stirring occasionally. Serve topped with sour cream or Cheddar cheese, if desired.

Makes 4½ cups

HINT: This recipe is perfect for leftover meat. Use 3½ cups shredded beef.

Quick Chunky Chili

163 MEATY CHILI

1 pound coarsely ground beef
¼ pound ground Italian sausage
2 medium ribs celery, diced
1 large onion, chopped
2 cloves garlic, minced
2 fresh jalapeño peppers*, chopped
1 can (28 ounces) whole peeled tomatoes, undrained, cut up
1 can (15 ounces) pinto beans, drained
1 can (12 ounces) tomato juice
1 cup water
¼ cup ketchup
1 teaspoon sugar
1 teaspoon chili powder
½ teaspoon salt
½ teaspoon ground cumin
½ teaspoon dried thyme leaves
⅛ teaspoon ground black pepper

Jalapeño peppers can sting and irritate the skin; wear rubber gloves when handling peppers and do not touch eyes. Wash your hands after handling.

Cook beef, sausage, celery, onion, garlic and jalapeño peppers in 5-quart Dutch oven over medium-high heat until meat is browned and onion is tender, stirring frequently. Drain.

Stir in tomatoes, beans, tomato juice, water, ketchup, sugar, chili powder, salt, cumin, thyme and black pepper. Bring to a boil over high heat. Reduce heat to medium-low; simmer, uncovered, 30 minutes, stirring occasionally.

Ladle into bowls. Garnish, if desired.

Makes 6 servings

164 TEXAS CHILI & BISCUITS

1 pound ground beef
1 package (about 1¾ ounces) chili seasoning mix
1 can (16 ounces) whole kernel corn, drained
1 can (14½ ounces) whole tomatoes, undrained and cut up
½ cup water
¾ cup biscuit baking mix
⅔ cup cornmeal
⅔ cup milk
1⅓ cups (2.8-ounce can) FRENCH'S® French Fried Onions, divided
½ cup (2 ounces) shredded Monterey Jack cheese

Preheat oven to 400°F. In medium skillet, brown beef; drain. Stir in chili seasoning, corn, tomatoes and water; bring to a boil. Reduce heat; simmer, uncovered, 10 minutes. Meanwhile, in medium bowl, combine baking mix, cornmeal, milk and ⅔ *cup* French Fried Onions; beat vigorously 30 seconds. Pour beef mixture into 2-quart casserole. Spoon biscuit dough in mounds around edge of casserole. Bake, uncovered, at 400°F for 15 minutes or until biscuits are light brown. Top biscuits with cheese and remaining ⅔ *cup* onions; bake, uncovered, 1 to 3 minutes or until onions are golden brown. *Makes 4 to 6 servings*

Meaty Chili

165 CHAMPIONSHIP CHILI

1 pound lean ground beef
½ cup chopped onion
½ cup chopped green bell pepper
¼ cup chopped celery
2 cans (15½ ounces each) light or dark
   red kidney beans, drained
1 can (14½ ounces) stewed tomatoes,
   undrained
1 cup tomato juice
1 package (1¼ ounces) chili seasoning mix

Cook beef, onion, green pepper and celery in
large saucepan over medium-high heat until
browned and vegetables are tender. Drain
excess fat. Stir in beans, tomatoes, tomato
juice and seasoning mix. Cover and simmer
30 minutes. Serve. *Makes 6 servings*

*Favorite recipe from **Canned Food Information
Council***

166 CHILI WITH RICE

1 pound lean ground beef
1 can (15½ ounces) kidney beans,
   undrained
1 can (15 ounces) tomato sauce
1 package (1¾ ounces) chili seasoning mix
2 cups MINUTE® Original Rice, uncooked
1 cup (4 ounces) shredded KRAFT®
   Natural Cheddar Cheese

1. BROWN meat in large skillet on medium
heat; drain.

2. ADD 2 cups water, kidney beans, tomato
sauce and seasoning mix. Bring to boil.

3. STIR in Minute® Rice. Sprinkle with
cheese; cover. Cook on low heat 5 minutes.
Makes 6 servings

Cook Time: 15 minutes

167 TWO–BEAN CHILI

1 pound sweet Italian sausage, removed
   from casing
1 pound ground beef
2 medium onions, chopped
1 large green bell pepper, chopped
3 cloves garlic, minced
¼ cup all-purpose flour
3 tablespoons chili powder
2 teaspoons ground cumin
2 teaspoons dried basil leaves
2 teaspoons dried oregano leaves
1 teaspoon salt
2 cans (28 ounces each) Italian-style
   tomatoes, undrained
3 tablespoons Worcestershire sauce
1¼ teaspoons TABASCO® pepper sauce
1 can (20 ounces) chick-peas, drained
1 can (15½ ounces) red kidney beans,
   drained
   Sliced ripe olives, chopped onion,
   chopped green bell pepper, chopped
   tomato, shredded cheese and cooked
   rice (optional)

In large heavy saucepan or Dutch oven, cook
sausage, beef, onions, bell pepper and garlic
about 20 minutes or until meats are browned
and vegetables are tender; drain fat. Stir in
flour, chili powder, cumin, basil, oregano and
salt; cook 1 minute. Add tomatoes; break up
with fork. Stir in Worcestershire sauce and
TABASCO® sauce. Cover and simmer 1 hour,
adding water if necessary; stir occasionally.
Stir in chick-peas and kidney beans. Cook
until heated through. Serve with olives,
onion, bell pepper, tomato, cheese and rice,
if desired. *Makes 8 servings*

168 QUICK AND SPICY PORK CHILI

1 pound ground pork
1 medium onion, coarsely chopped
1 clove garlic, minced
1 (14½-ounce) can kidney beans, drained
1 (14½-ounce) can Mexican-style diced tomatoes
1 (8-ounce) can tomato sauce
1 (8-ounce) can whole kernel corn, drained
2 tablespoons chili powder
1 tablespoon ground cumin
1 teaspoon salt
½ teaspoon black pepper

In large saucepan, cook and stir pork with onion and garlic until pork is cooked, about 6 minutes. Stir in remaining ingredients; bring to a boil. Cover and simmer 15 minutes, until flavors are blended and chili is hot. Serve with shredded Cheddar cheese and warmed flour tortillas, if desired.

Makes 6 servings

Prep Time: 10 minutes
Cook Time: 15 minutes

Favorite recipe from **National Pork Producers Council**

169 SOUL CITY CHILI

1 pound hot Italian sausage or kielbasa sausage
2 pounds ground beef
½ teaspoon LAWRY'S® Seasoned Salt
½ teaspoon LAWRY'S® Seasoned Pepper
2 cups water
1 can (15¼ ounces) kidney beans, undrained
1 can (14½ ounces) stewed tomatoes, undrained
2 packages (1.48 ounces each) LAWRY'S® Spices & Seasonings for Chili
½ cup hickory flavored barbecue sauce
¾ cup red wine

Place sausage in broiler; broil 7 minutes. In Dutch oven, brown beef; drain fat. Add Seasoned Salt and Seasoned Pepper; blend well. Stir in water, beans, tomatoes, Spices & Seasonings for Chili and barbecue sauce. Bring to a boil. Reduce heat; simmer, uncovered, 20 minutes. Meanwhile, cut sausage into bite-sized pieces and add to chili mixture. Stir in wine. Heat through.

Makes about 10 servings (9½ cups)

PRESENTATION: Top with diced green, yellow and red bell peppers and chopped onion. Perfect with crackers, too!

170 GLENN'S MAGIC CHILI

2½ pounds lean, coarsely ground beef
2 tablespoons CHEF PAUL
   PRUDHOMME'S Meat Magic®
2 tablespoons chili powder
1 tablespoon dried oregano leaves
1½ teaspoons ground cumin
1 teaspoon salt
2 cups chopped peeled tomatoes
2 cups minced onions
4 cups beef stock or water, divided
2 teaspoons minced garlic
1½ teaspoons CHEF PAUL PRUDHOMME'S
   Magic Pepper Sauce™
6 whole jalapeño peppers with stems,
   about 4 ounces*
1 tablespoon corn flour or all-purpose
   flour
2 cups cooked pinto or red beans
   (optional)

*If fresh jalapeños are unavailable, use jarred
jalapeño peppers, thoroughly rinsed and drained.
For a spicier chili, chop jalapeños before adding.*

In 4-quart saucepan, combine beef, Meat
Magic®, chili powder, oregano, cumin and
salt; stir well. Cover; cook over high heat 4
minutes. Stir well; re-cover and cook 1
minute. Stir in tomatoes and onions;
re-cover and cook 10 minutes, stirring
occasionally and scraping saucepan bottom
well each time. Add 2 cups beef stock, garlic
and Magic Pepper Sauce™, stirring well. Stir
in jalapeños. Bring to a boil; reduce heat to
low. Simmer 1 hour, stirring and scraping
saucepan bottom occasionally. Remove any
fat from top of chili mixture. In small bowl,
stir together flour and 2 tablespoons liquid
from chili mixture until well blended.

Add flour mixture, 1 cup beef stock and
beans to chili mixture, stirring well. Simmer
40 minutes, stirring frequently. Add
remaining 1 cup beef stock; cook and stir
20 minutes. Serve hot in bowls. Garnish as
desired.   *Makes 4 to 5 servings*

NOTE: If you make this a day ahead, remove
jalapeños and reserve. Add to chili before
reheating.

171 CHILI À LA MEXICO

2 pounds ground beef
2 cups finely chopped onions
2 cloves garlic, minced
1 can (28 ounces) whole peeled tomatoes,
   undrained, coarsely chopped
1 can (6 ounces) tomato paste
1½ to 2 tablespoons chili powder
1 teaspoon ground cumin
¼ teaspoon salt
¼ teaspoon ground red pepper (optional)
¼ teaspoon ground cloves (optional)
   Lime wedges and cilantro sprigs, for
   garnish

Brown beef in deep 12-inch skillet over
medium-high heat 6 to 8 minutes, stirring to
separate meat. Reduce heat to medium. Pour
off drippings. Add onions and garlic; cook
and stir 5 minutes or until onions are
softened.

Stir in tomatoes, tomato paste, chili powder,
cumin, salt, red pepper and cloves. Bring to
a boil over high heat. Reduce heat to low.
Cover and simmer 30 minutes, stirring
occasionally. Ladle into bowls. Garnish with
lime wedges and cilantro.
                        Makes 6 to 8 servings

Chili à la Mexico

172 CHILI

2 tablespoons vegetable oil
2 pounds ground beef
2 cups finely chopped white onions
1 to 2 dried de arbol chilies
2 cloves garlic, minced
1 teaspoon ground cumin
½ to 1 teaspoon salt
¼ teaspoon ground cloves
1 can (28 ounces) whole peeled tomatoes,
    undrained, coarsely chopped
½ cup fresh orange juice
½ cup tequila or water
¼ cup tomato paste
1 tablespoon grated orange peel
    Lime wedges and cilantro sprigs
    (optional)

Heat oil in deep 12-inch skillet over medium-high heat until hot. Crumble beef into skillet. Brown 6 to 8 minutes, stirring occasionally. Pour off drippings. Reduce heat to medium. Add onions; cook and stir 5 minutes or until tender.

Crush chilies into fine flakes in mortar with pestle. Add chilies, garlic, cumin, salt and cloves to skillet. Cook and stir 30 seconds.

Stir in tomatoes, orange juice, tequila, tomato paste and orange peel. Bring to a boil over high heat. Reduce heat to low. Cover and simmer 1½ hours, stirring occasionally.

Uncover skillet. Cook chili over medium-low heat 10 to 15 minutes or until thickened slightly, stirring frequently. Ladle into bowls. Garnish with lime wedges and cilantro if desired. *Makes 6 to 8 servings*

173 FAST 'N EASY CHILI

1½ pounds ground beef
1 can (15 to 19 ounces) red kidney or
    black beans, drained
1½ cups water
1 can (8 ounces) tomato sauce
1 envelope LIPTON® Recipe Secrets® Beefy
    Mushroom Soup Mix*
1 tablespoon chili powder

Also terrific with Lipton® Recipe Secrets® Onion, Onion-Mushroom or Beefy Onion Soup Mix.

• In 12-inch skillet, brown ground beef over medium-high heat; drain.

• Stir in remaining ingredients. Bring to a boil over high heat.

• Reduce heat to low and simmer covered, stirring occasionally, 20 minutes.

• Serve, if desired, over hot cooked rice.
Makes about 6 servings

VARIATIONS

FIRST ALARM CHILI: Add 4 teaspoons chili powder.

SECOND ALARM CHILI: Add 2 tablespoons chili powder.

THIRD ALARM CHILI: Add chili powder at your own risk.

174 7–SPICE CHILI WITH CORN BREAD TOPPING

1 pound ground turkey or lean beef
1 jar (16 ounces) Original or Spicy
    TABASCO® 7-Spice Chili Recipe
1 can (15.5 ounces) kidney beans, rinsed
    and drained
¾ cup water
1 package (12 ounces) corn muffin mix
1 can (7 ounces) whole kernel corn with
    sweet green and red peppers, drained
1 cup (4 ounces) shredded Cheddar
    cheese

In large skillet, brown turkey; drain. Stir in 7-Spice Chili Recipe, beans and water. Bring to a boil; reduce heat. Simmer 10 minutes.

Divide evenly among 6 (12-ounce) individual ramekins.

Meanwhile, prepare corn muffin mix according to package directions. Stir in corn and cheese until well blended.

Pour about ½ cup muffin mixture over top of each ramekin. Bake at 400°F 15 minutes or until corn bread topping is golden brown.

Makes 6 servings

7-Spice Chili with Corn Bread Topping

HEARTY SOUPS & SPICY CHILIES

175 CINCINNATI CHILI

1½ pounds ground beef*
 1 envelope LIPTON® Recipe Secrets®
    Onion Soup Mix**
 1 can (28 ounces) whole peeled tomatoes,
    undrained and chopped
 1 tablespoon chili powder
 ¼ teaspoon ground cinnamon
 ½ ounce (½ of 1-ounce square)
    unsweetened chocolate, chopped
 8 ounces spaghetti, cooked and drained

*Can substitute ground turkey for beef.

**Also terrific with Lipton® Recipe Secrets® Onion-Mushroom Soup Mix.

In 12-inch skillet, brown ground beef over medium-high heat; drain. Stir in onion soup mix blended with tomatoes, chili powder and cinnamon. Bring to a boil over high heat. Reduce heat to low and simmer uncovered, stirring occasionally, 15 minutes. Stir in chocolate until melted. Serve over hot spaghetti and, if desired, with shredded cheddar cheese, red kidney beans, chopped onion and oyster crackers.

Makes about 6 servings

176 CINCINNATI 5–WAY CHILI

12 ounces ground turkey
 1 cup chopped onion, divided
 3 cloves garlic, minced
 1 can (8 ounces) reduced-sodium tomato
    sauce
 ¾ cup water
 1 to 2 teaspoons cider vinegar
 1 tablespoon unsweetened cocoa
 1 to 2 tablespoons chili powder
 1 teaspoon ground cinnamon
 ½ teaspoon ground allspice
 ½ teaspoon paprika
 ⅛ teaspoon ground cloves (optional)
 1 bay leaf
 8 ounces spaghetti, cooked and kept warm
 ½ cup (2 ounces) shredded fat-free
    Cheddar cheese
 ½ cup rinsed drained canned red kidney
    beans

1. Cook and stir turkey in medium saucepan over medium heat about 5 minutes or until browned and no longer pink. Drain excess fat. Add ½ cup onion and garlic; cook about 5 minutes or until onion is tender.

2. Add tomato sauce, water, vinegar, cocoa, chili powder, cinnamon, allspice, paprika, cloves, if desired, and bay leaf; bring to a boil. Reduce heat and simmer, covered, 15 minutes, stirring occasionally. If thicker consistency is desired, simmer uncovered about 5 minutes more. Discard bay leaf; season to taste with salt and pepper, if desired.

3. Spoon spaghetti into bowls; spoon chili over and sprinkle with remaining ½ cup onion, cheese and beans.

Makes 4 servings

Cincinnati 5-Way Chili

177 TURKEY VEGETABLE CHILI MAC

Nonstick cooking spray
¾ **pound ground turkey breast**
½ **cup chopped onion**
2 **cloves garlic, minced**
1 **can (about 15 ounces) black beans,**
   rinsed and drained
1 **can (14½ ounces) Mexican-style stewed**
   tomatoes, undrained
1 **can (14½ ounces) no-salt-added diced**
   tomatoes, undrained
1 **cup frozen whole kernel corn**
1 **teaspoon Mexican seasoning**
½ **cup uncooked elbow macaroni**
⅓ **cup reduced-fat sour cream**

1. Spray large nonstick saucepan or Dutch oven with cooking spray; heat over medium heat until hot. Add turkey, onion and garlic; cook 5 minutes or until turkey is no longer pink, stirring to crumble.

2. Stir beans, tomatoes with liquid, corn and Mexican seasoning into saucepan; bring to a boil over high heat. Cover; reduce heat to low. Simmer 15 minutes, stirring occasionally.

3. Meanwhile, cook pasta according to package directions, omitting salt. Rinse; drain. Stir into saucepan. Simmer, uncovered, 2 to 3 minutes or until heated through.

4. Top each serving with dollop of sour cream before serving. Garnish as desired.

Makes 6 servings

178 TURKEY CHILI

2 **pounds ground raw turkey**
1 **tablespoon vegetable oil**
1 **cup chopped onion**
1 **cup chopped celery**
1 **cup chopped green pepper**
2 **cloves garlic, minced**
2 **cans (14½ ounces each) tomatoes,**
   undrained and cut into bite-size
   pieces
1 **can (8 ounces) tomato sauce**
1 **cup water**
½ **cup HEINZ® Tomato Ketchup**
1 **tablespoon chili powder**
1 **teaspoon salt**
½ **teaspoon ground cumin**
½ **teaspoon dried basil leaves, crushed**
¼ **teaspoon ground red pepper**
2 **cans (15½ to 17 ounces each) red**
   kidney beans, drained

In Dutch oven, cook turkey in oil 5 minutes or until no longer pink, stirring to crumble; remove with slotted spoon. Sauté onion, celery, green pepper and garlic in drippings until tender. Stir in turkey, tomatoes and next 8 ingredients. Cover; simmer 1 hour, stirring occasionally. Add kidney beans; simmer an additional 15 minutes. Serve in bowls, topped with shredded Cheddar cheese and sliced green onions, if desired.

Makes 10 to 12 servings (about 11 cups)

Turkey Vegetable Chili Mac

179 TURKEY CHILI

1 pound extra-lean ground turkey breast
1 cup chopped onion
1 cup chopped green bell pepper
3 cloves garlic, minced
3 cans (14½ ounces each) chopped
    tomatoes
½ cup water
1 tablespoon chili powder
1 teaspoon ground cinnamon
1 teaspoon ground cumin
½ teaspoon paprika
½ teaspoon dried oregano leaves, crushed
½ teaspoon black pepper
¼ teaspoon salt
1 can (15 ounces) pinto beans, rinsed and
    drained

1. Spray large skillet with nonstick cooking spray. Cook turkey, onion, bell pepper and garlic over medium-high heat about 5 minutes or until turkey begins to brown, stirring frequently and breaking up turkey with back of spoon.

2. Stir in tomatoes; cook 5 minutes. Add water, chili powder, cinnamon, cumin, paprika, oregano, black pepper and salt; mix well. Stir in beans.

3. Bring to a boil; reduce heat to medium-low. Simmer about 30 minutes or until chili thickens. Garnish, if desired.

Makes 4 servings

180 CHILI AND MORE

1 pound ground turkey or beef
¾ cup chopped onion
1 clove garlic, minced
1 can (14½ ounces) whole tomatoes,
    undrained
1½ cups Wheat CHEX® brand cereal
1 can (8 ounces) tomato sauce
1 cup shredded carrot
¼ cup chopped green bell pepper
2 to 3 teaspoons chili powder
¼ teaspoon ground cumin (optional)
1 can (15.5 ounces) kidney beans,
    undrained *or* 2 ounces dried kidney
    beans, cooked according to package
    directions, plus ¾ cup cooking liquid*

*¾ cup water may be substituted for cooking liquid.

Brown turkey, onion and garlic in saucepan over medium-high heat, stirring occasionally; drain. Stir in ½ cup water, tomatoes, cereal, tomato sauce, carrot, green pepper, chili powder and cumin. Cover and simmer 30 minutes, stirring occasionally to break up tomatoes. Add beans; simmer uncovered an additional 30 minutes, stirring occasionally. *Makes 6 servings*

Turkey Chili

181 SANTA FE SKILLET CHILI

1 to 1¼ pounds ground turkey (93% lean)
1 cup chopped onion
1 teaspoon bottled minced garlic
1 tablespoon chili powder
1 tablespoon ground cumin
¼ to ½ teaspoon ground red pepper
1 can (15½ ounces) chili beans in spicy sauce, undrained
1 can (14½ ounces) Mexican- or chili-style stewed or diced tomatoes, undrained
1 can (4 ounces) chopped green chilies, undrained

1. Spray large deep skillet with nonstick cooking spray. Cook turkey, onion and garlic over medium-high heat, breaking meat apart with wooden spoon.

2. Sprinkle chili powder, cumin and ground red pepper evenly over turkey mixture; cook and stir 3 minutes or until turkey is no longer pink.

3. Stir in beans, tomatoes and chilies. Reduce heat to medium; cover and simmer 10 minutes, stirring occasionally. Ladle chili into bowls. *Makes 4 servings*

Prep and Cook Time: 19 minutes

SERVING SUGGESTION: Offer a variety of toppings with the skillet chili, such as chopped fresh cilantro, sour cream, shredded Cheddar or Monterey Jack cheese and diced ripe avocado. Serve with warm corn tortillas or corn bread.

182 SOCK–IT–TO–'EM CHILI

1 tablespoon vegetable oil
¾ pound ground turkey or lean ground beef
1 (8-ounce) package mushrooms, sliced
2 medium carrots, peeled and diced
1 large green bell pepper, seeded and diced
1 medium onion, diced
2 garlic cloves, minced
1½ teaspoons chili powder
½ teaspoon ground cumin
1 (26-ounce) jar NEWMAN'S OWN® Sockarooni Spaghetti Sauce
2 (15- to 19-ounce) cans black beans, undrained
1 cup water
1 medium zucchini, diced

Heat oil in 5-quart Dutch oven over medium-high heat until hot. Add turkey; cook and stir until no longer pink. Add mushrooms, carrots, pepper, onion, garlic, chili powder and cumin; cook until onion is tender, stirring frequently.

Stir in Newman's Own® Sockarooni Spaghetti Sauce, beans with their liquid and water; bring to a boil. Reduce heat to low; cover and simmer 20 minutes. Add zucchini; cook over medium-low heat, uncovered, 10 minutes or until zucchini is just tender. Serve hot. *Makes 6 servings*

Santa Fe Skillet Chili

183 CONFETTI CHICKEN CHILI

1 pound 90% fat free ground chicken or 93% fat free ground turkey
1 large onion, chopped
2 carrots, chopped
1 large Anaheim or 1 medium green bell pepper, chopped
2 Italian tomatoes, chopped
1 jalapeño pepper*, finely chopped
1 can (15 ounces) Great Northern beans, rinsed and drained
2 cans (about 14 ounces each) defatted ⅓-less-salt chicken broth
2 teaspoons chili powder
½ teaspoon ground red pepper

Jalapeño peppers can sting and irritate the skin; wear rubber gloves when handling peppers and do not touch eyes. Wash hands after handling jalapeño peppers.

1. Heat large nonstick saucepan over medium heat until hot. Add chicken and onion; cook and stir 5 minutes or until chicken is browned. Drain fat from saucepan.

2. Add remaining ingredients to saucepan. Bring to a boil. Reduce heat to low and simmer 15 minutes. *Makes 5 servings*

Prep and Cook Time: 30 minutes

184 CHICKEN CHILI

1 pound ground chicken
1 medium onion, chopped
½ cup chopped green bell pepper
1 clove garlic, minced
1 can (28 ounces) whole peeled tomatoes, with juice, broken up
1 can (16 ounces) kidney beans, undrained
1 cup water
1 can (6 ounces) tomato paste
4 teaspoons chili powder
1 teaspoon salt
1 teaspoon sugar
1 teaspoon ground cumin
¼ teaspoon ground red pepper

Spray nonstick Dutch oven with nonstick cooking spray; heat over medium-high heat. Add chicken, onion, bell pepper and garlic; cook, stirring, until meat is browned. Add tomatoes with juice, beans, water, tomato paste, chili powder, salt, sugar, cumin and red pepper; stir well. Reduce heat to low; simmer, uncovered, stirring occasionally, about 30 minutes. *Makes 6 servings*

*Favorite recipe from **Delmarva Poultry Industry, Inc.***

Confetti Chicken Chili

Casseroles &
Skillet Dinners

185 TACO POT PIE

1 pound ground beef
1 package (1.25 ounces) taco seasoning
    mix
1 can (8 ounces) kidney beans, rinsed and
    drained
1 cup chopped tomato
¾ cup frozen corn, thawed
¾ cup frozen peas, thawed
1½ cups (6 ounces) shredded Cheddar
    cheese
1 package (11.5 ounces) refrigerated corn
    bread sticks

1. Preheat oven to 400°F. Brown meat in medium ovenproof skillet over medium-high heat, stirring to separate meat. Drain drippings. Add seasoning mix and ¼ cup water to skillet. Cook over medium-low heat 3 minutes or until most of liquid is absorbed, stirring occasionally.

2. Stir in beans, tomato, corn and peas. Cook 3 minutes or until mixture is hot. Remove from heat; stir in cheese.

3. Unwrap corn bread dough; separate into 16 strips. Twist strips, cutting to fit skillet. Arrange attractively over meat mixture. Press ends of dough lightly to edges of skillet to secure. Bake 15 minutes or until corn bread is golden brown and meat mixture is bubbly.

Makes 4 to 6 servings

Prep and Cook Time: 30 minutes

Taco Pot Pie

CASSEROLES & SKILLET DINNERS

186 BEEF MOLE TAMALE PIE

1½ pounds ground chuck
1 medium onion, chopped
1 green bell pepper, chopped
2 cloves garlic, minced
1¼ cups medium-hot salsa
1 package (10 ounces) frozen whole
    kernel corn, partially thawed
1 tablespoon unsweetened cocoa powder
2 teaspoons ground cumin
1 teaspoon dried oregano leaves
1½ teaspoons salt, divided
¼ teaspoon ground cinnamon
2 cups (8 ounces) shredded Monterey Jack
    or Cheddar cheese
⅓ cup chopped fresh cilantro
1 cup all-purpose flour
¾ cup yellow cornmeal
3 tablespoons sugar
2 teaspoons baking powder
⅔ cup milk
3 tablespoons butter, melted
1 egg, beaten
    Cilantro leaves, chili pepper and sour
    cream for garnish

Preheat oven to 400°F. Spray 11×7-inch baking dish with nonstick cooking spray. Brown ground chuck with onion, bell pepper and garlic in large deep skillet or Dutch oven over medium heat until meat just loses its pink color. Pour off drippings. Stir in salsa, corn, cocoa, cumin, oregano, 1 teaspoon salt and cinnamon. Bring to a boil. Reduce heat to medium-low; simmer, uncovered, 8 minutes, stirring occasionally. Remove from heat; stir in cheese and cilantro. Spread in prepared dish.

Combine flour, cornmeal, sugar, baking powder and remaining ½ teaspoon salt in large bowl. Add milk, butter and egg; stir just until dry ingredients are moistened. Drop by spoonfuls evenly over meat mixture; spread batter evenly with spatula.

Bake 15 minutes. *Reduce oven temperature to 350°F.* Bake 20 minutes or until topping is light brown and filling is bubbly. Let stand 5 minutes before serving. Garnish, if desired.

Makes 6 servings

187 COWPOKE ENCHILADAS

1⅓ cups tomato salsa
1 cup HEINZ® Tomato Ketchup
½ pound lean ground beef
½ cup chopped onion
½ cup chopped green bell pepper
1 can (15½ ounces) pinto or kidney beans,
    drained
6 (8-inch) flour tortillas, warmed
1¼ cups shredded Cheddar cheese, divided

In small bowl, combine salsa and ketchup. Pour ½ cup salsa mixture into bottom of 13×9-inch baking pan; set remainder aside. In large nonstick skillet, brown beef with onion and bell pepper; drain fat. Add beans and ⅓ cup salsa mixture; mix well. Spoon ½ cup beef mixture onto each tortilla; sprinkle with 2 tablespoons cheese. Roll tortillas; place seam side down in prepared baking pan. Spoon remaining salsa mixture over tortillas; sprinkle with remaining ½ cup cheese. Cover; bake in 350°F oven, 35 to 40 minutes or until hot. *Makes 6 servings*

Beef Mole Tamale Pie

188 QUICK TAMALE CASSEROLE

1½ pounds ground beef
¾ cup sliced green onions
1 can (4 ounces) chopped green chilies, drained and divided
1 can (15¼ ounces) whole kernel corn, drained
1 can (10¾ ounces) condensed tomato soup
¾ cup salsa
1 can (2¼ ounces) chopped pitted ripe olives (optional)
1 tablespoon Worcestershire sauce
1 teaspoon chili powder
¼ teaspoon garlic powder
4 slices (¾ ounce each) American cheese, halved
4 corn muffins, cut into ½-inch cubes
   Mexican Sour Cream Topping (recipe follows) (optional)

In skillet, brown ground beef with green onions. Drain. Reserve 2 tablespoons chilies for Mexican Sour Cream Topping, if desired. Stir in remaining chilies, corn, tomato soup, salsa, olives, Worcestershire sauce, chili powder and garlic powder until well blended. Place in 2-quart casserole. Top with cheese, then evenly spread muffin cubes over cheese. Bake at 350°F for 5 to 10 minutes or until cheese is melted. Serve with Mexican Sour Cream Topping, if desired.

Makes 6 servings

MEXICAN SOUR CREAM TOPPING

1 cup sour cream
2 tablespoons chopped green chilies, reserved from above
2 teaspoons chopped jalapeño peppers (optional)
2 teaspoons lime juice

Combine all ingredients in small bowl; mix until well blended. *Makes about 1 cup*

189 TAMALE PIE

1 tablespoon olive or vegetable oil
1 small onion, chopped
1 pound ground beef
1 envelope LIPTON® Recipe Secrets® Onion Soup Mix*
1 can (14½ ounces) stewed tomatoes, undrained
½ cup water
1 can (15 to 19 ounces) red kidney beans, rinsed and drained
1 package (8½ ounces) corn muffin mix

*Also terrific with Lipton® Recipe Secrets® Onion-Mushroom, Beefy Onion or Beefy Mushroom Soup Mix.

• Preheat oven to 400°F.

• In 12-inch skillet, heat oil over medium heat and cook onion, stirring occasionally, 3 minutes or until tender. Stir in ground beef and cook until browned. Drain.

• Stir in onion soup mix blended with tomatoes and water. Bring to a boil over high heat, stirring with spoon to crush tomatoes. Reduce heat to low and stir in beans. Simmer uncovered, stirring occasionally, 10 minutes. Turn into 2-quart casserole.

• Prepare corn muffin mix according to package directions. Spoon evenly over casserole.

• Bake uncovered 15 minutes or until topping is golden and filling is hot.

Makes about 6 servings

Quick Tamale Casserole

CASSEROLES & SKILLET DINNERS

190 TAMALE PIE

1 pound lean ground beef
1 package (10 ounces) frozen whole
    kernel corn, thawed
1 can (14½ ounces) diced tomatoes,
    undrained
1 can (4 ounces) sliced black olives,
    drained
1 package (1¼ ounces) taco seasoning mix
1 package (6 ounces) corn muffin or corn
    bread mix plus ingredients to prepare
    mix
¼ cup (1 ounce) shredded Cheddar cheese
1 green onion, thinly sliced

1. Preheat oven to 400°F. Place meat in large skillet; cook over high heat 6 to 8 minutes or until meat is no longer pink, breaking meat apart with wooden spoon. Pour off drippings. Add corn, tomatoes, olives and seasoning mix to meat. Bring to a boil over medium-high heat, stirring constantly. Pour into deep 9-inch pie plate; smooth top with spatula.

2. Prepare corn muffin mix according to package directions. Spread evenly over meat mixture. Bake 8 to 10 minutes or until golden brown. Sprinkle with cheese and onion. Let stand 10 minutes before serving. Garnish as desired.   *Makes 6 servings*

Prep and Cook Time: 20 minutes

SERVING SUGGESTION: Serve with papaya wedges sprinkled with lime juice.

191 LEAN PICADILLO PIE

1½ pounds lean ground pork
  ½ cup *each* chopped onion and green
    pepper
  1 clove garlic, minced
  1 can (14½ ounces) whole tomatoes,
    undrained, cut up
  ¾ cup chopped dried apricots or raisins
12 pimiento-stuffed green olives, sliced
  3 tablespoons chili powder
  2 tablespoons chopped almonds
  2 cans (14½ ounces each) chicken broth
  2 cups cornmeal

Heat large nonstick skillet over medium heat; cook and stir pork, onion, green pepper and garlic 5 minutes or until pork is lightly browned. Pour off any drippings. Stir in tomatoes, dried apricots, olives, chili powder and almonds. Cover and simmer 10 minutes. Bring chicken broth to a boil in large saucepan. Gradually stir in cornmeal; mix well. Spoon cornmeal mixture into 13×9-inch baking dish sprayed with nonstick cooking spray. Top with pork mixture. Cover with foil. Bake at 350°F for 30 minutes. Cut into squares to serve.

Makes 12 servings

Prep Time: 20 minutes
Cook Time: 30 minutes

*Favorite recipe from **National Pork Producers Council***

Tamale Pie

192 TAMALE PIE

BISCUIT TOPPING
- ½ cup white or yellow cornmeal
- ½ cup buttermilk
- ⅓ cup all-purpose flour
- 1 egg white, slightly beaten
- 1 tablespoon sugar
- ½ jalapeño pepper*, seeded, chopped
- 1 teaspoon baking powder

FILLING
- Nonstick cooking spray
- 1 green bell pepper, chopped
- ¾ cup chopped green onions
- 2 cloves garlic, finely chopped
- 1½ cups canned crushed tomatoes
- 1 can (about 15 ounces) pinto beans, rinsed and drained
- ¼ pound cooked ground turkey breast
- 2 teaspoons chili powder
- 1 teaspoon ground cumin
- ¼ teaspoon ground black pepper

Jalapeño peppers can sting and irritate the skin. Wear rubber gloves when handling peppers and do not touch eyes.

1. Preheat oven to 425°F. Spray 9-inch pie plate with nonstick cooking spray; set aside.

2. For topping, combine all topping ingredients in large bowl until well blended; set aside.

3. For filling, spray large nonstick skillet with cooking spray. Heat over medium heat until hot. Add bell pepper, onions and garlic. Cook and stir 5 minutes or until vegetables are tender. Add tomatoes, beans, turkey, chili powder, cumin and black pepper. Cook and stir 5 minutes or until heated through.

4. Spoon filling into prepared pie plate. Drop heaping tablespoonfuls topping around outer edge of filling; flatten with back of spoon to form biscuits.

5. Bake 25 minutes or until biscuits are golden brown. Let stand 5 minutes before serving. *Makes 4 servings*

193 STUFFED BEEF & BLACK BEAN TAMALE PIE

- 1 pound lean ground beef
- 1 packet (1¼ ounces) taco seasoning mix
- 1 can (15 to 16 ounces) black beans, rinsed, drained
- ½ cup water
- 1 can (8¾ ounces) whole kernel corn, very well drained
- ¾ cup light dairy sour cream
- ¾ cup shredded Co-Jack or Cheddar cheese
- ⅓ cup thinly sliced green onions

CRUST
- 1 package (8½ ounces) corn muffin mix
- ¾ cup shredded Co-Jack or Cheddar cheese
- ¾ cup light dairy sour cream
- ½ cup thinly sliced green onions

1. Heat oven to 400°F. Heat large nonstick skillet over medium heat until hot. Add ground beef; brown 5 to 7 minutes, stirring occasionally. Pour off drippings. Stir in seasoning mix, beans and water. Bring to a boil; reduce heat. Simmer 5 minutes, stirring occasionally; set aside.

Stuffed Beef & Black Bean Tamale Pie

2. Meanwhile in medium bowl, combine crust ingredients, mixing just until dry ingredients are moistened. (Batter will be stiff.) Using spoon dipped in water, spread slightly more than ½ the batter onto bottom and up side of 9-inch pie pan.

3. Arrange corn over batter; top with beef mixture. Spoon remaining batter over beef, along outer edge of pie. Carefully spread batter toward center, leaving a 3-inch circle uncovered. Bake in 400°F oven 23 to 25 minutes or until top is golden brown.

4. To serve, dollop ¾ cup sour cream over top; sprinkle with ¾ cup cheese and ⅓ cup green onions. Cut into wedges.

Makes 4 servings

Prep and Cook Time: 50 minutes

*Favorite recipe from **National Cattlemen's Beef Association***

194 BEEFY NACHO CRESCENT BAKE

1 pound lean ground beef
½ cup chopped onion
¼ teaspoon salt
⅛ teaspoon black pepper
1 tablespoon chili powder
1 teaspoon ground cumin
1 teaspoon dried oregano leaves
1 can (11 ounces) condensed nacho
   cheese soup, undiluted
1 cup milk
1 can (8 ounces) refrigerated crescent roll
   dough
¼ cup (1 ounce) shredded Cheddar cheese
   Chopped fresh cilantro (optional)
   Salsa (optional)

Preheat oven to 375°F. Spray 13×9-inch baking dish with nonstick cooking spray.

Place beef and onion in large skillet; season with salt and pepper. Brown beef over medium-high heat until no longer pink, stirring to separate meat. Drain fat. Stir in chili powder, cumin and oregano. Cook and stir 2 minutes; remove from heat.

Combine soup and milk in medium bowl, stirring until smooth. Pour soup mixture into prepared dish, spreading evenly.

Separate crescent dough into 4 rectangles; press perforations together firmly. Roll each rectangle to 8×4 inches. Cut each rectangle in half crosswise to form 8 (4-inch) squares.

Spoon about ¼ cup beef mixture in center of each square. Lift 4 corners of dough up over filling to meet in center; pinch and twist firmly to seal. Place squares in dish.

Bake, uncovered, 20 to 25 minutes or until crusts are golden brown. Sprinkle cheese over squares. Bake 5 minutes or until cheese melts. To serve, spoon soup mixture in dish over each serving; sprinkle with cilantro, if desired. Serve with salsa, if desired.

Makes 4 servings

195 TORTILLA LASAGNA

1 tablespoon vegetable oil
1 large onion, chopped
1 medium green pepper, chopped
1 large clove garlic, minced
1 pound ground beef
1 teaspoon dried oregano leaves
1 can (14½ ounces) tomatoes, drained,
   chopped
1 can (8 ounces) tomato sauce
1 cup sour cream
¾ teaspoon TABASCO® pepper sauce
10 corn tortillas, 5 inches in diameter
1 can (15 ounces) pinto beans, drained
2 cups (8 ounces) shredded Cheddar
   cheese

Preheat oven to 350°F. In large skillet heat oil; cook onion, green pepper and garlic 3 minutes or until tender. Add ground beef and oregano, breaking up meat with fork as it cooks until browned. Drain off fat; remove from heat.

In medium bowl combine tomatoes, tomato sauce, sour cream and TABASCO® sauce; mix well. Cut each tortilla in half. Arrange 10 halves in shallow 11×7-inch baking dish. Spread half the meat mixture over tortillas. Top with half the pinto beans, half the tomato mixture and 1 cup shredded cheese. Repeat with remaining ingredients. Bake 30 minutes or until heated through. Let stand 10 minutes before serving.

Makes 4 servings

Beefy Nacho Crescent Bake

CASSEROLES & SKILLET DINNERS

196 LAMB ENCHILADAS WITH GREEN SAUCE

1 can (13 ounces) tomatillos, drained and rinsed
1 can (4 ounces) chopped green chilies, drained
¼ cup chopped onion
2 sprigs cilantro or parsley
2 cloves garlic, minced, divided
½ cup chicken broth
1 teaspoon sugar
Dash pepper
½ pound lean ground American lamb
½ cup chopped green pepper
¼ cup chopped celery
8 (6-inch) flour tortillas
½ cup shredded mozzarella or Monterey Jack cheese (2 ounces)
Lite sour cream or plain yogurt
Sliced green onion

For Green Sauce, in blender container or food processor bowl combine tomatillos, chilies, chopped onion, cilantro and 1 clove garlic. Blend or process until smooth. Pour into small saucepan. Add broth, sugar and pepper. Bring to a boil; reduce heat. Simmer, covered, 10 minutes.

In skillet cook lamb, remaining 1 clove garlic, green pepper and celery until no pink remains and vegetables are crisp-tender. Drain off any fat. To soften tortillas, stack with white paper toweling between each tortilla. Microwave on HIGH (100% power) 1 to 2 minutes or until tortillas are pliable. (Or, if desired, wrap tortillas in foil. Heat in 350°F oven about 10 minutes or until pliable). Spoon meat mixture onto each tortilla, then roll up.

Place filled tortillas, seam side down, in 11×7-inch baking dish. Top with Green Sauce. Cover with foil. Bake in 350°F oven for 20 minutes. Uncover; sprinkle with cheese. Return to oven for 5 minutes. Serve garnished with sour cream and green onion.

Makes 4 servings

RED SAUCE OPTION: Substitute salsa or taco sauce for Green Sauce. Prepare and serve as directed.

*Favorite recipe from **American Lamb Council***

197 SANTA FE CASSEROLE BAKE

1 pound lean ground beef
1 package (1.0 ounce) LAWRY'S® Taco Spices & Seasonings
2 cups chicken broth
¼ cup all-purpose flour
1 cup dairy sour cream
1 can (7 ounces) diced green chilies
1 package (11 ounces) corn or tortilla chips
2 cups (8 ounces) shredded Monterey Jack or Cheddar cheese
½ cup sliced green onions with tops

In medium skillet, brown meat; drain fat. Add Taco Spices & Seasonings; blend well. In small bowl, combine broth and flour. Add to meat mixture; bring to a boil to slightly thicken liquid. Remove from heat. Stir in sour cream and chilies; blend well. In 13×9×2-inch greased baking dish, place ½ of chips. Top with ½ of beef mixture, ½ of cheese and ½ of green onions. Layer again with remaining ingredients ending with green onions. Bake, uncovered, in 375°F oven for 20 minutes. Let stand 5 minutes before cutting. *Makes 6 servings*

Santa Fe Casserole Bake

MICROWAVE DIRECTIONS: In 1-quart glass bowl, crumble beef. Microwave on HIGH 5 to 6 minutes, stirring once; drain fat. Add Taco Spices & Seasonings; blend well and set aside. In 1-quart glass measuring cup, combine broth and flour. Microwave on HIGH 5 minutes or until bubbling and thick, stirring once. Stir in sour cream and chilies. In 13×9×2-inch lightly greased microwave-safe baking dish, layer as stated above. Cover with waxed paper; microwave on 50% power 15 to 18 minutes rotating dish after 7 minutes. Let stand 5 minutes before cutting.

HINT: Top with guacamole for additional flavor.

198 TACO PIE

1 pound ground beef
½ cup chopped onion
1 teaspoon dried cilantro leaves
½ teaspoon ground cumin
½ teaspoon salt
½ teaspoon pepper
1 can (4 ounces) chopped green chilies, drained
1 fresh jalapeño pepper, minced
1 can (14.5 ounces) FRANK'S or SnowFloss Original Style Diced Tomatoes, drained slightly
1 can (15½ ounces) red kidney beans, rinsed, drained
1¼ cups milk
1 package (8½ ounces) corn bread mix
3 eggs
1 cup shredded Cheddar cheese
Tortilla chips, any style
Sour cream
Shredded lettuce

1. Preheat oven to 400°F. Brown ground beef and onion. Drain grease. Stir in seasonings.

2. Spread meat mixture in well-greased shallow 10-inch baking dish.

3. Layer chilies, jalapeño pepper, diced tomatoes and kidney beans over meat.

4. Beat milk, corn bread mix and eggs 1 minute with mixer. Pour over ingredients in baking dish.

5. Bake 30 minutes. Top with cheese and bake 10 minutes. Serve with tortilla chips, sour cream and lettuce.

Makes 4 servings

Prep Time: 15 minutes
Cook Time: 40 minutes

199 CHILI CORN BREAD FIESTA

1 pound ground beef
1 package (1.48 ounces) LAWRY'S® Spices & Seasonings for Chili
2 teaspoons LAWRY'S® Seasoned Salt
1 can (17 ounces) whole kernel corn, drained
1 can (14½ ounces) whole tomatoes, cut up, undrained
1 package (16 ounces) corn muffin mix, divided
1 egg
⅓ cup milk
1 cup (4 ounces) shredded Cheddar cheese

In medium skillet, brown beef until crumbly; drain fat. Add Spices & Seasonings for Chili, Seasoned Salt, corn and tomatoes; blend well. Place in 9-inch shallow casserole. Place 1½ cups corn muffin mix in medium bowl; add egg and milk. Stir with fork just until moistened. If mixture is too moist, add additional 1 tablespoon muffin mix. Spread evenly over beef mixture. Bake, uncovered, in 350°F oven 30 minutes. Top with cheese. Bake 5 minutes or until cheese is melted.

Makes 6 servings

PRESENTATION: Cut into squares for serving.

HINT: If available, use 1 package (8 ounces) corn muffin mix, prepared according to package directions.

CASSEROLES & SKILLET DINNERS

200 CHILI BEEF AND CORN CASSEROLE

1 (13¾-fluid-ounce) can COLLEGE INN®
    Beef Broth, divided
1 (6-ounce) can tomato paste
1 (1¼-ounce) package taco seasoning mix
¾ cup uncooked rice
1 pound ground beef
1 cup chopped onion
1 (17-ounce) can whole kernel sweet
    corn, drained
    Corn chips (optional)
    Diced fresh tomato (optional)

In small bowl, blend 1 cup beef broth, tomato paste and taco seasoning mix; set aside. In saucepan, over high heat, combine remaining broth and enough water to equal 1¾ cups liquid; heat to a boil. Add rice and cook according to package directions.

In large skillet, over medium-high heat, brown beef and cook onion until done; pour off fat. In 2-quart casserole, layer ⅓ each of the rice, corn, meat mixture and reserved sauce; repeat layers twice, combining the last portion of meat and sauce for the top layer. Cover; bake at 375°F for 40 to 45 minutes or until hot. Garnish with corn chips and diced tomato, if desired.

Makes 4 to 6 servings

MICROWAVE DIRECTIONS: Combine first 3 ingredients as above. In 1½-quart microwave-proof bowl, combine remaining broth and enough water to equal 1¾ cups liquid. Stir in rice; cover. Microwave on HIGH (100% power) for 15 to 17 minutes, stirring after 7 minutes.

Crumble beef in 1½-quart microwave-proof bowl. Microwave, uncovered, on HIGH for 2 minutes; stir in onion. Microwave, uncovered, on HIGH for 2 to 3 minutes; pour off fat. In 2-quart microwave-proof casserole, layer as above; cover. Microwave on HIGH for 15 to 17 minutes, rotating casserole ½ turn after 7 minutes. Let stand, covered, for 5 minutes before serving.

CASSEROLES & SKILLET DINNERS

201 TURKEY–TORTILLA BAKE

9 (6-inch) corn tortillas
½ pound 93% fat free ground turkey
½ cup chopped onion
¾ cup mild or medium taco sauce
1 can (4 ounces) chopped green chilies, drained
½ cup frozen whole kernel corn, thawed
½ cup (2 ounces) shredded reduced-fat Cheddar cheese

1. Preheat oven to 400°F. Place tortillas on large baking sheet, overlapping tortillas as little as possible. Bake 4 minutes; turn tortillas. Continue baking 2 minutes or until crisp. Cool completely on wire rack.

2. Heat medium nonstick skillet over medium heat until hot. Add turkey and onion. Cook and stir 5 minutes or until turkey is browned and onion is tender. Add taco sauce, chilies and corn. Reduce heat and simmer 5 minutes.

3. Break 3 tortillas and arrange over bottom of 1½-quart casserole. Spoon half the turkey mixture over the tortillas; sprinkle with half the cheese. Repeat layers. Bake 10 minutes or until cheese is melted and casserole is heated through. Break remaining tortillas and sprinkle over casserole. Garnish with reduced-fat sour cream, if desired.

Makes 4 servings

Prep and Cook Time: 30 minutes

202 NACHOS CASSEROLE

1 cup chunky taco sauce
1 can (4 ounces) green chilies, chopped
1 pound lean ground turkey
½ cup chopped onions
¼ teaspoon ground cumin
1 cup refried beans
½ cup (4 ounces) non-fat plain yogurt
1 cup (4 ounces) shredded reduced-fat Cheddar cheese, divided
¼ cup water
4 cups KELLOGG'S® CORN FLAKES® cereal, divided
Vegetable cooking spray

OPTIONAL GARNISH
Chopped tomatoes
Chopped green onions
Sliced olives
Reduced-fat sour cream

1. Combine taco sauce and chilies. Set aside.

2. In large frypan, cook turkey and onions until meat is browned. Drain off fat. Add cumin, beans, yogurt, ½ cup of the cheese, half of the taco sauce mixture and water.

3. Pour 2 cups Kellogg's® Corn Flakes® cereal into a 2-quart baking dish coated with cooking spray. Cover with meat mixture. Top with remaining taco sauce mixture. Sprinkle with remaining cereal.

4. Bake at 350°F about 35 minutes or until thoroughly heated. Sprinkle with remaining cheese. Bake just until cheese melts, about 5 minutes. Garnish with tomatoes, green onions, olives and sour cream.

Makes 6 servings

Turkey-Tortilla Bake

CASSEROLES & SKILLET DINNERS

203 EASY TEX–MEX BAKE

8 ounces uncooked thin mostaccioli
1 pound ground turkey breast
²/₃ cup bottled medium or mild salsa
1 package (10 ounces) frozen corn, thawed, drained
1 container (16 ounces) low-fat cottage cheese
1 egg
1 tablespoon minced fresh cilantro
½ teaspoon ground white pepper
¼ teaspoon ground cumin
½ cup (2 ounces) shredded Monterey Jack cheese

1. Cook pasta according to package directions, omitting salt. Drain and rinse well; set aside.

2. Spray large nonstick skillet with nonstick cooking spray. Add turkey; cook until no longer pink, about 5 minutes. Stir in salsa and corn. Remove from heat.

3. Preheat oven to 350°F. Combine cottage cheese, egg, cilantro, white pepper and cumin in small bowl.

4. Spoon ½ turkey mixture in bottom of 11×7-inch baking dish. Top with pasta. Spoon cottage cheese mixture over pasta. Top with remaining turkey mixture. Sprinkle cheese over casserole.

5. Bake 25 to 30 minutes or until heated through. *Makes 6 servings*

204 FIESTA CORN CASSEROLE

1 tablespoon butter
3 cups corn flakes, divided
1 pound lean ground beef
1 can (8 ounces) tomato sauce
1 package (1.0 ounce) LAWRY'S® Taco Spices & Seasonings
½ teaspoon LAWRY'S® Seasoned Salt
1 can (17 ounces) whole kernel corn, drained (reserve ¼ cup liquid)
2 cups (8 ounces) shredded Cheddar cheese

MICROWAVE DIRECTIONS: In 1½-quart shallow glass casserole, place butter and microwave on HIGH 30 seconds. Sprinkle 2 cups corn flakes over butter. Crush remaining 1 cup corn flakes and set aside. In separate baking dish, microwave ground beef on HIGH 5 minutes, stirring to crumble after 3 minutes. Drain fat and crumble beef. Add tomato sauce, Taco Spices & Seasonings, Seasoned Salt and ¼ cup corn liquid; blend well. Layer half each of corn, meat mixture and cheese over buttered corn flakes; repeat layers. Sprinkle remaining 1 cup crushed corn flakes over top in diagonal strips. Microwave on HIGH 12 to 15 minutes. *Makes 4 to 6 servings*

PRESENTATION: Serve with buttered green vegetable, sliced tomatoes and cucumbers and fresh fruit.

HINT: May substitute 2 cups broken taco shell pieces and 1 cup crushed taco shells for corn flakes.

Easy Tex-Mex Bake

205 CHILI SPAGHETTI CASSEROLE

8 ounces uncooked spaghetti
1 pound lean ground beef
1 medium onion, chopped
¼ teaspoon salt
⅛ teaspoon black pepper
1 can (15 ounces) vegetarian chili with beans
1 can (14½ ounces) Italian-style stewed tomatoes, undrained
1½ cups (6 ounces) shredded sharp Cheddar cheese, divided
½ cup reduced-fat sour cream
1½ teaspoons chili powder
¼ teaspoon garlic powder

Preheat oven to 350°F. Spray 13×9-inch baking dish with nonstick cooking spray.

Cook pasta according to package directions until al dente. Drain and place in prepared dish.

Meanwhile, place beef and onion in large skillet; season with salt and pepper. Brown beef over medium-high heat until beef is no longer pink, stirring to separate meat. Drain fat. Stir in chili, tomatoes with juice, 1 cup cheese, sour cream, chili powder and garlic powder.

Add chili mixture to pasta; stir until pasta is well coated. Sprinkle with remaining ½ cup cheese.

Cover tightly with foil and bake 30 minutes or until hot and bubbly. Let stand 5 minutes before serving. *Makes 8 servings*

Chili Spaghetti Casserole

CASSEROLES & SKILLET DINNERS

206 ZESTY ZUCCHINI LASAGNA

1 package (1.5 ounces) LAWRY'S®
    Original Style Spaghetti Sauce Spices
    & Seasonings
1 can (6 ounces) tomato paste
1¾ cups water
2 tablespoons IMPERIAL® Margarine
1 pound ground beef
½ teaspoon dried basil leaves
⅛ teaspoon dried thyme leaves
2 cups ricotta cheese
1 egg, slightly beaten
4 medium zucchini, thinly sliced
    lengthwise
1 cup shredded mozzarella cheese (about
    4 ounces)

MICROWAVE DIRECTIONS: In 1-quart glass measure, combine Spaghetti Sauce Spices & Seasonings, tomato paste, water and margarine. Cover with wax paper; microwave at HIGH (Full Power) 15 minutes, stirring every 4 minutes. In 1-quart microwave-safe casserole, place ground beef. Microwave at HIGH 5 minutes or until no longer pink, stirring once. Drain fat; crumble beef. Stir in prepared spaghetti sauce, basil and thyme; set aside. In small bowl, combine ricotta cheese with egg. In 12×8-inch microwave-safe casserole, arrange zucchini; sprinkle with water. Cover with plastic wrap; vent one corner. Microwave at HIGH 2 minutes; drain liquid. In same dish, layer ½ *each* zucchini, ricotta mixture and meat sauce. Repeat layers. Cover with plastic wrap; vent one corner. Microwave at HIGH 14 minutes, turning dish once. Sprinkle with cheese; microwave uncovered at HIGH 3 minutes or until cheese is melted.

Makes about 6 servings

207 SOUPER QUICK "LASAGNA"

1½ pounds ground beef
1 envelope LIPTON® Recipe Secrets®
    Onion or Onion-Mushroom Soup Mix
3 cans (8 ounces each) tomato sauce
1 cup water
½ teaspoon dried oregano leaves (optional)
1 package (8 ounces) broad egg noodles,
    cooked and drained
1 package (16 ounces) mozzarella cheese,
    shredded

Preheat oven to 375°F.

In 12-inch skillet, brown ground beef over medium-high heat; drain. Stir in onion soup mix, tomato sauce, water and oregano. Simmer covered, stirring occasionally, 15 minutes.

In 2-quart oblong baking dish spoon enough sauce to cover bottom. Alternately layer noodles, ground beef mixture and cheese, ending with cheese. Bake 30 minutes or until bubbling.   *Makes about 6 servings*

MICROWAVE DIRECTIONS: In 2-quart casserole, microwave ground beef, uncovered, at HIGH (Full Power) 7 minutes, stirring once; drain. Stir in onion soup mix, tomato sauce, water and oregano. Microwave at MEDIUM (50% Power) 5 minutes, stirring once. In 2-quart oblong baking dish, spoon enough sauce to cover bottom. Alternately layer as above. Microwave covered at MEDIUM, turning dish occasionally, 10 minutes or until bubbling. Let stand covered 5 minutes.

208 NO–FUSS BEEF & SPINACH LASAGNA

1 pound lean ground beef
¼ teaspoon salt
1 jar or can (26 to 30 ounces) prepared low-fat spaghetti sauce
1 can (14½ ounces) Italian-style diced tomatoes, undrained
¼ teaspoon ground red pepper
1 carton (15 ounces) part-skim ricotta cheese
1 package (10 ounces) frozen chopped spinach, defrosted, well drained
¼ cup grated Parmesan cheese
1 egg, beaten
10 uncooked lasagna noodles
1½ cups shredded part-skim mozzarella cheese

1. Heat oven to 375°F. In large nonstick skillet, brown ground beef over medium heat 8 to 10 minutes or until no longer pink. Pour off drippings. Season with salt; add spaghetti sauce, tomatoes and red pepper, stirring to combine. Set aside.

2. Meanwhile in medium bowl, combine ricotta cheese, spinach, Parmesan cheese and egg. Spread 2 cups beef sauce over bottom of 13×9-inch baking dish. Arrange 5 lasagna noodles in single layer, completely covering bottom of dish; press noodles into sauce. Spread entire ricotta cheese mixture on top of noodles; sprinkle with 1 cup mozzarella cheese and top with 2 cups beef sauce. Arrange remaining noodles in single layer; press lightly into sauce. Top with remaining beef sauce.

3. Bake in 375°F oven 45 minutes or until noodles are tender. Sprinkle remaining mozzarella cheese on top; tent lightly with aluminum foil. Let stand 15 minutes before cutting.   *Makes 12 servings*

No-Fuss Beef & Spinach Lasagna

NOTE: There's no need to precook the noodles for this no-fuss lasagna—the noodles cook during baking.

Prep and Cook Time: 65 minutes

*Favorite recipe from **National Cattlemen's Beef Association***

209 WILD LASAGNA CASSEROLE

1 cup chopped onion
¾ cup chopped green pepper
1 can (14½ ounces) clear beef broth, divided
1 pound lean ground beef
½ teaspoon *each* salt, dried oregano leaves and garlic powder
1 can (6 ounces) tomato paste
4 cups cooked wild rice
1 package (16 ounces) frozen vegetable medley with broccoli, carrots, water chestnuts & red bell peppers, thawed and drained
1½ cups (6 ounces) shredded mozzarella cheese, divided
1 cup light ricotta cheese

Preheat oven to 350°F. In large skillet, sauté onion and pepper in ⅓ cup broth until tender; remove and set aside. Brown beef and drain; stir in seasonings, remaining broth and tomato paste. Add onion mixture, wild rice, vegetables and 1 cup mozzarella cheese; toss to blend. Pour half of mixture into 3-quart casserole; dollop with ricotta cheese. Add remaining mixture. Top with remaining ½ cup mozzarella cheese. Cover and bake 40 minutes. Uncover and bake 10 minutes.   *Makes 8 to 10 servings*

*Favorite recipe from **Minnesota Cultivated Wild Rice Council***

CASSEROLES & SKILLET DINNERS

210 LASAGNA WITH WHITE AND RED SAUCES

Béchamel Sauce (recipe follows)
½ medium onion, sliced
1 clove garlic, minced
2 to 3 tablespoons vegetable oil
1 pound lean ground beef
1 can (28 ounces) crushed tomatoes or
    1 can (28 ounces) whole tomatoes,
    chopped, undrained
½ cup thinly sliced celery
½ cup thinly sliced carrot
1 teaspoon dried basil, crushed
1 package (1 pound) lasagna noodles,
    cooked, drained
6 ounces BEL PAESE® cheese,* thinly sliced
6 hard-cooked eggs, sliced (optional)
2 tablespoons butter or margarine, cut
    into small pieces
1 cup (about 2 ounces) freshly grated
    Parmigiano-Reggiano or Grana
    Padano cheese

Remove wax coating and moist, white crust from cheese.

Prepare Béchamel Sauce; set aside. Cook and stir onion and garlic in hot oil in Dutch oven over medium-high heat until tender. Add ground beef and cook until no longer pink, stirring occasionally. Add tomatoes, celery, carrot and basil. Reduce heat to low. Cover and simmer 45 minutes. Remove cover and simmer 15 minutes more.

Arrange ⅓ of the lasagna noodles in bottom of buttered 13×9-inch baking dish. Add ½ of the Bel Paese® and ½ of the eggs. Spread with meat sauce. Repeat layers of noodles, Bel Paese® and eggs. Spread with Béchamel Sauce. Top with layer of noodles. Dot with butter. Sprinkle with Parmigiana-Reggiano. Bake in preheated 350°F oven 30 to 40 minutes or until heated through. Let stand 10 minutes before cutting.

Makes 6 servings

BÉCHAMEL SAUCE: Melt 2 tablespoons butter or margarine in small saucepan over medium-low heat. Stir in 2 tablespoons all-purpose flour. Gradually blend in ¾ cup milk. Season to taste with white pepper. Cook until thick and bubbly, stirring constantly. Makes ¾ cup sauce.

Lasagna with White and Red Sauces

CASSEROLES & SKILLET DINNERS

211 LASAGNA ROLL–UPS

1 pound ground beef
1 (16-ounce) jar spaghetti sauce
¼ cup A.1.® Steak Sauce
½ teaspoon dried basil leaves
1 (15-ounce) container ricotta cheese
1 egg, beaten
¼ cup grated Parmesan cheese, divided
8 lasagna noodles, cooked
2 cups shredded mozzarella
    cheese (8 ounces)

In skillet, over medium-high heat, brown beef, stirring occasionally to break up meat; drain. In small bowl, mix spaghetti sauce, steak sauce and basil; stir half the sauce mixture into beef. In another bowl, mix ricotta cheese, egg and 2 tablespoons Parmesan cheese.

On each lasagna noodle, spread about ¼ cup ricotta mixture. Top with about ⅓ cup beef mixture and ¼ cup mozzarella cheese. Roll up each noodle from short end; stand on end in greased 2-quart casserole. Pour remaining sauce over noodles. Sprinkle with remaining Parmesan cheese. Bake at 350°F for 45 minutes or until hot and bubbly. Serve with additional Parmesan cheese if desired.

Makes 4 to 6 servings

MICROWAVE DIRECTIONS: In 2-quart microwave-safe casserole, crumble beef; cover. Microwave at HIGH (100% power) for 5 to 6 minutes or until browned; drain. Mix spaghetti sauce, steak sauce and basil; stir half the sauce mixture into beef. Fill lasagna rolls as above; arrange in same 2-quart casserole. Top with remaining sauce and Parmesan cheese; cover. Microwave at HIGH for 10 to 12 minutes or until hot and bubbly, rotating dish ½ turn after 5 minutes. Let stand 3 minutes before serving.

212 ZUCCHINI LASAGNA

1½ pounds ground beef
¾ pound sweet Italian sausage, casing
    removed
3 tablespoons FILIPPO BERIO® Olive Oil
1½ cups coarsely chopped mushrooms
1 large onion, chopped
1 large clove garlic, minced
1 can (14½ ounces) tomatoes, chopped,
    undrained
1 jar (15 ounces) marinara sauce
1 teaspoon salt
1 teaspoon dried basil leaves, crushed
½ teaspoon Italian herb seasoning
1 container (24 ounces) ricotta cheese
1 package (8 ounces) mozzarella cheese,
    cubed, divided
¼ cup chopped Italian parsley
2 eggs, beaten
6 unpeeled zucchini, cut lengthwise into
    thin slices about 8 inches long

Cook beef and sausage in hot oil in large skillet over medium-high heat until meats are no longer pink. Add mushrooms, onion and garlic. Cook several minutes, stirring frequently. Add tomatoes with juice, marinara sauce, salt, basil and Italian seasoning. Combine ricotta, ¾ of the mozzarella, parsley and eggs in medium bowl. Spoon 1 cup of the sauce onto bottom of 13×9-inch baking dish. Top with ⅓ of the zucchini, ⅓ of the cheese mixture and then 1 cup of the sauce. Repeat layers twice, ending with sauce. Cover with foil. Bake at 350°F for 45 minutes. Sprinkle with remaining mozzarella. Bake, uncovered, 10 minutes more or until cheese melts. Let stand 10 minutes before cutting. Heat remaining sauce and serve with lasagna.

Makes 8 servings

CASSEROLES & SKILLET DINNERS

213 MOM'S LEAN LASAGNA

1 cup chopped onion
1 tablespoon vegetable oil
½ pound extra lean ground beef or ground
     turkey breast
1 (26-ounce) jar HEALTHY CHOICE®
     Traditional Pasta Sauce
1 (15-ounce) carton part-skim ricotta
     cheese
¼ cup grated Parmesan cheese
½ teaspoon dried basil leaves
½ teaspoon dried oregano leaves
6 lasagna noodles, cooked, drained
1½ cups HEALTHY CHOICE® Fat Free
     Mozzarella Shreds

In large nonstick saucepan, sauté onion in hot oil until tender. Add ground beef and brown until cooked through. Stir in pasta sauce; heat through. In small bowl, mix together ricotta and Parmesan cheeses with basil and oregano. In 13×9×2-inch baking dish, layer 3 noodles, half of cheese mixture, half of sauce and half of mozzarella cheese. Repeat layers. Bake at 350°F for 30 minutes.
Makes 8 servings

Mom's Lean Lasagna

214 TUSCAN POT PIE

¾ pound sweet or hot Italian sausage
1 jar (26 to 28 ounces) prepared chunky vegetable or mushroom spaghetti sauce
1 can (19 ounces) cannellini beans, rinsed and drained
½ teaspoon dried thyme leaves
1½ cups (6 ounces) shredded mozzarella cheese
1 package (8 ounces) refrigerated crescent dinner rolls

1. Preheat oven to 425°F. Remove sausage from casings. Brown sausage in medium ovenproof skillet, stirring to separate meat. Drain drippings.

2. Add spaghetti sauce, beans and thyme to skillet. Simmer uncovered over medium heat 5 minutes. Remove from heat; stir in cheese.

3. Unroll crescent dough; divide into triangles. Arrange spiral fashion with points of dough toward center, covering sausage mixture completely. Bake 12 minutes or until crust is golden brown and meat mixture is bubbly.   *Makes 4 to 6 servings*

Prep and Cook Time: 27 minutes

215 PIZZA HOT DISH

1½ to 2 pounds ground beef
¼ cup chopped onion
1 package (10 ounces) egg noodles
2 jars (15½ ounces each) pizza sauce
1 can (10¾ ounces) condensed Cheddar cheese soup
2 cups (8 ounces) shredded mozzarella cheese

1. In large skillet brown ground beef with onion. Drain.

2. Prepare egg noodles according to package directions.

3. Add sauce, soup and cooked egg noodles to ground beef; mix well. Spoon into 13×9-inch baking pan or large casserole. Bake at 350°F for 30 minutes. Sprinkle with mozzarella cheese and bake an additional 15 minutes.   *Makes 8 to 12 servings*

*Favorite recipe from **North Dakota Beef Commission***

Tuscan Pot Pie

CASSEROLES & SKILLET DINNERS

216 LAYERED NOODLE BAKE

1 can (26½ ounces) DEL MONTE®
Spaghetti Sauce with Green Peppers
and Mushrooms
1 package (12 ounces) extra wide noodles,
cooked
4 Italian Meat Loaf Patties, cooked and
cut bite-size (page 240)
1 pint (16 ounces) ricotta or cottage
cheese
1 package (8 ounces) shredded mozzarella
cheese

1. Preheat oven to 350°F.

2. Onto bottom of shallow 3-quart or 13×9-
inch baking pan, spread thin layer of sauce.
Arrange half of noodles over sauce; cover
with half of remaining sauce. Cover with
meat, ricotta cheese and half of mozzarella
cheese; top with layers of remaining
noodles, sauce and mozzarella cheese.

3. Bake, uncovered, about 25 minutes or
until heated through. Garnish, if desired.

Makes 4 to 6 servings

217 CHEESY TURKEY AND SPAGHETTI

1 pound ground turkey
1 tablespoon vegetable oil
1 can (15 ounces) VEG-ALL® Mixed
Vegetables, undrained
1 can (10¾ ounces) condensed cream of
chicken soup
1 can (10¾ ounces) condensed cream of
mushroom soup
1 cup milk
¼ cup dry sherry wine
12 ounces spaghetti or linguini, cooked
1 cup sliced mushrooms
¾ cup Parmesan cheese, divided

1. In large skillet cook turkey in oil until no
longer pink.

2. Drain Veg-All®, reserving liquid. Combine
liquid with soups, milk and wine.

3. Add soup mixture to spaghetti and mix
with turkey, vegetables, mushrooms and ½
cup Parmesan cheese. Spoon into 2-quart
casserole. Sprinkle with remaining ¼ cup
Parmesan cheese.

4. Bake at 400°F for 30 minutes.

Makes 8 servings

Layered Noodle Bake

218 TURKEY MEATBALL & OLIVE CASSEROLE

2 cups uncooked rotini
½ pound ground turkey
¼ cup plus 3 tablespoons Italian-style dry bread crumbs, divided
1 egg, slightly beaten
2 teaspoons dried minced onion
2 teaspoons white wine Worcestershire sauce
½ teaspoon dried Italian seasoning
½ teaspoon salt
⅛ teaspoon black pepper
1 tablespoon vegetable oil
1 can (10¾ ounces) condensed cream of celery soup, undiluted
½ cup low-fat plain yogurt
¾ cup pimiento-stuffed green olives, sliced
1 tablespoon margarine or butter, melted Paprika (optional)

Preheat oven to 350°F. Spray 2-quart round casserole with nonstick cooking spray.

Cook pasta according to package directions until al dente. Drain and set aside.

Meanwhile, combine turkey, ¼ cup bread crumbs, egg, onion, Worcestershire, Italian seasoning, salt and pepper in medium bowl. Shape mixture into 1-inch meatballs.

Heat oil in medium skillet over high heat until hot. Add meatballs in single layer; cook until lightly browned on all sides and still pink in centers, turning frequently. *Do not overcook.* Remove from skillet; drain on paper towels.

Mix soup and yogurt in large bowl. Add pasta, meatballs and olives; stir gently to combine. Transfer to prepared dish.

Combine remaining 3 tablespoons bread crumbs and margarine in small bowl; sprinkle evenly over casserole. Sprinkle lightly with paprika, if desired.

Bake, covered, 30 minutes. Uncover and bake 12 minutes or until meatballs are no longer pink in centers and casserole is hot and bubbly.   *Makes 6 to 8 servings*

219 DELICIOUS GROUND BEEF MEDLEY

1 pound ground beef
½ cup chopped onion
¼ cup chopped celery
2 cups uncooked elbow macaroni
1 can (10¾ ounces) condensed cream of chicken soup
1 can (10¾ ounces) condensed cream of mushroom soup
⅔ cup milk
½ teaspoon salt
Dash of pepper
1 can (15¼ ounces) whole kernel corn, drained
½ cup chopped green pepper

1. Brown ground beef with onion and celery. Drain.

2. Cook macaroni according to package directions. Drain.

3. In 2½-quart casserole dish, combine soups with milk, salt and pepper. Add ground beef, macaroni, corn and green pepper. Bake at 350°F for 30 minutes.
      Makes 8 servings

Favorite recipe from **North Dakota Beef Commission**

Turkey Meatball & Olive Casserole

CASSEROLES & SKILLET DINNERS

220 BEEF STROGANOFF CASSEROLE

1 pound lean ground beef
¼ teaspoon salt
⅛ teaspoon black pepper
1 teaspoon vegetable oil
8 ounces sliced mushrooms
1 large onion, chopped
3 cloves garlic, minced
¼ cup dry white wine
1 can (10¾ ounces) condensed cream of
   mushroom soup, undiluted
½ cup sour cream
1 tablespoon Dijon mustard
4 cups cooked egg noodles
   Chopped fresh parsley (optional)

Preheat oven to 350°F. Spray 13×9-inch baking dish with nonstick cooking spray.

Place beef in large skillet; season with salt and pepper. Brown beef over medium-high heat until no longer pink, stirring to separate beef. Drain fat from skillet; set beef aside.

Heat oil in same skillet over medium-high heat until hot. Add mushrooms, onion and garlic; cook and stir 2 minutes or until onion is tender. Add wine. Reduce heat to medium-low and simmer 3 minutes. Remove from heat; stir in soup, sour cream and mustard until well combined. Return beef to skillet.

Place noodles in prepared dish. Pour beef mixture over noodles; stir until noodles are well coated.

Bake, uncovered, 30 minutes or until heated through. Sprinkle with parsley, if desired. Garnish as desired.   *Makes 6 servings*

221 WILD RICE TETRAZZINI

1 cup chopped green pepper
1 cup chopped onion
1 jar (8 ounces) sliced mushrooms,
   drained
4 tablespoons butter or margarine
1 package (about 1¼ pounds) fresh lean
   ground turkey
½ cup grated Parmesan cheese
3 tablespoons all-purpose flour
2 teaspoons garlic powder
1 teaspoon salt
1 teaspoon pepper
2 cups chicken broth
2 cups cream or milk
½ cup cooking sherry
2 cups cooked and drained spaghetti
3 cups cooked wild rice
2 cups shredded mozzarella cheese,
   divided
   Parsley flakes

Preheat oven to 350°F. Sauté green pepper, onion and mushrooms in butter. Add turkey; brown. Add Parmesan cheese, flour and seasonings; stir and cook 5 minutes. Gradually add broth, cream and sherry. Heat thoroughly. Place spaghetti and wild rice in greased 5-quart casserole. Mix in 1 cup mozzarella cheese. Pour turkey mixture in casserole; lightly mix. Top with remaining 1 cup mozzarella cheese and parsley. Cover with foil. Bake 30 minutes. Remove foil; continue baking 10 minutes or until lightly browned.   *Makes 8 to 10 servings*

*Favorite recipe from **Minnesota Cultivated Wild Rice Council***

Beef Stroganoff Casserole

CASSEROLES & SKILLET DINNERS

222 PASTITSIO

8 ounces uncooked elbow macaroni
½ cup cholesterol-free egg substitute
¼ teaspoon ground nutmeg
¾ pound lean ground lamb, beef or turkey
½ cup chopped onion
1 clove garlic, minced
1 can (8 ounces) tomato sauce
¾ teaspoon dried mint leaves
½ teaspoon dried oregano leaves
½ teaspoon ground black pepper
⅛ teaspoon ground cinnamon
2 teaspoons reduced-calorie margarine
3 tablespoons all-purpose flour
1½ cups skim milk
2 tablespoons grated Parmesan cheese

Cook pasta according to package directions, omitting salt. Drain and transfer to medium bowl; stir in egg substitute and nutmeg.

Lightly spray bottom of 9-inch square baking dish with nonstick cooking spray. Spread pasta mixture in bottom of baking dish. Set aside.

Preheat oven to 350°F. Cook ground lamb, onion and garlic in large nonstick skillet over medium heat until lamb is no longer pink. Stir in tomato sauce, mint, oregano, black pepper and cinnamon. Reduce heat and simmer 10 minutes; spread over pasta.

Melt margarine in small nonstick saucepan. Add flour. Stir constantly for 1 minute. Whisk in milk. Cook, stirring constantly, until thickened, about 6 minutes; spread over meat mixture. Sprinkle with Parmesan cheese. Bake 30 to 40 minutes or until set.

Makes 6 servings

223 COUNTRY WILD RICE CASSEROLE

1 cup chopped onion
¼ cup butter or margarine
1¼ pounds fresh lean ground turkey
¼ teaspoon pepper
4 cups frozen potatoes O'Brien with onions and peppers
3 cups cooked wild rice (1 cup raw)
2 cups shredded mild Cheddar cheese, divided
1 can (10¾ ounces) condensed cream of chicken soup
1 cup sour cream
⅓ cup bread crumbs

Preheat oven to 350°F. In large skillet, sauté onion in butter; remove from skillet. In same skillet brown turkey with pepper. Sprinkle potatoes in greased 13×9-inch baking pan. Mix onion, turkey, wild rice, 1½ cups of the cheese, soup and sour cream. Spread over potatoes. Sprinkle remaining ½ cup cheese and bread crumbs on top. Bake 40 minutes.

Makes 8 servings

Favorite recipe from **Minnesota Cultivated Wild Rice Council**

Pastitsio

CASSEROLES & SKILLET DINNERS

224 TURKEY RICE BAKE

½ cup uncooked rice
¾ pound ground turkey
¼ cup chopped onion
1 to 3 teaspoons garlic powder
1 teaspoon ground red pepper, divided
½ teaspoon dried sage leaves, crushed
¼ teaspoon ground black pepper
     Salt to taste
1 teaspoon hot pepper sauce
½ teaspoon tostada or burrito seasoning
     mix
1 can (14.5 ounces) FRANK'S or
     SnowFloss Italian Style Diced
     Tomatoes
1 can (15½ ounces) chili-style beans,
     drained
     Mozzarella, Cheddar or hot pepper
     cheese, shredded

1. Preheat oven to 350°F. Place uncooked rice in bottom of casserole dish.

2. Mix ground turkey with onion, garlic powder, ½ teaspoon red pepper, sage, black pepper and salt to taste. Place mixture on top of rice.

3. Add remaining ½ teaspoon red pepper, hot pepper sauce and seasoning mix to diced tomatoes and pour over turkey and rice.

4. Pour beans over casserole. Sprinkle cheese on top.

5. Bake for 45 minutes.

Makes 6 servings

Prep Time: 20 minutes
Bake Time: 45 minutes

225 BAKED BEEF AND RICE MARINARA

1 pound lean ground beef
¾ cup sliced fresh mushrooms
½ cup *each* chopped onions, chopped
     celery and diced green pepper
2 cups cooked rice
¾ teaspoon ground oregano
½ teaspoon *each* salt, dried basil leaves
     and garlic powder
1 can (15 ounces) tomato sauce
3 slices American cheese

Combine crumbled beef and vegetables in plastic colander; place colander over 2-quart microwave-safe baking dish. Cook, uncovered, on HIGH (maximum power) 4 minutes; stir after 2 minutes. Drain beef; place mixture in baking dish. Stir in remaining ingredients except cheese. Cook on HIGH 2 minutes. Arrange cheese slices on top; cook on HIGH 2 minutes. Let stand 5 minutes.   *Makes 4 servings*

CONVENTIONAL DIRECTIONS: Cook beef and vegetables over medium-high heat in large skillet until meat is no longer pink and vegetables are crisp-tender, stirring frequently; drain. Combine meat mixture with remaining ingredients except cheese in buttered 2-quart baking dish; arrange cheese slices on top. Bake at 350°F 20 to 25 minutes.

*Favorite recipe from **USA Rice Council***

226 SPINACH–POTATO BAKE

1 pound extra-lean (90% lean) ground beef
½ cup sliced fresh mushrooms
1 small onion, chopped
2 cloves garlic, minced
1 package (10 ounces) frozen chopped spinach, thawed, well drained
½ teaspoon grated nutmeg
1 pound russet potatoes, peeled, cooked, mashed
¼ cup light sour cream
¼ cup skim milk
    Salt and freshly ground pepper
½ cup (2 ounces) shredded Cheddar cheese

Preheat oven to 400°F. Spray deep 9-inch casserole dish with nonstick cooking spray.

Brown ground beef in large skillet. Drain. Add mushrooms, onion and garlic; cook until tender. Stir in spinach and nutmeg; cover. Heat thoroughly, stirring occasionally.

Combine potatoes, sour cream and milk. Add to ground beef mixture; season with salt and pepper to taste. Spoon into prepared casserole dish; sprinkle with cheese.

Bake 15 to 20 minutes or until slightly puffed and cheese is melted.   *Makes 6 servings*

227 TEXAS RANCH CHILI BEANS

1 pound lean ground beef
1 can (28 ounces) whole peeled tomatoes, undrained
2 cans (15½ ounces each) chili beans
1 cup chopped onions
1 cup water
1 package (1 ounce) HIDDEN VALLEY RANCH® Milk Recipe Original Ranch® salad dressing mix
1 teaspoon chili powder
1 bay leaf

In Dutch oven, brown beef over medium-high heat; drain off fat. Add tomatoes, breaking up with spoon. Stir in beans, onions, water, salad dressing mix, chili powder and bay leaf. Bring to boil; reduce heat and simmer, uncovered, 1 hour, stirring occasionally. Remove bay leaf just before serving.   *Makes 8 servings*

228 RED CLOUD BEEF AND ONIONS

2¼ cups nonfat milk
1½ cups water
1½ cups yellow cornmeal
½ cup grated Parmesan cheese
1 tablespoon butter or margarine
4 medium yellow onions, sliced (1 pound 6 ounces)
2 teaspoons vegetable oil
1 pound lean ground beef or pork
2 to 3 teaspoons chili powder (to taste)
½ cup canned whole pimientos or roasted red bell peppers, cut into ½-inch strips
2 cans (4 ounces each) whole green chilies, cut into ½-inch strips

For cornmeal base, combine milk, water and cornmeal in saucepan. Place over medium heat and cook, stirring, until mixture bubbles. Continue cooking 30 to 60 seconds or until mixture is consistency of soft mashed potatoes. Remove from heat; stir in cheese and butter. Spoon into 2½-quart casserole. Sauté onions in oil in large skillet until soft and tender. Spoon into casserole in ring around edge. In same skillet, sauté beef until browned; drain. Stir in chili powder. Spoon into center of casserole. Arrange pimientos and chilies in latticework pattern over top. Cover and bake at 400°F for 25 to 30 minutes or until hot in center. Serve with dollops of sour cream, if desired.

Makes 6 servings

Favorite recipe from **National Onion Association**

229 ARTICHOKE CASSEROLE

¾ pound extra-lean (90% lean) ground beef
½ cup sliced mushrooms
¼ cup chopped onion
1 clove garlic, minced
1 can (14 ounces) artichoke hearts, drained, rinsed, chopped
½ cup dry bread crumbs
¼ cup (1 ounce) grated Parmesan cheese
2 tablespoons chopped fresh rosemary *or* 1 teaspoon dried rosemary leaves
1½ teaspoons chopped fresh marjoram *or* ½ teaspoon dried marjoram leaves
Salt and freshly ground pepper
3 egg whites

Preheat oven to 400°F. Spray 1-quart casserole with nonstick cooking spray.

Brown ground beef in medium skillet. Drain. Add mushrooms, onion and garlic; cook until tender.

Combine ground beef mixture, artichokes, crumbs, cheese, rosemary and marjoram; mix lightly. Season with salt and pepper to taste.

Beat egg whites until stiff peaks form; fold into ground beef mixture. Spoon into prepared casserole.

Bake 20 minutes or until lightly browned around edges.

Makes 4 servings

Red Cloud Beef and Onions

CASSEROLES & SKILLET DINNERS

230 MOUSSAKA

1 large eggplant
2½ teaspoons salt, divided
2 large zucchini
2 large russet potatoes, peeled
½ to ¾ cup olive oil, divided
5 tablespoons butter or margarine, divided
1 large onion, chopped
1½ pounds ground beef or lamb
2 cloves garlic, minced
1 cup chopped tomatoes
½ cup dry red or white wine
¼ cup chopped fresh parsley
¼ teaspoon ground cinnamon
⅛ teaspoon black pepper
1 cup grated Parmesan cheese, divided
⅓ cup all-purpose flour
¼ teaspoon ground nutmeg
2 cups milk

Cut eggplant lengthwise into ½-inch-thick slices. Place in large colander set over bowl; sprinkle with 1 teaspoon salt. Drain 30 minutes. Cut zucchini lengthwise into ⅜-inch-thick slices. Cut potatoes lengthwise into ¼-inch-thick slices.

Heat ¼ cup oil in large skillet over medium heat until hot. Add potatoes in single layer. Cook 5 minutes per side or until tender and lightly browned. Remove potatoes from skillet; drain on paper towels. Add more oil to skillet, if needed. Cook zucchini 2 minutes per side or until tender. Drain on paper towels. Add more oil to skillet. Cook eggplant 5 minutes per side or until tender. Drain on paper towels. Drain oil from skillet; discard.

Melt 1 tablespoon butter in same skillet over medium heat. Add onion. Cook and stir 5 minutes. Add beef and garlic to skillet. Cook and stir 10 minutes or until meat is no longer pink. Pour off drippings. Stir in tomatoes, wine, parsley, 1 teaspoon salt, cinnamon and pepper. Bring to a boil over high heat. Reduce heat to low. Simmer 10 minutes or until liquid is evaporated.

Preheat oven to 325°F. Grease 13×9-inch baking dish. Arrange potatoes in bottom; sprinkle with ¼ cup cheese. Top with zucchini and ¼ cup cheese, then eggplant and ¼ cup cheese. Spoon meat mixture over top.

To prepare sauce, melt remaining 4 tablespoons butter in medium saucepan over low heat. Blend in flour, remaining ½ teaspoon salt and nutmeg with wire whisk. Cook 1 minute, whisking constantly. Gradually whisk in milk. Cook over medium heat, until mixture boils and thickens, whisking constantly. Pour sauce evenly over meat mixture in dish; sprinkle with remaining ¼ cup cheese. Bake 30 to 40 minutes or until hot and bubbly. Garnish as desired. *Makes 6 to 8 servings*

Moussaka

CASSEROLES & SKILLET DINNERS

231 CHILI MEATLOAF & POTATO CASSEROLE

MEATLOAF
1½ pounds lean ground beef
¾ cup finely chopped onion
⅓ cup saltine cracker crumbs
1 egg, slightly beaten
3 tablespoons milk
1 tablespoon chili powder
¾ teaspoon salt

POTATO TOPPING
3 cups prepared mashed potatoes
1 can (11 ounces) whole kernel corn with red and green peppers, drained
¼ cup thinly sliced green onions
½ to 1 cup shredded taco seasoned cheese

1. Heat oven to 375°F. In large bowl, combine meatloaf ingredients, mixing lightly but thoroughly; gently press into bottom of 9-inch square baking pan. Bake in 375°F oven 20 to 25 minutes or until no longer pink and juices run clear. Carefully pour off drippings.

2. Meanwhile in medium bowl, combine all topping ingredients except cheese. Spread over meatloaf to edges of pan; sprinkle with cheese. Broil 3 to 4 inches from heat 3 to 5 minutes or until top is lightly browned; cut into 6 rectangular servings.

Makes 6 servings

*Favorite recipe from **National Cattlemen's Beef Association***

232 CAPTAIN'S CHOICE BAKED BEANS

1 pound ground beef
1 can (16 ounces) baked beans
1 can (15½ ounces) dark red kidney beans, drained
1 can (15½ ounces) butter beans, drained
½ cup MISSISSIPPI Barbecue Sauce
1 onion, chopped
½ cup packed brown sugar
1 tablespoon Worcestershire sauce
2 tablespoons prepared mustard
3 to 4 strips bacon (optional)

1. Preheat oven to 350°F. Brown ground beef; drain fat.

2. In 2-quart casserole, combine ground beef and all remaining ingredients except bacon. Place bacon strips on top.

3. Bake at 350°F for 1¼ hours.

Makes 6 servings

Prep Time: 20 minutes
Bake Time: 1¼ hours

Chili Meatloaf & Potato Casserole

CASSEROLES & SKILLET DINNERS

233 STEAMED PORK AND HAM

6 dried Oriental mushrooms
1 slice (4 ounces) smoked or baked ham
3 green onions with tops
1 pound ground pork
¼ cup chopped water chestnuts
1 tablespoon cornstarch
1 tablespoon sesame oil
1 tablespoon soy sauce
1 teaspoon minced fresh ginger
½ teaspoon sugar

Place mushrooms in small bowl; cover with hot water. Let stand 30 minutes; drain. Squeeze excess water from mushrooms. Cut stems off; discard. Cut caps into thin strips; place in medium bowl. Set aside.

Cut ham into julienned strips. Reserve 2 tablespoons ham strips. Finely chop remaining ham; add to mushrooms. Cut onions diagonally into thin slices. Reserve 1 tablespoon onion slices and stir remaining slices into mushroom mixture.

Add pork, water chestnuts, cornstarch, oil, soy sauce, ginger and sugar to mushroom-ham mixture; mix lightly. Spread mixture into greased 9-inch shallow ovenproof serving dish or pie plate.

To steam pork mixture, place wire rack in wok. Add water to 1 inch *below* rack. Cover wok; bring water to a boil over high heat. Carefully place dish with pork on rack. Cover and reduce heat to medium. Steam pork mixture about 25 to 30 minutes until firm. Carefully remove dish from wok.

Sprinkle dish with reserved ham and onion slices. Garnish as desired. Serve immediately.   *Makes 4 servings*

234 ONE–POT DINNER

1 pound ground turkey, browned
¾ pound bacon, cooked, cut into small pieces
1 can (16 ounces) pork & beans, undrained
1 can (15¼ ounces) lima or green beans, undrained
1 can (15½ ounces) kidney beans, undrained
1 cup chopped onion (microwaved 3 minutes, if desired)
1 cup ketchup
¾ cup pearl barley
½ cup water
¼ cup packed brown sugar
3 tablespoons white vinegar
1 teaspoon liquid smoke (optional)

Combine all ingredients and cook in slow cooker on HIGH 4 to 9 hours. Or, place in casserole dish and microwave, covered, on MEDIUM (50% power) 30 minutes, stirring occasionally.   *Makes 8 servings*

NOTE: This dish is even better when served the next day. When reheating, add more water.

Favorite recipe from **North Dakota Barley Council**

CASSEROLES & SKILLET DINNERS

235 BROCCOLI AND BEEF PASTA

1 pound lean ground beef
2 cloves garlic, minced
1 can (14½ ounces) beef broth
1 medium onion, thinly sliced
1 cup uncooked rotini pasta
½ teaspoon dried basil leaves
½ teaspoon dried oregano leaves
½ teaspoon dried thyme leaves
1 can (14½ ounces) Italian-style tomatoes, undrained
2 cups broccoli florets *or* 1 package (10 ounces) frozen chopped broccoli, thawed
3 ounces shredded Cheddar cheese or grated Parmesan cheese

1. Combine meat and garlic in large nonstick skillet; cook over high heat 6 to 8 minutes or until meat is no longer pink, breaking meat apart with wooden spoon. Pour off drippings. Place meat mixture in large bowl; set aside.

2. Add broth, onion, pasta, basil, oregano and thyme to skillet. Bring to a boil. Reduce heat to medium-high and boil 10 minutes; add tomatoes and their juice. Increase heat to high and bring to a boil; stir in broccoli. Cook, uncovered, 6 to 8 minutes, stirring occasionally, until broccoli is crisp-tender and pasta is tender. Return meat to skillet and stir 3 to 4 minutes or until heated through.

3. With slotted spoon, transfer meat mixture to serving platter. Sprinkle with cheese. Cover with lid or tent with foil several minutes until cheese melts. Meanwhile, bring juice left in skillet to a boil over high heat. Boil until thick and reduced to 3 to 4 tablespoons. Spoon over meat mixture.

Makes 4 servings

Prep and Cook Time: 30 minutes

SERVING SUGGESTION: Serve with garlic bread.

236 QUICK BEEF STROGANOFF

1 pound ground beef
1 package LIPTON® Noodles & Sauce— Butter
2¼ cups water
1 jar (4½ ounces) sliced mushrooms, drained
2 tablespoons finely chopped pimiento
⅛ teaspoon garlic powder
½ cup sour cream

In 10-inch skillet, brown ground beef; drain. Stir in remaining ingredients except sour cream. Bring to a boil, then simmer, stirring frequently, 7 minutes or until noodles are tender. Stir in sour cream; heat through but do not boil. *Makes about 2 servings*

MICROWAVE DIRECTIONS: In 2-quart casserole, cook ground beef at HIGH (Full Power) 4 to 6 minutes. Add noodles & sauce—butter, water, mushrooms, pimiento and garlic powder. Heat at HIGH 10 minutes or until noodles are tender, stirring occasionally. Stir in sour cream.

Broccoli and Beef Pasta

237 CURRY BEEF

12 ounces wide egg noodles *or* 1⅓ cups
    long-grain white rice
1 tablespoon olive oil
1 medium onion, thinly sliced
1 tablespoon curry powder
1 teaspoon ground cumin
2 cloves garlic, minced
1 pound lean ground beef
1 cup (8 ounces) sour cream
½ cup 2% milk
½ cup raisins, divided
1 teaspoon sugar
¼ cup chopped walnuts, almonds or
    pecans

1. Cook noodles or rice according to package directions. Meanwhile, heat oil in large skillet over medium-high heat until hot. Add onion; cook and stir 3 to 4 minutes. Add curry powder, cumin and garlic; cook 2 to 3 minutes longer or until onion is tender. Add meat; cook 6 to 8 minutes or until meat is no longer pink, breaking meat apart with wooden spoon.

2. Stir in sour cream, milk, ¼ cup raisins and sugar. Reduce heat to medium, stirring constantly, until heated through. Spoon over drained noodles or rice. Sprinkle with remaining ¼ cup raisins and nuts.

Makes 4 servings

Prep and Cook Time: 30 minutes

SERVING SUGGESTION: Serve with sliced cucumber sprinkled with sugar and vinegar or plain yogurt topped with brown sugar, chopped bananas and green onions.

238 PORK PASTA FAGIOLI

½ pound lean ground pork
1 small onion, diced
1 clove garlic, minced
1 can (15 ounces) cannellini (white kidney
    beans), drained
1 can (14½ ounces) chicken broth
1 can (14½ ounces) Italian-style chopped
    tomatoes
½ cup small pasta shells or macaroni
1 teaspoon dried oregano leaves
½ teaspoon salt
½ teaspoon crushed fennel seed
½ teaspoon coarsely ground black pepper
¼ teaspoon crushed red pepper flakes

In large heavy saucepan brown and crumble ground pork. Stir in onion and garlic; cook and stir until onion is soft, about 3 minutes. Stir in all remaining ingredients; bring to a boil, reduce heat and simmer 10 to 12 minutes or until pasta is tender.

Makes 6 (1-cup) servings

Prep Time: 20 minutes

Favorite recipe from **National Pork Producers Council**

Curry Beef

CASSEROLES & SKILLET DINNERS

239 PORK AND PASTA SKILLET SUPPER

1 pound ground pork
1 medium onion, chopped
1 can (14½ ounces) pasta-ready tomatoes
1 can (8 ounces) tomato sauce
1 small yellow summer squash or zucchini, thinly sliced
1½ cups (4 ounces uncooked) hot cooked penne pasta, or other small shape pasta

1. Heat nonstick skillet over medium-high heat. Add pork and onion; cook and stir until evenly browned. Drain any excess drippings.

2. Stir in tomatoes and tomato sauce; bring to a boil. Reduce heat to low; cook 5 minutes.

3. Stir in squash and pasta. Cook 2 to 5 minutes or until heated through.

Makes 4 servings

NOTE: Serve with a crisp green salad and French bread.

Prep Time: 15 minutes

Favorite recipe from **National Pork Producers Council**

240 SKILLET ITALIANO

1 pound ground beef
½ medium onion, chopped
1 package (1.5 ounces) LAWRY'S® Original Style Spaghetti Sauce Spices & Seasonings
1 can (14½ ounces) whole tomatoes, cut up, undrained
1 package (10 ounces) frozen Italian-cut green beans, thawed
LAWRY'S® Seasoned Salt to taste
1 cup (4 ounces) shredded Cheddar cheese

In large skillet, brown ground beef and onion until beef is crumbly; drain fat. Add Spaghetti Sauce Spices & Seasonings, tomatoes and beans; blend well. Bring to a boil. Reduce heat; cover and simmer 20 minutes. Add Seasoned Salt to taste. Top with cheese; cover and heat until cheese melts.

Makes 4 to 6 servings

PRESENTATION: Serve with warm bread and a tossed fruit salad.

CASSEROLES & SKILLET DINNERS

241 SZECHWAN BEEF

1 pound ground beef
1 tablespoon vegetable oil
1 cup sliced carrots
1 cup frozen peas
$\frac{1}{3}$ cup water
3 tablespoons soy sauce
2 tablespoons cornstarch
$\frac{1}{4}$ teaspoon ground ginger
1 jar (7 ounces) baby corn, drained
1 medium onion, thinly sliced
   Sliced mushrooms and olives as desired
$\frac{1}{4}$ cup shredded Cheddar cheese
$1\frac{1}{3}$ cups uncooked instant rice

1. In wok or large skillet, brown ground beef; remove from wok and set aside. Drain fat.

2. Add oil to wok or skillet and return to medium heat. Add carrots and peas and stir-fry about 3 minutes.

3. In small cup combine water and soy sauce with cornstarch and ginger. Add to vegetables in wok.

4. Return ground beef to wok along with baby corn, onion, mushrooms, olives and cheese. Cook over medium heat until all ingredients are heated through.

5. Prepare instant rice according to package directions. Serve beef and vegetables over rice. *Makes 4 to 5 servings*

*Favorite recipe from **North Dakota Beef Commission***

242 WESTERN SKILLET NOODLES

1 pound ground beef
$2\frac{1}{3}$ cups water
1 package LIPTON® Noodles & Sauce— Beef Flavor
2 teaspoons chili powder
1 can (12 ounces) whole kernel corn with sweet peppers, drained
1 cup shredded cheddar cheese (about 4 ounces), divided

In 10-inch skillet, brown beef; drain. Add water and bring to a boil; stir in noodles & sauce—beef flavor and chili powder. Continue boiling over medium heat, stirring occasionally, 7 minutes. Add corn and $\frac{2}{3}$ cup cheese. Simmer 5 minutes or until cheese is melted. Top with remaining $\frac{1}{3}$ cup cheese.
Makes about 4 servings

243 BEAN THREADS WITH MINCED PORK

4 ounces bean threads or Chinese rice
    vermicelli
3 dried mushrooms
1 small red or green hot chili pepper
3 green onions, divided
2 tablespoons minced fresh ginger
2 tablespoons hot bean sauce
1½ cups chicken broth
1 tablespoon soy sauce
1 tablespoon dry sherry
2 tablespoons vegetable oil
6 ounces lean ground pork
2 cilantro sprigs for garnish

Place bean threads and dried mushrooms in separate bowls. Cover each with hot water. Let stand 30 minutes; drain. Cut bean threads into 4-inch pieces. Squeeze out excess water from mushrooms. Cut off and discard stems; cut caps into thin slices.

Cut chili pepper in half and scrape out seeds.* Finely mince chili pepper. Thinly slice 2 of the onions. Cut remaining onion into 1½-inch slivers and reserve for garnish. Combine ginger and hot bean sauce in small bowl. Combine chicken broth, soy sauce and sherry in medium bowl.

Heat oil in wok or large skillet over high heat. Add pork and stir-fry until meat is no longer pink, about 2 minutes. Add chili pepper, sliced onions and ginger-bean sauce mixture. Stir-fry until meat absorbs color from bean sauce, about 1 minute.

Add chicken broth mixture, bean threads and mushrooms. Simmer, uncovered, until most of the liquid is absorbed, about 5 minutes. Garnish with onion slivers and cilantro sprigs. *Makes 4 servings*

*Chili peppers can sting and irritate the skin; wear rubber gloves when handling peppers and do not touch eyes. Wash hands after handling.

244 BEEF WITH SNOW PEAS & BABY CORN

¾ pound extra-lean (90% lean) ground
    beef
1 clove garlic, minced
1 teaspoon vegetable oil
6 ounces snow peas, halved lengthwise
1 red bell pepper, cut into strips
1 can (15 ounces) baby corn, drained,
    rinsed
1 tablespoon soy sauce
1 teaspoon sesame oil
    Salt and freshly ground black pepper
2 cups cooked rice

Brown ground beef in wok or large skillet. Drain. Add garlic; cook until tender. Set aside. Wipe out wok with paper towel.

Heat vegetable oil in wok over medium-high heat. Add snow peas and red bell pepper; stir-fry 2 to 3 minutes or until vegetables are crisp-tender. Stir in ground beef mixture, baby corn, soy sauce and sesame oil. Season with salt and black pepper to taste. Serve over rice. *Makes 4 servings*

Beef with Snow Peas & Baby Corn

CASSEROLES & SKILLET DINNERS

245 THREE–TOPPED RICE

1 ounce Pickled Ginger Slices (recipe
   follows) (optional)
2½ cups short-grain rice
4¼ cups water, divided
1 teaspoon salt, divided
1½ cups fresh or frozen green peas
1 piece fresh ginger (about 1 inch square),
   grated
2 tablespoons sugar, divided
2 tablespoons sake or dry sherry, divided
1 tablespoon plus 1 teaspoon soy sauce,
   divided
8 ounces ground chicken
4 eggs, lightly beaten

Prepare Pickled Ginger Slices, if desired.
Place rice in large bowl; add cold water to
cover. Stir rice gently with fingers. (Water
will become cloudy.) Drain rice in colander.
Repeat washing and draining 3 or 4 times
until water remains almost clear. Place rice
in large, heavy saucepan with tight-fitting lid.
Add 2¾ cups water; soak 30 minutes. Gently
stir ½ teaspoon salt into rice. Cover and
bring to a boil over medium-high heat.
Reduce heat to low; simmer about 15
minutes or until liquid is absorbed. Do not
lift lid during cooking. Remove pan from
heat; let stand, covered, 15 minutes. Gently
fluff rice with wooden spoon or paddle. Lay
dry kitchen towel over saucepan; cover
towel with lid. Let stand 10 minutes to
absorb excess moisture.

Cut Pickled Ginger Slices into thin strips; set
aside. Place peas, remaining 1½ cups water
and ½ teaspoon salt in small saucepan. Bring
to a boil over medium-high heat; boil 4
minutes or until peas are tender. Drain well.
Squeeze grated ginger between thumb and
fingers to extract juice into cup. Squeeze
enough ginger to measure 1 teaspoon ginger
juice. Combine 1 tablespoon sugar, 1
tablespoon sake, 1 tablespoon soy sauce and
ginger juice in medium saucepan; bring to a
boil over high heat. Add chicken; cook and
stir 3 to 4 minutes or until chicken is no
longer pink. Turn off heat.

Place eggs, remaining 1 tablespoon sugar,
1 tablespoon sake and 1 teaspoon soy sauce
in medium skillet. Cook 3 to 5 minutes over
medium-low heat, stirring constantly with
fork until eggs are set but still moist.
Remove from heat.

Divide rice among four individual serving
bowls. Place equal amounts of chicken, eggs
and peas over rice in triangular patterns.
Garnish with Pickled Ginger.

Makes 4 servings

PICKLED GINGER SLICES

4 ounces fresh ginger, peeled
1 cup boiling water
½ cup rice vinegar
2 tablespoons sugar
½ teaspoon salt

Cut ginger crosswise into thin slices. Place
in small bowl; add boiling water. Let stand
30 seconds; drain well. Place vinegar, sugar
and salt in small glass or ceramic bowl; stir
until sugar is dissolved. Add ginger; stir to
coat well. Cover bowl; let stand at room
temperature at least 1 hour. Refrigerate,
covered, until well chilled. To serve, remove
slices from pickling liquid.

Makes about ¾ cup

Three-Topped Rice

CASSEROLES & SKILLET DINNERS

246 THAI CHICKEN WITH BASIL

1 small bunch fresh basil
2 cups vegetable oil
6 large shallots, chopped
5 cloves garlic, minced
1 piece fresh ginger (about 1 inch square),
    cut into very thin strips
1 pound ground chicken or turkey
2 fresh Thai or jalapeño chilies* (1 red and
    1 green or 2 green), seeded and cut
    into thin slices
2 teaspoons brown sugar
½ teaspoon salt
    Boston lettuce leaves

Chilies can sting and irritate the skin; wear rubber gloves when handling chilies and do not touch eyes. Wash hands after handling chilies.

Set aside 8 basil sprigs. Stem remaining basil leaves and cut into ¼-inch-thick strips to equal ½ cup; set aside. Heat oil in wok over medium-high heat until oil registers 375°F on deep-fry thermometer. Add 1 basil sprig and deep-fry** about 15 seconds or until basil is glossy and crisp. Remove fried sprig with slotted spoon to paper towels; drain. Repeat with remaining 7 sprigs, reheating oil between batches.

Let oil cool slightly. Pour off oil, reserving ¼ cup. Return ¼ cup oil to wok and heat over medium-high heat 30 seconds or until hot. Add shallots, garlic and ginger; cook and stir 1 minute. Add chicken and stir-fry about 4 minutes or until lightly browned. Push chicken up side of wok, letting juices remain in bottom.

Continue to cook about 5 to 7 minutes until all juices evaporate. Add chili slices, brown sugar and salt to chicken and cook 1 minute. Stir in reserved basil strips. Remove from heat.

Line serving plate with lettuce. Spoon chicken mixture on top. Garnish as desired. Top with fried basil and serve immediately.
Makes 4 servings

**Use long-handled tongs since oil may splatter.*

247 BEEF FRIED RICE

¾ pound extra-lean (90% lean) ground
    beef
6 green onions, chopped
3 large stalks celery, chopped
8 ounces bean sprouts
½ cup chopped fresh mushrooms
½ cup finely chopped red bell pepper
1 teaspoon grated gingerroot
3 cups cooked rice
2 tablespoons soy sauce
    Salt and freshly ground black pepper

Brown ground beef in large skillet. Drain. Stir in onions, celery, bean sprouts, mushrooms, red bell pepper and gingerroot. Cook over medium-high heat 5 minutes or until vegetables are crisp-tender, stirring frequently. Stir in rice and soy sauce. Season with salt and black pepper to taste. Heat thoroughly, stirring occasionally.
Makes 4 servings

Thai Chicken with Basil

CASSEROLES & SKILLET DINNERS

248 MA–PO BEAN CURD

1 tablespoon Szechuan peppercorns
    (optional)
¾ cup chicken broth
1 tablespoon soy sauce
1 tablespoon dry sherry
2 tablespoons vegetable oil
4 ounces ground pork
1 tablespoon hot bean sauce*
2 cloves garlic, minced
2 teaspoons minced fresh ginger
12 to 14 ounces bean curd (tofu), drained
    and cut into ½-inch cubes
2 green onions, thinly sliced
3 tablespoons water
4½ teaspoons cornstarch
1 teaspoon Oriental sesame oil

Available in the Oriental section of large supermarkets or in specialty grocery stores.

Place peppercorns in small skillet; shake over medium-low heat, until fragrant, about 2 minutes. Let cool. Crush peppercorns with mortar and pestle or place between paper towels and crush with hammer; set aside. (Wear rubber gloves when crushing.)

Combine chicken broth, soy sauce and sherry in small bowl; set aside. Heat vegetable oil in wok or large skillet over high heat. Add pork and stir-fry until pork is no longer pink, about 2 minutes. Add hot bean sauce, garlic and ginger. Stir-fry until meat absorbs color from bean sauce, about 1 minute. Add chicken broth mixture and bean curd to wok. Simmer, uncovered, 5 minutes. Stir in onions. Blend water and cornstarch in small cup. Add to wok; cook and stir until sauce boils and thickens slightly. Stir in sesame oil. Pass crushed peppercorns to sprinkle over individual servings, if desired.

Makes 3 to 4 servings

249 BEEF & VEGETABLE FRIED RICE

1 pound lean ground beef
2 cloves garlic, crushed
1 teaspoon grated fresh ginger *or*
    ¼ teaspoon ground ginger
2 tablespoons water
1 red bell pepper, cut into ½-inch pieces
1 package (6 ounces) frozen pea pods
3 cups cold cooked rice
3 tablespoons soy sauce
2 teaspoons dark sesame oil
¼ cup thinly sliced green onions

1. In large nonstick skillet, brown ground beef, garlic and ginger over medium heat 8 to 10 minutes or until beef is no longer pink, breaking up into ¾-inch crumbles. Remove with slotted spoon; pour off drippings.

2. In same skillet, heat water over medium-high heat until hot. Add bell pepper and pea pods; cook 3 minutes or until bell pepper is crisp-tender, stirring occasionally. Add rice, soy sauce and sesame oil; mix well. Return beef to skillet; heat through, about 5 minutes. Stir in green onions before serving.

Makes 4 (1½-cup) servings

Prep and Cook Time: 25 minutes

*Favorite recipe from **National Cattlemen's Beef Association***

Beef & Vegetable Fried Rice

250 SWEET AND SOUR BEEF

1 pound lean ground beef
1 small onion, thinly sliced
2 teaspoons minced fresh ginger
1 package (16 ounces) frozen mixed
    vegetables (snap peas, carrots, water
    chestnuts, pineapple and red pepper)
6 to 8 tablespoons bottled sweet and sour
    sauce or sauce from frozen mixed
    vegetables
Hot cooked rice

1. Place meat, onion and ginger in large skillet; cook over high heat 6 to 8 minutes or until no longer pink, breaking meat apart with wooden spoon. Pour off drippings.

2. Stir in frozen vegetables and sauce. Cook, covered, 6 to 8 minutes, stirring every 2 minutes or until vegetables are heated through. Serve over rice. Garnish as desired.

Makes 4 servings

Prep and Cook Time: 15 minutes

SERVING SUGGESTION: Serve with sliced Asian apple-pears.

251 BEEF & BROCCOLI

1 pound lean ground beef
4 tablespoons soy sauce
2 tablespoons dry sherry
1 tablespoon all-purpose flour
1 tablespoon sugar
1 tablespoon seasoned rice vinegar
2 teaspoons grated gingerroot *or*
    1 teaspoon ground ginger
1 pound fresh broccoli, stems sliced, tops
    broken into flowerets (about 6 cups)
1 medium onion, sliced crosswise,
    separated into rings
Dash of hot pepper sauce
Salt and freshly ground pepper
Hot cooked rice

MICROWAVE DIRECTIONS: Crumble ground beef into large microwave-safe bowl. Stir together soy sauce, sherry, flour, sugar, vinegar and gingerroot in 2-cup glass measure. Add to ground beef; mix well. Cover; chill 30 minutes.

Microwave marinated ground beef mixture, uncovered, on HIGH (100%) 6 minutes or until ground beef is no longer pink, stirring twice during cooking. Drain; keep meat warm.

Combine broccoli and onion in microwave-safe casserole dish. Cover with plastic wrap; vent. Microwave on HIGH 5 to 6 minutes or until crisp-tender. Add to meat with hot pepper sauce; mix lightly. Season with salt and pepper to taste. Serve with rice.

Makes 4 servings

Favorite recipe from **USA Rice Council**

Sweet and Sour Beef

CASSEROLES & SKILLET DINNERS

252 MALAYSIAN CURRIED BEEF

2 tablespoons vegetable oil
2 large yellow onions, chopped
1 piece fresh ginger (about 1 inch square), minced
2 cloves garlic, minced
2 tablespoons curry powder
1 teaspoon salt
2 large baking potatoes (1 pound), peeled and cut into 1-inch chunks
1 cup beef broth
1 pound ground beef chuck
2 ripe tomatoes (12 ounces), peeled, seeded and chopped
   Hot cooked rice

Heat wok or large skillet over medium-high heat 1 minute or until hot. Drizzle oil into wok. Add onions and stir-fry 2 minutes. Add ginger, garlic, curry and salt to wok. Cook and stir about 1 minute or until fragrant. Add potatoes; cook and stir 3 minutes. Add broth to potato mixture. Cover and bring to a boil. Reduce heat to low; simmer about 20 minutes or until potatoes are fork-tender.

Stir ground chuck into potato mixture. Cook and stir about 5 minutes or until beef is browned and no pink remains; spoon off fat if necessary. Add tomato chunks and stir gently until thoroughly heated. Spoon beef mixture into serving dish. Top center with rice. Garnish as desired.

Makes 4 servings

253 SPANISH RICE

4 slices bacon, diced
1 medium green bell pepper, diced
1 small onion, chopped
1 large clove garlic, crushed
½ pound ground beef
2 cups canned stewed tomatoes
1 cup long-grain rice, uncooked
1 cup water
1½ teaspoons TABASCO® pepper sauce
1 teaspoon salt

• In 12-inch skillet over medium-high heat, cook bacon until crisp, stirring occasionally. With slotted spoon, remove to paper towels; set aside. In drippings remaining in skillet over medium heat, cook green pepper, onion and garlic until tender-crisp, about 5 minutes. Remove to bowl.

• In same skillet over medium-high heat, cook ground beef until well browned on all sides, stirring frequently. Drain. Add tomatoes with their liquid, rice, water, Tabasco® sauce, salt and green pepper mixture. Over high heat, bring to a boil; reduce heat to low. Cover and simmer 20 minutes or until rice is tender, stirring occasionally.

• To serve, sprinkle mixture with cooked bacon.   *Makes 4 servings*

Malaysian Curried Beef

CASSEROLES & SKILLET DINNERS

254 WHITE CHILI PILAF

Nonstick cooking spray
½ pound lean ground beef
½ pound bulk turkey sausage
1 cup finely chopped green bell pepper
2 to 3 tablespoons seeded, minced jalapeño peppers*
2 teaspoons minced garlic
2 teaspoons ground cumin
½ teaspoon dried oregano leaves
2 teaspoons chicken flavor bouillon granules
1 cup uncooked white basmati rice
1 cup rinsed, drained canned Great Northern beans
1 cup sliced green onions
½ cup minced fresh cilantro
6 tablespoons nonfat sour cream
¾ cup diced seeded tomato
½ cup plus 1 tablespoon shredded reduced-fat Colby-Jack cheese

Jalapeño peppers can sting and irritate the skin; wear rubber gloves when handling peppers and do not touch eyes.

1. Spray large nonstick skillet with cooking spray; heat over medium heat until hot. Add beef and sausage; cook 5 minutes or until meat is no longer pink, stirring to crumble. Remove meat from skillet.

2. Spray large saucepan with cooking spray; add peppers and garlic. Cook and stir over medium heat 5 minutes or until peppers are tender. Stir in cumin and oregano; cook and stir 1 minute. Stir in 2¼ cups water and bouillon granules; bring to a boil over high heat. Stir in rice. Cover; reduce heat to medium-low. Simmer 15 minutes.

3. Add meat, beans and onions to saucepan; cover. Simmer 5 minutes or until rice is tender. Remove saucepan from heat; stir in cilantro. Cover; let stand 5 minutes. Top each serving evenly with sour cream, tomato and cheese before serving.

Makes 6 servings

255 SPANISH SKILLET SUPPER

1 pound ground beef
1⅔ cups water
1 can (8¾ ounces) whole kernel corn, undrained
1 package LIPTON® Rice & Sauce— Spanish
¾ cup shredded cheddar cheese (about 3 ounces), divided

In 12-inch skillet, brown ground beef; drain. Add water and bring to a boil; stir in corn and rice & sauce—Spanish. Reduce heat and simmer uncovered, stirring occasionally, 10 minutes or until rice is tender. Stir in ½ cup cheese until melted; top with remaining ¼ cup cheese.

Makes 4 servings

White Chili Pilaf

CASSEROLES & SKILLET DINNERS

256 SPANISH–STYLE COUSCOUS

1 cup couscous
1 pound lean ground beef
½ medium onion, chopped
2 cloves garlic, minced
1 teaspoon ground cumin
½ teaspoon dried thyme leaves
1 can (14½ ounces) beef broth
½ cup pimiento-stuffed green olives, sliced
1 small green bell pepper, seeded and cut into ½-inch pieces

1. Bring 1⅓ cups water to a boil over high heat in 1-quart saucepan. Stir in couscous. Cover; remove from heat.

2. Place meat in large skillet; cook over high heat 6 to 8 minutes or until meat is no longer pink, breaking meat apart with wooden spoon. Pour off drippings. Add onion, garlic, cumin and thyme; cook and stir 30 seconds or until onion and garlic are tender. Add beef broth and olives; bring to a boil. Boil, uncovered, 5 minutes. Add pepper; cover and simmer 5 minutes more or until broth is reduced by half. Fluff couscous with fork. Spoon couscous onto plates or into serving bowls. Spoon meat mixture and broth over couscous. *Makes 4 servings*

Prep and Cook Time: 20 minutes

SERVING SUGGESTION: Serve with carrot sticks.

257 TURKEY JAMBALAYA

1 teaspoon vegetable oil
1 cup chopped onion
1 green bell pepper, chopped
½ cup chopped celery
3 cloves garlic, finely chopped
1¾ cups ⅓-less-salt chicken broth
1 cup chopped seeded tomato
¼ pound cooked ground turkey breast
¼ pound cooked turkey sausage
3 tablespoons tomato paste
1 bay leaf
1 teaspoon dried basil leaves
¼ teaspoon ground red pepper
1 cup uncooked white rice
¼ cup chopped fresh parsley

1. Heat oil in large nonstick skillet over medium-high heat until hot. Add onion, bell pepper, celery and garlic. Cook and stir 5 minutes or until vegetables are tender.

2. Add chicken broth, tomato, turkey, turkey sausage, tomato paste, bay leaf, basil and red pepper. Stir in rice. Bring to a boil over high heat, stirring occasionally. Reduce heat to medium-low. Simmer, covered, 20 minutes or until rice is tender.

3. Remove skillet from heat. Remove and discard bay leaf. Top servings evenly with parsley. Serve immediately.
Makes 4 servings

Spanish-Style Couscous

CASSEROLES & SKILLET DINNERS

258 SLOPPY JOES WITH RICE

¾ pound ground beef
1 small onion, sliced
1 small red or green pepper, cut into strips
1 cup barbecue sauce
1½ cups water
½ teaspoon salt
1½ cups MINUTE® Original Rice, uncooked
Shredded cheddar cheese (optional)

BROWN meat, onion and pepper in large skillet on medium heat. Drain. Stir in barbecue sauce. Bring to boil. Reduce heat to low; cover and simmer 5 minutes.

MEANWHILE, bring water and salt to boil in medium saucepan. Stir in rice; cover. Remove from heat. Let stand 5 minutes. Fluff with fork. Serve meat mixture over rice. Sprinkle with cheese, if desired.

Makes 4 servings

Prep Time: 5 minutes
Cook Time: 15 minutes

259 TEX–MEX SKILLET SUPPER

1 pound lean ground pork
2 cloves garlic, minced
1 can (15 ounces) black beans, drained
1 can (12 ounces) whole kernel corn, drained
1 jar (12 ounces) salsa
½ cup water
1 teaspoon dried oregano leaves, crushed
½ teaspoon ground cumin
¼ teaspoon salt (optional)
6 (6-inch) flour tortillas, cut in half and then into 1-inch strips
2 ounces shredded Cheddar cheese

In large skillet, cook pork and garlic over medium-high heat until pork is lightly browned. Drain off any fat. Stir in remaining ingredients except cheese; bring to a boil, cover and simmer 10 to 12 minutes. Uncover; top with cheese and cook 2 minutes more, until cheese is melted. Serve hot with sour cream, green onions and tortilla chips, if desired.

Makes 6 servings

Prep Time: 15 minutes

Favorite recipe from **National Pork Producers Council**

260 SOUTHWESTERN SKILLET DINNER

1 pound ground beef
2 teaspoons chili powder
1 jar (16 ounces) thick and chunky salsa
1½ cups BIRDS EYE® frozen Corn
¾ cup shredded Cheddar cheese

• Cook ground beef in large skillet over high heat until well browned, about 8 minutes; drain. Stir in chili powder; cook 1 minute.

• Add salsa and corn; bring to boil. Reduce heat to medium; cover and cook 4 minutes.

• Sprinkle with cheese; cover and cook until cheese melts. *Makes about 4 servings*

Prep Time: 5 minutes
Cook Time: 20 minutes

SERVING SUGGESTION: Serve with rice or tortilla chips. Or, serve as a taco filling.

Sloppy Joes with Rice

CASSEROLES & SKILLET DINNERS

261 QUICK AND EASY SPANISH RICE AND BEEF

¾ pound ground beef
1 can (14½ ounces) stewed tomatoes
1 cup water
1 package (10 ounces) frozen corn or mixed vegetables
½ teaspoon salt
½ teaspoon dried oregano leaves
½ teaspoon chili powder
¼ teaspoon garlic powder
⅛ teaspoon pepper
1½ cups uncooked MINUTE® Original Rice

Brown meat in large skillet. Add tomatoes, water, corn and seasonings. Bring to a boil and boil about 2 minutes. Stir in rice. Cover; remove from heat. Let stand 5 minutes. Fluff with fork. *Makes 4 servings*

262 CORN & ZUCCHINI MEDLEY

¾ pound extra-lean (90% lean) ground beef
1 (10-ounce) package frozen whole kernel corn, thawed
2 small zucchini (about ½ pound), chopped
1 large tomato, chopped
½ cup chopped onion
1 tablespoon chopped fresh basil *or* 1 teaspoon dried basil leaves
1½ teaspoons chopped fresh thyme *or* ½ teaspoon dried thyme leaves
Salt and freshly ground pepper

Brown ground beef in large skillet. Drain. Reduce heat to medium-low. Stir in corn, zucchini, tomato, onion, basil and thyme; cover. Cook 10 minutes or until zucchini is tender. Season with salt and pepper to taste.
Makes 4 servings

263 LEMONY BEEF, VEGETABLES & BARLEY

1 pound lean ground beef
8 ounces mushrooms, sliced
1 medium onion, chopped
1 clove garlic, crushed
1 can (14 ounces) ready-to-serve beef broth
½ cup quick-cooking barley
½ teaspoon salt
¼ teaspoon pepper
1 package (10 ounces) frozen peas and carrots, defrosted
1 teaspoon grated lemon peel

1. In large nonstick skillet, cook and stir ground beef, mushrooms, onion and garlic over medium heat 8 to 10 minutes or until beef is no longer pink, breaking beef up into ¾-inch crumbles. Pour off drippings.

2. Stir in broth, barley, salt and pepper. Bring to a boil; reduce heat to medium-low. Cover tightly; simmer 10 minutes.

3. Add peas and carrots; continue cooking 2 to 5 minutes or until barley is tender. Stir in lemon peel.

Makes 4 (1½-cup) servings

Prep & Cook Time: 30 minutes

*Favorite recipe from **National Cattlemen's Beef Association***

Lemony Beef, Vegetables & Barley

264 MEAT AND POTATO STIR–FRY

1 tablespoon vegetable oil
1 large baking potato, peeled and cut into ½-inch cubes
2 medium carrots, peeled and thinly sliced
1 medium onion, halved and sliced
⅔ cup beef broth
1 teaspoon salt, divided
1 pound lean ground beef round
1 large clove garlic, minced
1 tablespoon dried parsley flakes
1 teaspoon paprika
½ teaspoon ground cinnamon
½ teaspoon ground cumin
¼ teaspoon pepper

1. Heat oil in wok or large skillet over medium-high heat until hot. Add potato, carrots and onion; cook and stir 3 minutes. Stir in broth and ½ teaspoon salt. Reduce heat to medium. Cover and cook 6 to 7 minutes more or until potato is tender, stirring once or twice. Remove vegetables from wok; set aside. Wipe out wok with paper towel.

2. Heat wok over medium-high heat until hot. Add beef and garlic; stir-fry 3 minutes or until meat is no longer pink. Add parsley, paprika, cinnamon, cumin, remaining ½ teaspoon salt and pepper; cook and stir 1 minute. Add vegetables; heat through.

Makes 4 servings

Prep and Cook Time: 25 minutes

265 MID–EASTERN SKILLET DINNER

½ pound ground lamb
½ pound ground raw turkey
1 teaspoon garlic powder
1 teaspoon Italian seasoning, crushed, *or* ½ teaspoon *each* dried oregano and basil leaves, crushed
2 cups cooked garbanzo beans (chick-peas) or cooked white beans*
2 medium tomatoes, chopped
Juice of 1 SUNKIST® Lemon
2 tablespoons tomato paste mixed with ¼ cup water
2 teaspoons sugar
1 teaspoon dried mint leaves, crushed
Grated peel of ½ SUNKIST® Lemon

Thoroughly combine lamb, turkey, garlic powder and Italian seasoning. Shape into 8 small patties. In large, lightly oiled nonstick skillet, brown patties on both sides over medium-high heat (10 to 12 minutes). Pour off fat. Add remaining ingredients except lemon peel. Bring to boil; cover and cook over low heat 25 minutes, stirring occasionally. Uncover last 5 minutes to slightly thicken sauce. Add lemon peel.

Makes 4 servings

To cook dry beans: For every 1 cup dry beans/peas, bring to boil in 6 to 8 cups water. Boil 2 minutes. Cover; remove from heat and let stand 1 hour. Drain beans and replace water. Bring to boil; cover and cook over low heat 1½ to 2 hours or until beans are tender. One cup dry beans yields about 2¾ cups cooked beans.

Meat and Potato Stir-Fry

CASSEROLES & SKILLET DINNERS

266 JOE'S SPECIAL

1 pound lean ground beef
2 cups sliced mushrooms
1 small onion, chopped
2 teaspoons Worcestershire sauce
1 teaspoon dried oregano leaves
1 teaspoon ground nutmeg
½ teaspoon garlic powder
½ teaspoon salt
1 package (10 ounces) frozen chopped
   spinach, thawed
4 large eggs, lightly beaten
⅓ cup grated Parmesan cheese

1. Spray large skillet with nonstick cooking spray. Combine meat, mushrooms and onion; cook over medium-high heat 6 to 8 minutes or until onion is tender, breaking meat apart with wooden spoon. Add Worcestershire, oregano, nutmeg, garlic powder and salt. Cook until meat is no longer pink.

2. Drain spinach (do not squeeze dry); stir into meat mixture. Push mixture to one side of pan. Reduce heat to medium. Pour eggs into other side of pan; cook, without stirring, 1 to 2 minutes or until set on bottom. Lift eggs to allow uncooked portion to flow underneath. Repeat until softly set. Gently stir into meat mixture and heat through. Stir in cheese. *Makes 4 to 6 servings*

Prep and Cook Time: 20 minutes

SERVING SUGGESTION: Serve with salsa and toast.

267 SKILLET SAUSAGE AND PEPPERS

1 pound bulk Italian sausage
1 medium onion, cut into wedges
1 small green pepper, cut into strips
1 small red pepper, cut into strips
1 can (8 ounces) tomato sauce
1 can (8 ounces) whole tomatoes,
   undrained
½ teaspoon dried oregano leaves
2 cups STOVE TOP® Chicken Flavor
   Stuffing Mix in the Canister

BROWN sausage in large skillet on medium-high heat. Stir in onion, peppers, tomato sauce, tomatoes and oregano. Bring to boil. Reduce heat to low; cover and simmer 5 minutes or until vegetables are tender-crisp.

STIR in stuffing mix just to moisten; cover. Remove from heat. Let stand 5 minutes.
Makes 4 servings

Prep Time: 15 minutes
Cook Time: 15 minutes

Joe's Special

Meat Loaves & Meatballs

268 ITALIAN–STYLE MEAT LOAF

1 egg
1½ pounds lean ground beef or turkey
8 ounces hot or mild Italian sausage, casings removed
1 cup CONTADINA® Seasoned Bread Crumbs
1 cup (8-ounce can) CONTADINA® Tomato Sauce, divided
1 cup finely chopped onion
½ cup finely chopped green bell pepper

In large bowl, beat egg lightly. Add ground beef, sausage, bread crumbs, *¾ cup* tomato sauce, onion and bell pepper; mix well. Press into ungreased 9×5-inch loaf pan. Bake, uncovered, in preheated 350°F. oven for 60 minutes. Spoon *remaining* tomato sauce over meat loaf. Bake for an additional 15 minutes or until no longer pink in center; drain. Let stand for 10 minutes before serving.   *Makes 8 servings*

269 "SOUPERIOR" MEAT LOAF

2 pounds ground beef
1½ cups fresh bread crumbs
1 envelope LIPTON® Recipe Secrets® Onion Soup Mix*
2 eggs
¾ cup water
⅓ cup ketchup

• Preheat oven to 350°F.

• In large bowl, combine all ingredients.

• In 13×9-inch baking or roasting pan, shape mixture into loaf.

• Bake uncovered 1 hour or until done. Let stand 10 minutes before serving.
      Makes about 8 servings

*Also terrific with Lipton® Recipe Secrets® Beefy Onion, Onion-Mushroom, Beefy Mushroom or Savory Herb with Garlic Soup Mix.

Italian-Style Meat Loaf

MEAT LOAVES & MEATBALLS

270 PINWHEEL MEAT LOAF

½ cup milk
1½ cups crustless Italian or French bread
    cubes
1½ pounds ground beef
½ pound sweet Italian sausage, removed
    from casings and crumbled
2 eggs, slightly beaten
2 tablespoons finely chopped parsley
1 tablespoon finely chopped garlic
1 teaspoon salt
½ teaspoon pepper
2 cups water
1 tablespoon butter or margarine
1 package LIPTON® Rice & Sauce—Cajun-
    Style
2 packages (10 ounces each) frozen
    chopped spinach, thawed and
    squeezed dry

In small bowl, pour milk over bread cubes; mash with fork until bread is soaked.

In large bowl, thoroughly combine bread mixture, ground beef, sausage, eggs, parsley, garlic, salt and pepper. Place on 12×12-inch sheet of aluminum foil moistened with water. Cover with 12×14-inch sheet of waxed paper moistened with water. Using hands or rolling pin, press into 12×12-inch rectangle. Refrigerate 2 hours or until well chilled.

In medium saucepan, bring 2 cups water, butter and rice & sauce—Cajun-style to a boil. Continue boiling over medium heat, stirring occasionally, 10 minutes or until rice is tender. Refrigerate 2 hours or until well chilled.

Pinwheel Meat Loaf

Preheat oven to 350°F. Remove waxed paper from ground beef mixture. If desired, season spinach with additional salt and pepper. Spread spinach over ground beef mixture leaving 1-inch border. Spread rice evenly over spinach. Roll, starting at long end and using foil as guide, jelly-roll style, removing foil while rolling; seal edges tightly. In 13×9-inch baking pan, place meat loaf seam side down. Bake, uncovered, 1 hour or until done. Let stand 15 minutes before serving. Cut into 1-inch slices.

Makes about 8 servings

271 TANGY MEAT LOAF

½ cup ketchup
2 tablespoons packed brown sugar
½ teaspoon dry mustard
4 teaspoons Worcestershire sauce
2 teaspoons seasoned salt (optional)
1½ teaspoons onion powder
¼ teaspoon garlic powder
¼ teaspoon ground black pepper
1 egg
1½ cups Wheat CHEX® brand cereal
2 tablespoons finely chopped green pepper
1½ pounds lean ground beef

Preheat oven to 350°F. In large bowl combine ketchup, brown sugar and mustard. Reserve 4 tablespoons mixture for topping. Add Worcestershire, salt, if desired, onion powder, garlic powder, black pepper and egg. Blend well. Stir in cereal and green pepper. Let stand 5 minutes. Break up cereal. Add ground beef; mix well. Shape into loaf in shallow baking pan. Bake 65 minutes. Spread top with reserved ketchup mixture. Bake additional 15 minutes. *Makes 6 servings*

272 MEDITERRANEAN MICROWAVE MEAT LOAF

1 pound lean ground beef
¼ pound Italian sausage
½ cup dry bread crumbs
¼ cup grated Parmesan cheese
1 large egg
⅓ cup plus 2 tablespoons prepared pasta sauce, divided
2 tablespoons lemon juice, divided
½ teaspoon ground allspice
¼ teaspoon black pepper

1. In large bowl, combine ground beef, sausage (if in links, remove casing), bread crumbs, cheese, egg, ⅓ cup pasta sauce, 1 tablespoon lemon juice, allspice and pepper. Mix until blended. Pat into ball. Place in 9-inch glass pie plate or shallow microwavable casserole 9 to 10 inches in diameter. Press into 7-inch circle.

2. Microwave, uncovered, on HIGH 8 minutes. Pour off drippings. Meanwhile, combine remaining 2 tablespoons pasta sauce and 1 tablespoon lemon juice; spread over top of meat loaf. Microwave 3 to 5 minutes more or until meat loaf registers 150°F in center. Let stand 5 minutes before serving. *Makes 4 servings*

Prep and Cook Time: 20 minutes

SERVING SUGGESTION: Serve with frozen stuffed potatoes heated according to package directions and tossed green salad.

273 GRILLED MEAT LOAF

1½ **pounds ground chuck or ground sirloin**
½ **cup seasoned dry bread crumbs**
⅔ **cup chili sauce, divided**
⅓ **cup grated onion**
1 **egg**
½ **teaspoon pepper**
¼ **teaspoon salt**
2 **tablespoons packed light brown sugar**
1 **tablespoon spicy brown or Dijon-style mustard**

Prepare barbecue grill for direct cooking. Combine beef, bread crumbs, ⅓ cup chili sauce, onion, egg, pepper and salt in large bowl; mix well. On cutting board or cookie sheet, shape mixture into 9×5-inch oval loaf, 1½ inches thick.

Combine remaining ⅓ cup chili sauce, sugar and mustard in small bowl; mix well. Set aside. Place meat loaf on grid. Grill meat loaf, on covered grill, over medium-hot coals 10 minutes. Carefully turn meat loaf over using 2 large spatulas.

Brush chili sauce mixture over top of meat loaf. Continue to grill, covered, 10 to 12 minutes for medium-well or until desired doneness is reached. (If desired, insert instant-read thermometer* into center of thickest part of meat loaf. Thermometer should register 160°F for medium-well.) Let stand 10 minutes before slicing. Serve with mashed potatoes and peas and carrots, if desired. *Makes 4 to 6 servings*

Do not leave instant-read thermometer in meat loaf during grilling since thermometer is not heatproof.

274 PIZZA MEAT LOAF

1 **can (10½ ounces) pizza sauce with cheese, divided**
3 **cups Corn CHEX® brand cereal, crushed to 1 cup**
⅓ **cup finely chopped green pepper**
1 **egg, slightly beaten**
2 **teaspoons seasoned salt**
¾ **teaspoon onion powder**
½ **to ¾ teaspoon dried oregano leaves, crushed**
⅛ **teaspoon ground black pepper**
2 **pounds ground beef**
½ **cup (2 ounces) shredded mozzarella cheese**

Preheat oven to 350°F. Place ⅓ cup pizza sauce in small bowl; set aside. Combine remaining pizza sauce, cereal, green pepper, egg, seasoned salt, onion powder, oregano and black pepper in large bowl; mix in ground beef. Shape into loaf in shallow baking dish. Bake 65 minutes. Brush on reserved sauce; sprinkle cheese on top. Bake an additional 15 to 20 minutes or until no longer pink. Let stand 5 minutes before serving. *Makes 8 servings*

NOTE: Meat mixture may be shaped into two loaves. Bake 45 minutes. Brush on reserved sauce; sprinkle cheese on top. Bake additional 15 minutes or until no longer pink. Let stand 5 minutes before serving.

Grilled Meat Loaf

275 ITALIAN MEAT LOAF PATTIES

1 package (12 ounces) extra wide noodles
1 tablespoon butter or margarine, melted
1 can (15 ounces) DEL MONTE® Original Sloppy Joe Sauce
2 pounds ground beef or turkey
1 cup dry bread crumbs
2 eggs, beaten
1 tablespoon dried minced onions

1. Preheat oven to 375°F.

2. Cook noodles according to package directions; drain. Toss with butter; keep hot.

3. Set aside half of sauce to brush on patties. In large bowl, combine remaining sauce with remaining ingredients; mix with fork. On large, greased baking sheet, shape meat mixture into 8 (1-inch-thick) oblong patties. Brush reserved sauce over patties.

4. Bake 20 minutes or until no longer pink in center. (Cool, cover and refrigerate half of cooked patties for Layered Noodle Bake, page 186.) Serve remaining patties with hot, buttered noodles. Garnish, if desired.

Makes 4 servings

TIP: Omit reserving half of patties for Layered Noodle Bake. Double noodles and butter to make 8 servings.

Prep Time: 5 minutes
Cook Time: 20 minutes

276 MEAT LOAF SURPRISE

1½ pounds ground beef
2 cups Wheat CHEX® brand cereal, crushed to 1 cup
1 can (8 ounces) tomato sauce
1 egg
¼ cup chopped onion
2 teaspoons Italian seasoning
1 teaspoon seasoned salt (optional)
½ teaspoon pepper
1 cup (4 ounces) diced Cheddar cheese*

*Try other types of cheese for variety.

Preheat oven to 350°F. Combine beef, cereal, tomato sauce, egg, onion, Italian seasoning, seasoned salt and pepper in large bowl. Place half of mixture in ungreased 8-inch square baking pan. Place cheese evenly over meat. Top with remaining meat mixture. Bake 45 to 50 minutes or until done.

Makes 8 servings

MICROWAVE DIRECTIONS: Combine beef, cereal, tomato sauce, egg, onion, Italian seasoning, seasoned salt and pepper in large bowl. Place half of mixture in ungreased 1½-quart microwave-safe dish. Place cheese evenly over meat to within 1 inch from edge of dish. Top with remaining meat mixture. Microwave, uncovered, on HIGH for 18 to 20 minutes or until no longer pink, rotating dish ½ turn after 10 minutes. Remove from oven. Let stand 10 minutes to firm before serving.

Italian Meat Loaf Patties

277 COUNTRY MEAT LOAF

1 tablespoon vegetable oil
2 stalks celery, minced
1 medium onion, minced
1 large clove garlic, crushed
1 jar (16 ounces) TABASCO® 7-Spice Chili
    Recipe
1 pound lean ground beef
1 pound ground turkey
1 large egg
½ cup fresh bread crumbs
1 tablespoon TABASCO® pepper sauce
1½ teaspoons salt
1½ teaspoons dried thyme leaves
1 teaspoon ground cumin

In 10-inch skillet over medium heat in hot oil, cook celery, onion and garlic until tender, about 5 minutes, stirring occasionally.

Set aside ½ cup TABASCO® 7-Spice Chili Recipe. In large bowl combine remaining chili recipe, ground beef, ground turkey, egg, bread crumbs, TABASCO® sauce, salt, thyme, cumin and cooked celery mixture until well mixed.

Preheat oven to 350°F. In 12×8-inch baking dish shape mixture into 10×4-inch oval loaf. Brush top with reserved ½ cup TABASCO® 7-Spice Chili Recipe. Bake 1 hour.

Makes 8 servings

SERVING SUGGESTION: Serve meat loaf with roasted new potatoes and vegetables, such as baby carrots, broccoli, cauliflower and green beans.

278 CHEESY SPINACH STUFFED MEATLOAF

MEATLOAF
1½ pounds lean ground beef
¾ cup soft bread crumbs
1 egg
1 teaspoon salt
⅛ teaspoon pepper

FILLING
1 package (10 ounces) frozen chopped
    spinach, defrosted, well drained
½ cup shredded part-skim mozzarella
    cheese
3 tablespoons grated Parmesan cheese
1 teaspoon dried Italian seasoning
¼ teaspoon salt
⅛ teaspoon garlic powder

TOPPING
3 tablespoons ketchup
¼ cup shredded part-skim mozzarella
    cheese
Dried Italian seasoning (optional)

1. Heat oven to 350°F. In medium bowl, combine filling ingredients; mix well. Set aside. In large bowl, combine meatloaf ingredients, mixing lightly but thoroughly.

2. Place beef mixture on waxed paper and pat into 14×10-inch rectangle. Spread filling over beef, leaving ¾-inch border around edges. Starting at short end, roll up jelly-roll fashion. Press beef mixture over spinach filling at both ends to seal. Place seam side down on rack in open roasting pan.

Cheesy Spinach Stuffed Meatloaf

3. Bake in 350°F oven 1 hour. Spread ketchup over loaf; return to oven and continue baking 15 minutes. Top loaf with ¼ cup mozzarella cheese. Sprinkle with additional Italian seasoning, if desired.

4. To serve, cut into 1-inch-thick slices.

Makes 6 servings

COOK'S TIP: To make soft bread crumbs, place torn bread slices in food processor, fitted with steel blade, or blender container. Cover; process 30 seconds, pulsing on and off, until fine crumbs form. One and a half slices will yield 1 cup soft bread crumbs.

NOTE: Thick potato wedges seasoned with herbs can bake alongside meatloaf.

Total Prep and Cook Time: 1½ hours

*Favorite recipe from **National Cattlemen's Beef Association***

MEAT LOAVES & MEATBALLS

279 MEAT LOAF OLÉ

1½ pounds lean ground beef
¾ cup unseasoned dry bread crumbs
1 egg, beaten
1 can (4 ounces) diced green chiles, drained
½ cup (2 ounces) shredded Cheddar cheese
1 package (1.0 ounce) LAWRY'S® Taco Spices & Seasonings
1 medium tomato, chopped
½ cup sliced green onions
2 tablespoons ketchup
1 tablespoon salsa
½ teaspoon LAWRY'S® Seasoned Salt

In large bowl, combine ground beef, bread crumbs, egg, chiles, Cheddar cheese and Taco Spices & Seasonings; blend well. Pat meat mixture into 9×5×3-inch loaf pan. Bake, uncovered, in 350°F oven about 1 hour or until meat is cooked through. Let stand 10 minutes before draining fat and removing meat loaf from pan. In small bowl, combine remaining ingredients. Slice meat loaf into ½-inch slices and spoon tomato mixture over slices. *Makes 6 servings*

PRESENTATION: Serve with Mexican rice.

280 HUNT'S® MARVELOUS MEATLOAF

1½ pounds ground beef
12 ounces pork sausage, casings removed
1 cup finely chopped onion
¾ cup fine dry bread crumbs
½ cup finely chopped celery
1 (8-ounce) can HUNT'S® Tomato Sauce, divided
1 egg
1 teaspoon garlic salt
½ teaspoon rubbed sage
½ cup HUNT'S® Tomato Ketchup

In large bowl, combine ground beef, sausage, onion, bread crumbs, celery, ½ cup tomato sauce, egg, garlic salt and sage until well blended. Place mixture in shallow baking pan; form into loaf. Bake, uncovered, at 375°F for 1 hour 15 minutes; drain. Meanwhile, in small bowl, stir together *remaining* tomato sauce and ketchup. Spoon over loaf, coating well. Bake 15 minutes longer. Serve immediately.

Makes 8 servings

MEAT LOAVES & MEATBALLS

281 HAM LOAF

1 pound ground pork
½ pound ham, ground
¾ cup milk
½ cup fresh bread crumbs
1 egg
1 tablespoon instant tapioca
½ teaspoon prepared horseradish
3 to 4 drops red food color (optional)

SAUCE
½ cup ketchup
2 tablespoons packed brown sugar
1 tablespoon Worcestershire sauce

In large bowl, mix together pork, ham, milk, crumbs, egg, tapioca, horseradish and food color with hands until well blended. Place mixture in loaf pan and bake at 325°F for 1 hour. Stir together Sauce ingredients. Pour Sauce over Ham Loaf and bake for another 30 minutes, basting occasionally with Sauce. Remove from oven; let stand 10 minutes before removing from pan. Slice to serve.

Makes 6 servings

Prep Time: 10 minutes
Cook Time: 90 minutes

*Favorite recipe from **National Pork Producers Council***

282 SANTA FE MEAT LOAF

2 pounds lean ground pork
1 teaspoon vegetable oil
2 medium onions, finely chopped
4 cloves garlic, crushed
½ cup finely chopped parsley
½ cup dry bread crumbs
½ cup skim milk
¼ cup minced sun-dried tomatoes
1 jalapeño pepper, seeded and minced*
1 tablespoon chili powder
1½ teaspoons salt
1 teaspoon ground cumin
1 teaspoon dried thyme leaves
½ teaspoon ground cayenne

Wear rubber gloves when handling jalapeño peppers.

In large nonstick skillet heat oil over medium-high heat. Sauté onions and garlic until soft, about 10 minutes; cool slightly and transfer to large bowl. Add all remaining ingredients and mix thoroughly. Place mixture in 9×5×2½-inch loaf pan and bake in 350°F oven for 1½ hours. Remove from oven and allow to rest 10 minutes before removing from pan. Slice to serve warm, or wrap well and refrigerate for sandwiches.

Makes 8 servings

Prep Time: 15 minutes
Cook Time: 90 minutes

*Favorite recipe from **National Pork Producers Council***

MEAT LOAVES & MEATBALLS

283 HOMESTYLE MEATLOAF

½ cup ketchup
2 teaspoons brown sugar
1 teaspoon dry mustard
1 pound BOB EVANS FARMS® Original
    Recipe Roll Sausage
1 pound lean ground beef
1 cup uncooked quick oats
½ cup chopped onion
1 egg, beaten
1 teaspoon salt
¼ teaspoon black pepper

Preheat oven to 350°F. Combine ketchup, brown sugar and mustard in small bowl; set aside. Combine ⅓ cup ketchup mixture and remaining ingredients in large bowl; mix well. Shape mixture into loaf in large shallow baking dish. Bake 1 hour; remove from oven. Pour remaining ketchup mixture over loaf; bake 10 minutes more. Let stand 5 minutes before slicing. Serve hot. Refrigerate leftovers.

Makes 6 to 8 servings

284 COUNTRY PICNIC LOAF

2 pounds ground pork
1½ pounds lean ground beef
3 cups coarse fresh bread crumbs
⅔ cup ketchup
3 eggs, beaten
1 package (1 ounce) LAWRY'S® Au Jus
    Gravy Mix
2 cups diced cooked ham
⅔ cup chopped walnuts
1 jar (4½ ounces) sliced mushrooms,
    drained
2 tablespoons LAWRY'S® Minced Onion
    with Green Onion Flakes
1 teaspoon ground allspice
½ teaspoon LAWRY'S® Garlic Powder with
    Parsley
½ teaspoon dried thyme

In large bowl, combine ground meats and bread crumbs; blend well. In small bowl, combine ketchup, eggs and Au Jus Gravy Mix; blend well. Add to meat mixture; mix well. Stir in ham, walnuts, mushrooms, Minced Onion with Green Onion Flakes, allspice, Garlic Powder with Parsley and thyme. Press mixture into 2-quart casserole dish. Bake, uncovered, in 325°F oven 1½ hours or until meat pulls away from sides of pan; drain fat. Let stand 10 minutes before slicing.   *Makes about 12 servings*

MEAT LOAVES & MEATBALLS

285 CARAWAY LAMB MEATLOAF

1 pound lean ground American lamb
¾ cup rye bread crumbs (about 1 slice, torn)
½ cup canned cream-style corn
½ cup finely chopped onion
2 egg whites *or* 1 whole egg
1 tablespoon dried parsley flakes
1 teaspoon caraway seeds
¼ teaspoon black pepper

In bowl combine bread crumbs, corn, onion, egg whites, parsley flakes, caraway seeds and pepper. Mix well. Stir in ground lamb until well mixed. Shape into loaf about 7×3½ inches. Place in loaf pan. Bake in 350°F oven for 45 to 50 minutes. (Or, if desired, shape into 4 loaves, each 4×2 inches. Place in individual loaf pans. Bake 35 to 40 minutes.) Remove meatloaf from pan and let stand 5 minutes before slicing.

Makes 4 servings

*Favorite recipe from **American Lamb Council***

Caraway Lamb Meatloaf

286 MUSHROOM AND ORANGE–STUFFED LAMB LOAVES

1 pound lean ground American lamb
⅓ cup dry bread crumbs
¼ cup orange juice
¼ cup snipped fresh parsley
1 egg white
½ teaspoon salt
¼ teaspoon pepper
¼ teaspoon dried thyme leaves, crushed

FILLING
4 ounces fresh mushrooms, coarsely chopped (1½ cups)
¼ cup chopped onion
½ teaspoon bottled minced garlic *or* 1 clove garlic, minced
Dash of salt
Dash of cayenne pepper
¼ cup orange marmalade
2 tablespoons dry bread crumbs

For filling, combine mushrooms, onion, garlic, dash of salt and cayenne pepper in small skillet. Cook and stir over medium heat until liquid evaporates, about 5 minutes. Stir in marmalade and 2 tablespoons bread crumbs; set aside.

In large bowl, combine ⅓ cup bread crumbs, orange juice, parsley, egg white, salt, pepper and thyme. Add lamb; mix well. Divide meat mixture into four equal parts. Flatten each to a 5-inch circle. Place ¼ of the mushroom filling mixture on each circle. Bring edges up and around filling to form a small loaf; seal.

Place loaves, seam side down, on microwave-safe plate. Cover with waxed paper. Microwave on HIGH (100%) 7 to 10 minutes or until no longer pink in center; turning plate once. If desired, spread additional marmalade on loaves just before serving. *Makes 4 servings*

Favorite recipe from American Lamb Council

287 MINI TURKEY LOAVES

1 pound ground turkey
1 small apple, chopped
½ small onion, chopped
½ cup uncooked rolled oats
2 teaspoons Dijon-style mustard
1 teaspoon dried rosemary leaves
1 teaspoon salt
Dash of pepper
Cranberry sauce
Vegetable Stir-Fry (recipe follows)
Mashed potatoes (optional)

Preheat oven to 425°F. Grease 12 (2½-inch) muffin cups. Combine turkey and next 7 ingredients in large bowl. Press into prepared muffin cups. Bake 20 minutes or until no longer pink in center. Top with cranberry sauce. Garnish as desired. Serve with Vegetable Stir-Fry and mashed potatoes, if desired. *Makes 4 servings*

VEGETABLE STIR-FRY
1 tablespoon vegetable oil
3 to 4 carrots, diagonally sliced
2 zucchini, diagonally sliced
3 tablespoons orange juice
Salt and pepper

Heat oil in skillet over medium heat. Add carrots; stir-fry 3 minutes. Add zucchini and juice; stir-fry 4 minutes or until vegetables are crisp-tender. Season with salt and pepper.

Mini Turkey Loaves

288 MEAT LOAF WITH PARMESAN CRUST

1 tablespoon vegetable oil
1 cup chopped yellow onion
1 cup chopped green bell pepper
2 teaspoons minced garlic
2 pounds ground lean turkey or ground beef round
1/4 cup egg substitute *or* 1 large egg, beaten
1/3 cup bottled chili sauce
2 cups seasoned bread crumbs, divided
1/2 teaspoon freshly ground black pepper
3/4 cup (3 ounces) shredded ALPINE LACE® Fat Free Pasteurized Process Skim Milk Cheese Product—For Parmesan Lovers
1/2 cup firmly packed parsley leaves
3 strips turkey bacon (optional)

1. Preheat the oven to 350°F. Spray a 9×5×3-inch loaf pan with nonstick cooking spray. In a large skillet, heat the oil over medium-high heat. Add the onion, bell pepper and garlic and sauté for 5 minutes or until tender. Transfer to a large bowl.

2. Add the turkey, egg substitute (or the egg), chili sauce, 1½ cups of the bread crumbs and the black pepper to the onion mixture. Mix with your hands until well blended.

3. In a food processor or blender, process the Parmesan, parsley and the remaining ½ cup of bread crumbs for 30 seconds or until fine crumbs form. Mix into the turkey mixture.

4. Transfer the turkey mixture to the pan and pat into a loaf, mounding it slightly in the center. Place the bacon strips diagonally across the top of the loaf, if you wish.

5. Bake for 1 hour or until an instant-read thermometer inserted into the center registers 165°F. Loosely cover meat loaf with foil during the last 15 minutes. Transfer to a warm platter, let stand for 10 minutes, then slice and serve. *Makes 12 servings*

289 MEXICAN MEATLOAF

1½ pounds lean ground turkey or beef
1 cup GUILTLESS GOURMET® Salsa (mild, medium or hot), divided
1 cup (3.5 ounces) crushed GUILTLESS GOURMET® Baked Tortilla Chips (yellow or white corn)
1/2 medium onion, chopped
3 egg whites, slightly beaten
1/2 teaspoon coarsely ground black pepper

Preheat oven to 350°F. Mix turkey, ½ cup salsa, crushed chips, onion, egg whites and pepper in large bowl until lightly blended. Shape into loaf and place in 9×5-inch loaf pan.

Bake 1 hour or until firm. Pour remaining ½ cup salsa over top; bake 10 minutes more. Let stand 10 minutes before slicing and serving. *Makes 4 servings*

290 BUSY DAY TURKEY LOAF

1 cup KELLOGG'S® CROUTETTES®
 Stuffing Mix
½ cup skim milk
¼ cup finely chopped onion
2 egg whites
2 teaspoons Worcestershire sauce
½ teaspoon salt
1 pound lean ground turkey
¼ cup ketchup
2 teaspoons firmly packed brown sugar
1 teaspoon prepared mustard

1. Preheat oven to 350°F. Combine Kellogg's® Croutettes® stuffing mix and milk in large bowl. Let stand 5 minutes or until Croutettes® are softened. Add onion, egg whites, Worcestershire sauce and salt. Mix well. Add ground turkey. Mix until well combined.

2. Shape into loaf. Place in foil-lined shallow baking pan. Score loaf by making several diagonal grooves across top with spoon.

3. Combine ketchup, sugar and mustard in small bowl. Fill grooves with ketchup mixture.

4. Bake about 45 minutes or until browned and no longer pink in center.

Makes 6 servings

291 MINUTE MEN MEATBALLS

MEATBALLS
1 pound ground beef
⅓ cup chopped onion
⅓ cup fresh bread crumbs
1 egg
½ teaspoon salt
½ teaspoon pepper

SAUCE
1 package (1.5 ounces) spaghetti sauce
 mix
1 can (8 ounces) tomato sauce
⅔ cup water
1 can (4 ounces) mushrooms, drained
⅓ cup sliced beef pepperoni
2 tablespoons grated Parmesan cheese
½ teaspoon garlic powder
1 pound angel hair pasta
2 tablespoons vegetable oil
 Sliced celery and black olives for garnish

In medium bowl, combine ground beef, onion, bread crumbs, egg, salt and pepper. Shape into small meatballs. Place on baking sheet and bake in 350°F oven until cooked through.

In medium saucepan, combine sauce mix with tomato sauce and water. Stir in mushrooms, pepperoni, Parmesan cheese and garlic powder. Simmer 10 to 12 minutes. Add meatballs to sauce and simmer until heated through.

Prepare pasta according to package directions; drain. Toss with oil to prevent sticking. Serve meatballs and sauce over pasta. Garnish with celery and black olives.

Makes 4 servings

Favorite recipe from **North Dakota Beef Commission**

MEAT LOAVES & MEATBALLS

292 MEDITERRANEAN MEATBALLS AND COUSCOUS

1 can (about 14 ounces) defatted ⅓-less-salt chicken broth
2½ cups water
1½ cups precooked couscous*
¾ cup golden raisins
¼ cup chopped parsley
3 tablespoons lemon juice, divided
3 teaspoons grated lemon peel, divided
2 teaspoons ground cinnamon, divided
1 teaspoon turmeric
½ teaspoon ground cumin
1 pound ground beef round
½ cup crushed saltine crackers
¼ cup evaporated skim milk
½ teaspoon dried oregano leaves

Package label may not indicate couscous is precooked. Check ingredient list for "precooked semolina."

Pour chicken broth and water into 2-quart saucepan. Bring to a boil over high heat. Remove from heat. Add couscous, raisins, parsley, 2 tablespoons lemon juice, 2 teaspoons lemon peel, 1½ teaspoons cinnamon, turmeric and cumin. Cover and let stand 5 minutes.

Combine beef, crackers, milk, remaining 1 tablespoon lemon juice, 1 teaspoon lemon peel, ½ teaspoon cinnamon and oregano in large bowl. Mix until well blended. Shape into 24 meatballs. Place in large microwavable baking dish. Cover loosely with waxed paper. Microwave at HIGH 4 minutes or until meatballs are cooked through.

Stir couscous mixture and spoon onto serving platter. Arrange meatballs on couscous. Garnish with lemon wedges and fresh oregano, if desired.

Makes 6 servings

Prep and Cook Time: 25 minutes

293 MEATBALL SURPRISE

½ box (6.25 ounces) stuffing mix for chicken
1 pound ground beef
1 can (10¾ ounces) condensed cream of mushroom soup
1 can (10¾ ounces) condensed cream of celery soup
2 tablespoons dried onion soup mix
1 cup milk
2 cups hot cooked rice

Prepare stuffing according to package directions. Divide ground beef into 8 portions; flatten into thin patties. Spoon prepared stuffing onto middle of patties; roll into balls, sealing ground beef around stuffing. Place meatballs on baking sheet and bake at 350°F until cooked through.

In medium saucepan, combine soups, soup mix and milk. Stir over medium heat until hot. Spoon hot rice onto serving platter; top with meatballs and soup mixture.

Makes 4 servings

*Favorite recipe from **North Dakota Beef Commission***

Mediterranean Meatballs and Couscous

294 ITALIAN MEATBALLS

1½ pounds meat loaf mix* or lean ground
    beef
⅓ cup dry bread crumbs
⅓ cup milk
⅓ cup grated onion
¼ cup (1 ounce) freshly grated Parmesan
    cheese
1 egg
2 cloves garlic, minced
1½ teaspoons dried basil leaves
1 teaspoon salt
1 teaspoon dried oregano leaves
½ teaspoon rubbed sage
¼ teaspoon crushed red pepper flakes
    Marinara Sauce (recipe follows)
    Additional grated Parmesan cheese and
        hot cooked pasta (optional)

*Meat loaf mix is a combination of ground beef, pork
and veal; see your meat retailer or make your own
with 1 pound lean ground beef, ¼ pound ground pork
and ¼ pound ground veal.*

Preheat oven to 400°F. Spray broiler pan
with nonstick cooking spray. Combine all
ingredients except Marinara Sauce,
additional cheese and pasta in large bowl.
Mix lightly but thoroughly. Shape to form
meatballs using ⅓ cup meat mixture for each
meatball.

Place meatballs on prepared pan; bake 25 to
30 minutes until instant-read thermometer
inserted into meatballs registers 145°F.

Meanwhile, prepare Marinara Sauce. Add
cooked meatballs to Marinara Sauce;
simmer, uncovered, about 10 minutes or
until meatballs are cooked through and no
longer pink in centers, turning meatballs in
sauce once. (Internal temperature should
register 160° to 165°F.)

Serve meatballs in shallow bowls; top with
sauce. Serve with cheese and pasta. Garnish
as desired.   *Makes 5 to 6 servings*

MARINARA SAUCE
1½ tablespoons olive oil
3 cloves garlic, minced
1 can (28 ounces) Italian plum tomatoes,
    undrained
¼ cup tomato paste
2 teaspoons dried basil leaves
½ teaspoon sugar
¼ teaspoon salt
¼ teaspoon crushed red pepper flakes

Heat oil in large skillet over medium heat.
Add garlic; cook and stir 3 minutes. Stir in
remaining ingredients. Bring to a boil.
Reduce heat to low; simmer, uncovered,
10 minutes.   *Makes about 3½ cups*

TIP: If serving with pasta, double sauce
recipe.

Italian Meatballs

MEAT LOAVES & MEATBALLS

295 THAI MEATBALLS AND NOODLES

Thai Meatballs (recipe follows)
12 ounces uncooked egg noodles
2 cans (13¾ ounces each) reduced-sodium chicken broth
2 tablespoons packed brown sugar
2 tablespoons fish sauce or reduced-sodium soy sauce
1 small piece fresh ginger (about 1×½ inch), cut into thin strips
1 medium carrot, cut into matchstick-size strips
1 pound bok choy, cut into ½-inch-wide strips
½ cup slivered fresh mint or basil leaves or chopped cilantro

Prepare Thai Meatballs. While meatballs are cooking, cook noodles according to package directions; drain. Transfer noodles to large serving bowl; keep warm.

Heat chicken broth in large saucepan or wok over high heat. Add brown sugar, fish sauce and ginger; stir until sugar is dissolved. Add Meatballs and carrot to saucepan; bring to a boil. Reduce heat to medium-low; cover and simmer 15 minutes or until meatballs are heated through.

Add bok choy; simmer 4 to 5 minutes or until stalks are crisp-tender. Stir in mint; pour mixture over noodles in serving bowl. Garnish as desired.   *Makes 6 servings*

THAI MEATBALLS
1½ pounds ground beef or pork
¼ cup chopped fresh basil leaves
¼ cup chopped fresh mint leaves
2 tablespoons finely chopped fresh ginger
4 teaspoons fish sauce
6 cloves garlic, minced
1 teaspoon ground cinnamon
½ teaspoon fennel seeds, crushed
½ teaspoon pepper
2 tablespoons peanut oil, divided

Combine beef, basil, mint, ginger, fish sauce, garlic, cinnamon, fennel and pepper in large bowl; mix until well blended. Rub cutting board with 1 tablespoon oil. Pat meat mixture into 12×8-inch rectangle on board. Cut into 32 squares. Shape each square into a ball.

Heat remaining 1 tablespoon oil in large skillet or wok over medium-high heat. Add meatballs in single layer; cook 8 to 10 minutes or until no longer pink in center, turning to brown all sides. (Cook in several batches.) Remove meatballs with slotted spoon to paper towels; drain.
     Makes 32 meatballs

Thai Meatballs and Noodles

MEAT LOAVES & MEATBALLS

296 THREE EASY MEATBALL MEALS

1 pound lean ground beef
½ cup soft bread crumbs *or* ¼ cup dry
   bread crumbs
1 egg
2 tablespoons finely chopped onion
1 clove garlic, crushed
½ teaspoon salt
⅛ teaspoon pepper

1. Heat oven to 400°F. In large bowl, combine all ingredients, mixing lightly but thoroughly. Pinch off about 1½-inch pieces of beef mixture to make 20 meatballs; place in ungreased 15×10-inch jelly roll pan.

2. Bake in 400°F oven 10 to 13 minutes or until no longer pink and juices run clear. Use meatballs in one of the recipes below, proceeding as directed.

SPICY BEEF 'N ZUCCHINI SOUP: In large saucepan, combine 2 cups diced zucchini, 1 can (14 ounces) ready-to-serve beef broth, 1 cup prepared chunky salsa and 1 cup water; bring to a boil. Reduce heat; simmer 3 to 5 minutes or until zucchini is crisp-tender. Stir in meatballs and 1 tablespoon chopped fresh cilantro; heat through. Top with corn chips, if desired, immediately before serving.   *Makes 4 servings*
(serving size: 1½ cups)

Left to Right: Spicy Beef 'n Zucchini Soup, Italian Meatball Sandwich and Easy Meatball Stew

ITALIAN MEATBALL SANDWICHES: In large skillet, heat 1 teaspoon vegetable oil in large skillet over medium heat until hot. Cook and stir ¾ cup thin bell pepper strips and ¾ cup thin onion wedges 3 to 4 minutes or until tender. Reduce heat to medium-low; add meatballs and 1 jar (14 ounces) prepared spaghetti sauce. Cover; cook 5 to 6 minutes to heat through, stirring occasionally. Spoon equal amounts into 4 split hoagie rolls; sprinkle with shredded mozzarella cheese, if desired. *Makes 4 sandwiches*

EASY MEATBALL STEW: In large saucepan, combine 1 jar (12 ounces) brown beef gravy, 1 small can (8 ounces) stewed tomatoes (undrained), ¾ cup water, ¾ teaspoon dried thyme leaves and ⅛ teaspoon pepper; bring to a boil. Stir in 1 package (16 ounces) frozen vegetable (with potato) mixture. Reduce heat; simmer 10 to 15 minutes or until vegetables are tender. Stir in meatballs; heat through. Sprinkle with chopped parsley, if desired. *Makes 4 servings (serving size: 1½ cups)*

COOK'S TIP: To make soft bread crumbs, place 1 slice torn bread in food processor, fitted with steel blade, or blender container. Cover; process 30 seconds, pulsing on and off until fine crumbs form. Makes about ⅔ cup.

Total Prep & Cook Time: 30 to 40 minutes

*Favorite recipe from **National Cattlemen's Beef Association***

297 SPICY CARIBBEAN MEATBALLS

1 pound extra lean ground beef
½ cup fine dry bread crumbs
1 egg *or* ¼ cup egg substitute
1 can (10½ ounces) condensed beef consommé, divided
1 teaspoon pumpkin pie spice
Salt and pepper to taste
¼ cup finely chopped onion
¼ cup finely chopped green bell pepper
½ jalapeño pepper, finely chopped
Water

1. In large bowl combine bread crumbs, egg and ¼ cup consommé. Add pumpkin pie spice and salt and pepper to taste. Blend well.

2. Add ground beef, onion, bell pepper and jalapeño pepper to crumb mixture and mix lightly. Form into 1½- to 2-inch meatballs.

3. Place meatballs on baking sheet coated with nonstick cooking spray. Brown under preheated broiler, turning once.

4. Transfer meatballs to large skillet; add ¼ cup consommé and ¼ cup water. Bring to a simmer; cook about 15 minutes or until cooked through, adding water if necessary.
Makes 4 servings

TIPS: Remaining consommé can be used to make gravy if desired. Meatballs can be made smaller and served as an appetizer.

*Favorite recipe from **North Dakota Beef Commission***

MEAT LOAVES & MEATBALLS

298 SWEDISH MEATBALLS

1½ **cups fresh bread crumbs**
 1 **cup heavy cream**
 2 **tablespoons butter or margarine,**
   divided
 1 **small onion, chopped**
 1 **pound ground beef**
 ½ **pound ground pork**
 3 **tablespoons chopped fresh parsley,**
   divided
1½ **teaspoons salt**
 ¼ **teaspoon black pepper**
 ¼ **teaspoon ground allspice**
 1 **cup beef broth**
 1 **cup sour cream**
 1 **tablespoon all-purpose flour**

Combine bread crumbs and cream in small bowl; mix well. Let stand 10 minutes. Melt 1 tablespoon butter in large skillet over medium heat. Add onion. Cook and stir 5 minutes or until onion is tender. Combine beef, pork, bread crumb mixture, onion, 2 tablespoons parsley, salt, pepper and allspice in large bowl; mix well. Cover; refrigerate 1 hour.

Pat meat mixture into 1-inch-thick square on cutting board. Cut into 36 squares. Shape each square into a ball. Melt remaining 1 tablespoon butter in same large skillet over medium heat. Add meatballs. Cook 10 minutes or until browned on all sides and no longer pink in center. Remove meatballs from skillet; drain on paper towels.

Drain drippings from skillet; discard. Pour broth into skillet. Heat over medium-high heat, stirring frequently and scraping up any browned bits. Reduce heat to low.

Combine sour cream and flour; mix well. Stir sour cream mixture into skillet. Cook 5 minutes, stirring constantly. *Do not boil.* Add meatballs. Cook 5 minutes more. Sprinkle with remaining 1 tablespoon parsley. Garnish as desired.

Makes 5 to 6 servings

NOTE: Mashed potatoes, boiled red potatoes or broad egg noodles are wonderful accompaniments.

299 THE OTHER MEATBALLS AND SPAGHETTI

 1 **pound ground pork**
 ¼ **cup dry bread crumbs**
 1 **egg**
 1 **tablespoon finely minced onion**
 ¼ **teaspoon salt**
   Dash hot pepper sauce
 1 **jar (28 ounces) marinara sauce**
12 **ounces uncooked spaghetti, cooked,**
   drained

Mix pork, bread crumbs, egg, onion and seasonings. Shape meat mixture into ¾-inch diameter balls. Brown meatballs; drain. Heat marinara sauce in large skillet; add meatballs. Cover and simmer 10 to 12 minutes. Serve over hot spaghetti.

Makes 6 servings

Prep Time: 20 minutes
Cook Time: 15 minutes

*Favorite recipe from **National Pork Producers Council***

Swedish Meatballs

Spanish Rice and Meatballs

300 SPANISH RICE AND MEATBALLS

6 slices bacon
1 pound lean ground beef
½ cup soft bread crumbs
1 egg, slightly beaten
½ teaspoon salt
⅛ teaspoon pepper
½ cup chopped onion
½ cup sliced celery
⅔ cup uncooked white rice
1½ cups water
1 can (14½ ounces) whole peeled
  tomatoes, cut into bite-size pieces
⅓ cup HEINZ® 57 Sauce
¼ teaspoon pepper
⅛ teaspoon hot pepper sauce
1 green bell pepper, cut into ¾-inch
  chunks

In large skillet, cook bacon until crisp; remove, coarsely crumble and set aside. Drain drippings, reserving 1 tablespoon. In large bowl, combine beef, bread crumbs, egg, salt and ⅛ teaspoon pepper. Form into 20 meatballs, using a rounded tablespoon for each. In same skillet, brown meatballs in reserved drippings; remove. In same skillet, sauté onion and celery until tender-crisp; drain excess fat. Add rice, water, tomatoes, 57 Sauce, ¼ teaspoon pepper and hot pepper sauce. Cover; simmer 20 minutes. Stir in bacon, meatballs and green pepper. Cover; simmer an additional 10 minutes or until rice is tender and liquid is absorbed, stirring occasionally. *Makes 4 servings (4 cups rice mixture)*

MEAT LOAVES & MEATBALLS

301 PORK BALLS IN CURRY SAUCE

1½ **pounds lean ground pork**
¾ **cup soft bread crumbs**
¾ **cup finely chopped onion**
1 **egg, lightly beaten**
1 **teaspoon salt**
1 **tablespoon vegetable oil**
1 to 2 **tablespoons crushed dried red peppers**
1 **tablespoon curry powder**
1 **teaspoon ground ginger**
3 **cups chopped onion**
2 **cloves garlic, minced**
1 **cup tomato sauce**
1 **cup chicken broth**
⅔ **cup cider vinegar**
¾ **cup sour cream**

Combine ground pork, bread crumbs, ¾ cup onion, egg and salt. Shape into 1½-inch balls (about 30). Heat oil in large skillet. Add half of pork balls and cook, turning occasionally, to brown all sides. Remove browned pork balls from pan and repeat with remaining balls. Remove pork balls from pan; pour off fat, reserving 2 tablespoons in skillet. Add red peppers, curry powder and ginger to skillet; cook and stir about 1 minute. Add 3 cups onions, garlic, tomato sauce, chicken broth and vinegar; stir to blend. Bring to a boil. Add pork balls; cover. Reduce heat and simmer 45 minutes. Push balls to one side of pan; stir sour cream into sauce. *Do not boil.* Carefully mix sauce and balls. Serve with noodles or rice, if desired.

Makes 8 servings

Prep Time: 20 minutes
Cook Time: 45 minutes

Favorite recipe from **National Pork Producers Council**

302 PORK MEATBALLS STROGANOFF

1 **pound lean ground pork**
½ **cup soft bread crumbs**
1 **egg, beaten**
1 **teaspoon salt**
⅛ **teaspoon pepper**
2 **tablespoons vegetable oil**
8 **ounces fresh mushrooms, cut into quarters**
1 **small onion, chopped**
1 **tablespoon all-purpose flour**
½ **cup dry sherry**
½ **cup water**
½ **cup dairy sour cream**
   Hot cooked noodles
   Snipped parsley (optional)

In mixing bowl combine ground pork, bread crumbs, egg, salt and pepper; mix well. Shape into 12 meatballs. In large skillet brown meatballs in hot oil; remove. Pour off pan drippings, reserving 2 tablespoons in skillet. Cook mushrooms and onion in drippings until tender, about 3 minutes. Add flour; cook and stir for 1 to 2 minutes or until thickened and bubbly. Stir in sherry and water. Return meatballs to skillet. Simmer, covered, 20 minutes. Remove from heat; stir in sour cream. *Do not boil.* Serve over hot cooked noodles. Sprinkle with parsley, if desired. *Makes 4 servings*

Prep Time: 20 minutes
Cook Time: 20 minutes

Favorite recipe from **National Pork Producers Council**

303 BRAISED LION'S HEAD

MEATBALLS
- 1 pound lean ground pork
- 4 ounces shrimp, shelled, deveined and finely chopped
- 1/4 cup sliced water chestnuts, finely chopped
- 1 teaspoon minced fresh ginger
- 1 green onion with top, finely chopped
- 1 tablespoon soy sauce
- 1 tablespoon dry sherry
- 1/2 teaspoon salt
- 1/2 teaspoon sugar
- 1 tablespoon cornstarch
- 1 egg, lightly beaten
- 2 tablespoons vegetable oil

SAUCE
- 1 1/2 cups chicken broth
- 2 tablespoons soy sauce
- 1/2 teaspoon sugar
- 1 head napa cabbage (1 1/2 to 2 pounds)
- 2 tablespoons cornstarch
- 3 tablespoons cold water
- 1 teaspoon sesame oil

For meatballs, combine all meatball ingredients *except* vegetable oil in large bowl; mix well. Shape mixture into eight balls. Heat vegetable oil in wok or large nonstick skillet over medium-high heat. Add meatballs; cook 6 to 8 minutes until browned, stirring occasionally.

Transfer meatballs to 5-quart saucepan; discard drippings. Add chicken broth, 2 tablespoons soy sauce and 1/2 teaspoon sugar. Bring to a boil. Reduce heat to low; cover. Simmer 30 minutes. While meatballs are cooking, core cabbage. Cut base of leaves into 2-inch squares. Cut leafy tops in half. Place over meatballs; cover. Simmer an additional 10 minutes.

Using slotted spoon, transfer cabbage and meatballs to serving platter. Blend 2 tablespoons cornstarch and water. Gradually add to pan juices, stirring constantly; cook until slightly thickened. Stir in sesame oil. Serve over meatballs and cabbage. Garnish as desired.   *Makes 4 to 6 servings*

304 SWEET & SOUR MEATBALLS WITH VEGETABLES

- 1 pound ground turkey
- 2 cups Multi-Bran CHEX® brand cereal, crushed to 3/4 cup
- 1/4 cup chopped onion
- 2 tablespoons chopped fresh parsley
- 1 clove garlic, minced
- 1/4 teaspoon ground ginger
- 1/4 cup cholesterol-free egg product *or* 1 egg, beaten
- 1 teaspoon lite soy sauce
- 1 package (16 ounces) frozen Oriental or mixed vegetables, prepared according to package directions, drained
- 9 ounces (1 cup) prepared sweet and sour sauce
- Hot cooked rice (optional)

In medium bowl combine turkey, cereal, onion, parsley, garlic, ginger, egg product and soy sauce. Mix well. Shape meat mixture into 2-inch balls using 1 rounded tablespoon for each. Brown meatballs in lightly greased skillet over medium heat, turning often. Add 1/4 cup water; cover and cook over low heat 8 to 10 minutes or until no longer pink, stirring occasionally. Drain. Add vegetables and sauce. Stir gently over low heat until meatballs are coated and sauce and vegetables are warm. Serve over rice, if desired.   *Makes 6 servings*

Braised Lion's Head

MEAT LOAVES & MEATBALLS

305 KOFTAS (LAMB MEATBALLS IN SPICY GRAVY)

2 teaspoons Garam Masala (page 29)
1½ pounds ground lamb or ground beef
2 eggs
1½ cups finely chopped onions, divided
½ cup chopped cilantro
2 cloves garlic, minced
1 teaspoon minced fresh ginger
1½ teaspoons salt, divided
24 whole blanched almonds
1 tablespoon peanut oil
1 teaspoon ground coriander
1 teaspoon ground cumin
1 teaspoon chili powder
½ teaspoon turmeric
2 tomatoes, peeled, seeded and chopped
½ cup water
1 cup plain yogurt

Prepare Garam Masala. Place 2 teaspoons in medium bowl. Add lamb, eggs, ½ cup onion, cilantro, garlic, ginger and ½ teaspoon salt; mix well. Refrigerate at least 1 hour or overnight.

Shape mixture into 24 ovals or balls; insert 1 almond into each meatball. Heat oil in large skillet over medium-high heat. Add half the meatballs; cook 8 minutes or until brown, turning frequently. Remove meatballs from skillet. Repeat with remaining meatballs.

Reduce heat to medium. Add remaining 1 cup onion. Cook and stir 6 to 8 minutes or until browned. Stir in remaining 1 teaspoon salt, coriander, cumin, chili powder and turmeric. Add tomatoes. Cook 5 minutes or until tomatoes are tender. Add water; bring mixture to a boil over high heat. Add meatballs. Reduce heat to medium-low. Simmer 15 minutes or until thoroughly cooked. Remove meatballs from skillet to serving platter; keep warm.

Remove skillet from heat; place yogurt in small bowl. Stir in several spoonfuls hot mixture. Stir yogurt mixture into sauce in skillet. Cook over medium-low heat until sauce thickens. *Do not boil.* Pour sauce over meatballs. Garnish as desired.

Makes 6 servings

306 SWEDISH–STYLE MEATBALLS

1½ pounds ground pork
1 cup soft bread crumbs
2 cups half-and-half, divided
1 egg
¼ cup finely chopped onion
1 teaspoon salt
¼ teaspoon pepper
¼ teaspoon ground allspice
1 teaspoon vegetable oil
¼ cup all-purpose flour
1 can (14½ ounces) chicken broth
2 tablespoons snipped fresh dill

Combine pork, bread crumbs, ⅓ cup half-and-half, egg, onion and seasonings; mix well. Shape mixture into eighteen 2-inch balls. Heat oil in nonstick skillet. Brown meatballs over medium heat, turning carefully; remove from skillet with slotted spoon.

Reserve 2 tablespoons drippings in pan. Stir in flour; cook until thickened. Gradually add chicken broth; cook and stir until thickened. Stir in remaining 1⅔ cups half-and-half and dill; cook 2 minutes. Return meatballs to skillet; simmer 10 minutes.

Makes 6 servings

Prep Time: 25 minutes

*Favorite recipe from **National Pork Producers Council***

Koftas

The Main
Event

307 SALISBURY STEAKS WITH MUSHROOM–WINE SAUCE

1 pound lean ground beef sirloin
¾ teaspoon garlic salt or seasoned salt
¼ teaspoon pepper
2 tablespoons butter or margarine
1 package (8 ounces) sliced button mushrooms *or* 2 packages (4 ounces each) sliced exotic mushrooms
2 tablespoons sweet vermouth or ruby port wine
1 jar (12 ounces) *or* 1 can (10½ ounces) beef gravy

1. Heat large heavy nonstick skillet over medium-high heat 3 minutes or until hot.* Meanwhile, combine ground sirloin, garlic salt and pepper; mix well. Shape mixture into four ¼-inch-thick oval patties.

2. Place patties in skillet as they are formed; cook 3 minutes per side or until browned. Transfer to plate; keep warm. Pour off any drippings.

3. Melt butter in skillet; add mushrooms and cook 2 minutes, stirring occasionally. Add vermouth; cook 1 minute. Add gravy; mix well.

4. Return meat to skillet; simmer uncovered over medium heat 3 minutes for medium or until desired doneness, turning meat and stirring sauce once.   *Makes 4 servings*

*If pan is not heavy, use medium heat.

NOTE: For a special touch, sprinkle steaks with chopped parsley or chives.

Prep and Cook Time: 20 minutes

Salisbury Steak with Mushroom-Wine Sauce

THE MAIN EVENT

308 EASY PEPPER STEAK

1 pound lean ground beef
1 tablespoon chopped fresh thyme *or*
    1 teaspoon dried thyme leaves
1 teaspoon paprika
    Salt and freshly ground black pepper
3 tablespoons all-purpose flour
1¼ cups chicken broth
2 tablespoons dry white wine
1 teaspoon Worcestershire sauce
3 medium bell peppers (use 1 each red,
    green and yellow, if possible), cut into
    thin slices
1 medium onion, sliced, separated into
    rings

Crumble ground beef into large bowl. Stir in thyme, paprika, 1 teaspoon salt and dash of black pepper. Shape into four ½-inch-thick oval loaves. Place on microwave-safe rack; cover with waxed paper. Microwave on HIGH (100%) 4 to 5 minutes or to desired doneness, turning rack after 3 minutes. Reserve ⅓ cup meat drippings; keep meat warm. Mix together drippings and flour in medium microwave-safe bowl. Stir in broth, wine and Worcestershire sauce. Microwave on HIGH 2 to 3 minutes or until mixture thickens, stirring every minute. Season with salt and black pepper to taste. Add bell peppers and onions; cover. Microwave on HIGH 6 to 7 minutes or until vegetables are crisp-tender, stirring after 3 minutes. Serve over meat. *Makes 4 servings*

309 BACON–WRAPPED PORK AND APPLE PATTIES

1 pound lean ground pork
¾ cup quick-cooking rolled oats
    Salt
½ teaspoon ground sage
¼ teaspoon pepper
¼ teaspoon dried thyme leaves, crushed
⅓ cup applesauce
1 egg, slightly beaten
¼ cup minced green onions
4 slices bacon
1 large tart green apple, cut into thin
    wedges
½ medium yellow onion, cut into small
    wedges
1 tablespoon olive oil

In large bowl combine oats, ½ teaspoon salt, sage, pepper and thyme. Stir in applesauce, egg and green onions; mix well. Stir in ground pork until well blended. Form into 4 patties about ¾ to 1 inch thick. Wrap 1 bacon strip around each patty; secure with toothpick. Grill or broil patties 4 to 5 minutes on each side or until no longer pink.

Meanwhile in small skillet, cook and stir apple and onion wedges in hot oil until tender. Sprinkle lightly with salt. Serve with patties. *Makes 4 servings*

Favorite recipe from **National Pork Producers Council**

Easy Pepper Steak

THE MAIN EVENT

310 SALISBURY STEAK WITH MUSHROOM GRAVY

SALISBURY STEAK
 1 pound lean ground beef
 ⅓ cup finely chopped onion
 ¼ cup saltine cracker crumbs
 1 egg white, slightly beaten
 2 tablespoons milk
 1 tablespoon prepared horseradish
 ¼ teaspoon salt
 ⅛ teaspoon pepper

MUSHROOM GRAVY
 1 jar (12 ounces) brown beef gravy
 4 ounces mushrooms, sliced
 2 tablespoons water

1. In medium bowl, combine Salisbury steak ingredients, mixing lightly but thoroughly; shape into 4 oval ½-inch-thick patties.

2. Heat large nonstick skillet over medium heat until hot. Place beef patties in skillet; cook 7 to 8 minutes or until no longer pink and juices run clear, turning once. Remove from skillet; keep warm.

3. In same skillet, combine gravy ingredients; cook over medium heat 3 to 5 minutes or until mushrooms are tender. Serve over Salisbury steak and mashed potatoes, if desired.   *Makes 4 servings*

Total Prep & Cook Time: 25 minutes

COOK'S TIP: For zesty mashed potatoes, stir 1 teaspoon prepared horseradish into each cup of hot mashed potatoes.

*Favorite recipe from **National Cattlemen's Beef Association***

311 QUICK–MIX SAUSAGE

 1 pound lean ground pork
 Seasonings for desired variation*

Thoroughly mix ground pork and desired seasonings. Shape into patties and brown, or crumble and fry for use in a recipe.
      Makes 8 servings

***COUNTRY-STYLE SAUSAGE:** ¾ teaspoon ground sage, ½ teaspoon salt, ¼ teaspoon ground black pepper

***BREAKFAST SAUSAGE:** 1 teaspoon ground sage, ½ teaspoon salt, ½ teaspoon dried savory, ¼ teaspoon ground black pepper, ¼ teaspoon nutmeg

***SPICED BREAKFAST SAUSAGE:** to Breakfast Sausage add ¼ teaspoon *each* ground cloves and ground mace

***ITALIAN SAUSAGE:** 1 minced clove garlic, 1 teaspoon paprika, 1 teaspoon crushed thyme, ½ teaspoon salt, ½ teaspoon fennel seeds, ⅛ teaspoon cayenne

***MEXICAN CHORIZO:** 1 tablespoon ground red chiles, 1 teaspoon salt, ½ teaspoon ground coriander, ¼ teaspoon ground cloves, ¼ teaspoon ground black pepper, ¼ teaspoon ground oregano, ¼ teaspoon ground cumin, 2 minced cloves garlic

Prep Time: 5 minutes
Cook Time: 10 minutes

*Favorite recipe from **National Pork Producers Council***

Salisbury Steak with Mushroom Gravy

THE MAIN EVENT

312 HOMEMADE SAUSAGE PATTIES

1½ pounds ground pork
½ pound ground turkey
2 teaspoons rubbed sage
1½ teaspoons salt
1 to 1½ teaspoons black pepper
1 teaspoon dried thyme leaves
½ teaspoon fennel seeds, crushed
     (optional)

Combine pork, turkey, sage, salt, pepper, thyme and fennel seeds in large bowl; mix well. Cover and refrigerate at least 1 hour or up to 24 hours.

For each sausage patty, shape ¼ cup pork mixture into ½-inch-thick patty, about 2½ inches in diameter. Heat large skillet over medium-high heat until hot. Add enough sausage patties as will fit without crowding skillet. Cook sausage patties 4 minutes, turning halfway through cooking.

Reduce heat to medium-low and continue cooking sausage patties 6 to 8 minutes more or until no longer pink in center, turning halfway through cooking. Repeat with remaining sausage patties.

Makes 16 sausage patties

313 TURKEY WITH CHILI CRANBERRY SAUCE

1 pound ground raw turkey
¼ cup seasoned dry bread crumbs
¼ cup thinly sliced green onions
1 egg, slightly beaten
¼ teaspoon salt
¼ teaspoon pepper
1 tablespoon vegetable oil
⅔ cup whole berry cranberry sauce
⅓ cup HEINZ® Chili Sauce
2 tablespoons water
⅛ teaspoon ground cinnamon

Combine turkey, bread crumbs, green onions, egg, salt and pepper. Shape into 4 patties, about ½ inch thick. Slowly sauté patties in oil, about 4 to 5 minutes per side or until cooked through. Stir in cranberry sauce, chili sauce, water and cinnamon. Simmer, uncovered, 1 minute.

Makes 4 servings

Homemade Sausage Patties

THE MAIN EVENT

314 STUFFED SALISBURY STEAK WITH MUSHROOM & ONION TOPPING

2 pounds ground beef
$^{1}/_{4}$ cup FRENCH'S® Worcestershire Sauce
2$^{2}/_{3}$ cups (two 2.8-ounce cans) FRENCH'S® French Fried Onions, divided
1 teaspoon garlic salt
$^{1}/_{2}$ teaspoon ground black pepper
4 ounces Cheddar cheese, cut into 6 sticks (about 2×$^{1}/_{2}$×$^{1}/_{2}$ inches)
Mushroom Topping (recipe follows)

Combine beef, Worcestershire, *1$^{1}/_{3}$ cups* French Fried Onions, garlic salt and pepper. Divide meat evenly into 6 portions. Place 1 stick cheese in center of each portion, firmly pressing and shaping meat into ovals around cheese.

Place steaks on grid. Grill over medium-high coals 15 minutes or until meat thermometer inserted into beef reaches 160°F, turning once. Serve with Mushroom Topping and sprinkle with remaining *1$^{1}/_{3}$ cups* onions.

Makes 6 servings

MUSHROOM TOPPING
2 tablespoons butter or margarine
1 package (12 ounces) mushrooms, wiped clean and quartered
2 tablespoons FRENCH'S® Worcestershire Sauce

Melt butter in large skillet over medium-high heat. Add mushrooms; cook 5 minutes or until browned, stirring often. Add Worcestershire. Reduce heat to low. Cook 5 minutes, stirring occasionally.

Makes 6 servings

Prep Time: 25 minutes
Cook Time: 25 minutes

315 TURNIP SHEPHERD'S PIE

1 pound small turnips,* peeled, cut into $^{1}/_{2}$-inch cubes
1 pound lean ground turkey
$^{1}/_{3}$ cup dry bread crumbs
$^{1}/_{4}$ cup chopped onion
$^{1}/_{4}$ cup ketchup
1 egg
$^{1}/_{2}$ teaspoon *each* salt, pepper and beau monde seasoning
$^{1}/_{3}$ cup half-and-half
1 tablespoon butter or margarine
Salt and pepper
1 tablespoon chopped fresh parsley
$^{1}/_{4}$ cup shredded sharp Cheddar cheese

For Rutabaga Shepherd's Pie, use 1 pound rutabagas in place of turnips.

Preheat oven to 400°F. Place turnips in large saucepan; cover with water. Cover. Bring to a boil; reduce heat to medium-low. Simmer 20 minutes or until fork-tender.

Mix turkey, crumbs, onion, ketchup, egg and $^{1}/_{2}$ teaspoon each salt, pepper and seasoning. Pat on bottom and sides of 9-inch pie pan. Bake 20 to 30 minutes until turkey is no longer pink. Blot with paper towel to remove any drippings.

Drain cooked turnips. Mash turnips with electric mixer until smooth, blending in half-and-half and butter. Season with salt and pepper to taste. Fill meat shell with turnip mixture; sprinkle with parsley, then cheese. Return to oven until cheese melts. Garnish as desired.

Makes 4 main-dish servings

Turnip Shepherd's Pie

THE MAIN EVENT

316 HUNGARIAN BEEF ROLLS

Spicy Tomato Sauce (recipe follows)
4 bacon slices, finely chopped
½ cup finely chopped onion
1 small clove garlic, minced
¾ pound lean ground beef
2 eggs, beaten
1 tablespoon paprika, Hungarian if
  possible
Salt
Dash freshly ground pepper
1½ pounds beef top round, sliced ½ inch
  thick (about 12 slices)
2 tablespoons vegetable oil

Prepare Spicy Tomato Sauce; keep warm
while preparing beef rolls.

Cook bacon in medium skillet until partially
cooked. Add onion and garlic; continue
cooking until bacon is crisp and onion is
tender. Drain.

Combine bacon mixture, ground beef, eggs,
paprika, salt to taste and pepper in medium
bowl; mix lightly. Set aside.

Pound each beef slice to ¼-inch thickness.
Spoon approximately 2 tablespoons ground
beef mixture onto one end of one beef slice;
roll to enclose filling. Secure with wooden
pick or tie closed with kitchen string. Repeat
with remaining beef slices and ground beef
mixture.

Heat oil in large skillet. Add beef rolls in
batches; cook until browned on all sides.

Add to Spicy Tomato Sauce; bring to a boil.
Reduce heat; cover. Simmer 50 minutes or
until beef is tender. Remove wooden picks
before serving. *Makes 6 servings*

SPICY TOMATO SAUCE
1 tablespoon vegetable oil
1 medium onion, chopped
1 clove garlic, minced
1 can (14½ ounces) tomatoes, crushed,
  undrained
2 cups chicken broth
2 tablespoons tomato paste
1 teaspoon paprika, Hungarian if possible
  Bay leaves
½ teaspoon salt
  Dash freshly ground pepper

Heat oil in large saucepan. Add onion and
garlic; cook until tender. Stir in tomatoes
with juice and remaining ingredients. Bring
to a boil. Reduce heat; simmer until ready to
use. Remove bay leaves just before serving.

317 LEAN HOMEMADE SAUSAGE

1 pound lean ground pork
½ teaspoon ground rosemary
⅛ teaspoon salt
⅛ teaspoon ground thyme
⅛ teaspoon dried marjoram, crushed
⅛ teaspoon pepper

Combine all ingredients; mix well. Place in
an airtight container. Refrigerate 4 to 24
hours to allow flavors to blend.

Shape into ½-inch-thick patties. Cook patties
in large skillet over medium heat 4 to 5
minutes on each side or until done. Or, place
patties on unheated rack in broiler pan. Broil
5 inches from heat about 5 minutes on each
side. *Makes 8 servings*

Prep Time: 10 minutes
Cook Time: 10 minutes

Favorite recipe from **National Pork Producers Council**

THE MAIN EVENT

318 TOLUCA TATERS

1 package (1.48 ounces) LAWRY'S® Spices
    & Seasonings for Chili
1 pound ground turkey
1 can (15½ ounces) kidney beans,
    undrained
1 can (14½ ounces) whole peeled
    tomatoes, undrained and cut up
½ cup water
8 medium russet potatoes, washed and
    pierced with fork
1 cup (4 ounces) shredded Cheddar
    cheese
½ cup thinly sliced green onions

MICROWAVE DIRECTIONS: In large
glass bowl, prepare Spices & Seasonings for
Chili with ground turkey, kidney beans,
tomatoes and water according to package
microwave directions; keep warm.
Microwave potatoes on HIGH 25 minutes,
turning over after 12 minutes. Cut potatoes
lengthwise and stir inside with fork to fluff.
Top each potato with ½ to ¾ cup prepared
chili, 2 tablespoons cheese and 1 tablespoon
green onions. *Makes 8 servings*

PRESENTATION: Top with sour cream, if
desired. Serve with a mixed green salad and
fresh fruit.

HINT: This recipe is a great way to use
leftover chili.

Toluca Taters

THE MAIN EVENT

319 CHILI–STUFFED POBLANO PEPPERS

1 pound lean ground beef
4 large poblano peppers
1 can (15 ounces) chili-seasoned beans
1 can (14½ ounces) chili-style chunky tomatoes, undrained
1 tablespoon Mexican (adobo) seasoning
⅔ cup (about 2½ ounces) shredded Mexican cheese blend or Monterey Jack cheese

1. Preheat broiler. Cook ground beef in large nonstick skillet over medium-high heat 5 to 6 minutes or until no longer pink. Pour off drippings.

2. Meanwhile, bring 2 quarts water to a boil in 3-quart saucepan. Cut peppers in half lengthwise; remove seeds. Add 4 pepper halves to boiling water; cook 3 minutes or until bright green and slightly softened. Remove; drain upside down on plate. Repeat with remaining 4 halves. Set aside.

3. Add beans, tomatoes and Mexican seasoning to ground beef. Cook and stir over medium heat 5 minutes or until mixture thickens slightly.

4. Arrange peppers, cut sides up, in 13×9-inch baking dish. Divide chili mixture evenly among peppers; top with cheese. Broil 6 inches from heat 1 minute or until cheese is melted. Serve immediately.

Makes 4 servings

Prep and Cook Time: 26 minutes

SERVING SUGGESTION: Serve stuffed peppers with corn bread and chunky salsa.

320 STUFFED PEPPERS

6 medium green peppers
 Boiling salted water
1 pound ground beef
1 small onion, chopped
1 can (8 ounces) kidney beans, drained
1 can (6 ounces) tomato paste
2½ cups water, divided
1½ teaspoons salt, divided
1 teaspoon sugar
¾ teaspoon chili powder
¼ teaspoon garlic salt
⅓ cup shredded cheddar cheese (optional)
1 tablespoon butter or margarine (optional)
2¼ cups uncooked MINUTE® Original Rice

Cut slice from tops of peppers; remove seeds. Cook, uncovered, in enough salted water to cover peppers about 5 minutes; drain.

Brown beef and onion in large skillet; drain. Add beans, tomato paste, ¼ cup water, ¾ teaspoon salt, sugar, chili powder and garlic salt; mix well. Spoon into peppers and place in 13×9-inch baking dish. Add small amount of water to cover bottom of dish. Bake at 375°F for 25 minutes or until peppers are tender. Sprinkle with cheese.

Meanwhile, bring remaining 2¼ cups water, ¾ teaspoon salt and butter to a full boil in medium saucepan. Stir in rice. Cover; remove from heat. Let stand 5 minutes. Fluff with fork. Serve with peppers.

Makes 6 servings

Chili-Stuffed Poblano Peppers

THE MAIN EVENT

321 KOREAN BEEF–STUFFED ZUCCHINI

4 evenly shaped zucchini (8 inches long and about ½ pound each), ends trimmed
1½ teaspoons salt
3 small dried Oriental mushrooms
½ pound ground beef chuck
2 tablespoons diagonally sliced green onion
1 tablespoon soy sauce
2 teaspoons sesame oil
⅛ to ¼ teaspoon ground black pepper
1 egg yolk
2 cloves garlic, minced
1 large yellow onion, peeled, cut in half and sliced
1½ cups beef broth, divided
1 teaspoon sugar
Ground red pepper (optional)
2 teaspoons cornstarch (optional)
2 tablespoons slivered blanched almonds, toasted

Cut each zucchini crosswise into 4 (2-inch) lengths. Stand zucchini chunks, largest cut sides up, on cutting board. Make 2 cuts at right angles through each chunk to within ⅜ inch from bottom, being careful not to cut all the way through. Gently open cuts in each chunk and sprinkle surfaces lightly with salt. Let stand at room temperature 45 minutes to extract moisture. Place mushrooms in small bowl; add enough hot water to cover mushrooms completely. Let stand 30 minutes.

Meanwhile, combine ground chuck, green onion, soy sauce, oil, black pepper, egg yolk and garlic in large bowl; mix well. Drain mushrooms and squeeze out excess water. Cut stems off mushrooms; discard. Finely chop mushroom tops and stir into beef mixture.

Rinse zucchini chunks under cold running water. Gently squeeze to remove excess water and drain on paper towels. Gently open each zucchini and stuff about 1 rounded tablespoon meat mixture into cuts of zucchini.

Add onion slices, 1 cup broth and sugar to wok; mix well. Carefully arrange stuffed zucchini, cut sides up, in a single layer in onion mixture, placing larger chunks in center and smaller chunks around edge of wok. Sprinkle top of chunks lightly with red pepper. Cover; bring to a boil over high heat. Reduce heat to medium; simmer 10 minutes or until beef is firm and zucchini is crisp-tender. Add more broth if it evaporates.

Transfer zucchini to plate with slotted spoon, leaving onions in broth. Cover zucchini; keep warm. If thicker sauce is desired, combine cornstarch and 2 tablespoons broth in cup. Stir cornstarch mixture into onion mixture. Cook and stir until sauce boils and thickens. Spoon sauce over serving platter or individual serving plates. Place stuffed zucchini on top of sauce; sprinkle with almonds. Garnish as desired. Serve immediately.

Makes 4 main-dish servings

Korean Beef-Stuffed Zucchini

322 BEEF STROGANOFF AND ZUCCHINI TOPPED POTATOES

4 baking potatoes (8 ounces each)
¾ pound ground beef round
¾ cup chopped onion
1 cup sliced mushrooms
1 beef bouillon cube
2 tablespoons ketchup
1 teaspoon Worcestershire sauce
¼ teaspoon freshly ground black pepper
¼ teaspoon hot pepper sauce
1 medium zucchini, cut into julienned strips
½ cup low-fat sour cream, divided

1. Pierce potatoes in several places with fork. Place in microwave oven on paper towel. Microwave potatoes at HIGH 15 minutes or until softened. Wrap in paper towels. Let stand 5 minutes.

2. Heat large nonstick skillet over medium-high heat until hot. Add beef and onion. Cook and stir 5 minutes or until beef is browned. Add all remaining ingredients except zucchini and sour cream. Cover and simmer 5 minutes. Add zucchini. Cover and cook 3 minutes. Remove from heat. Stir in ¼ cup sour cream. Cover and let stand 5 minutes.

3. Cut potatoes open. Divide beef mixture evenly among potatoes. Top with remaining ¼ cup sour cream.   *Makes 4 servings*

Prep and Cook Time: 25 minutes

Beef Stroganoff and Zucchini Topped Potato

THE MAIN EVENT

323 PORK–STUFFED EGGPLANT

1 medium eggplant
½ pound lean ground pork
1 small green pepper, coarsely chopped
¼ cup chopped onion
1 clove garlic, minced
¼ cup water
⅛ teaspoon dried oregano leaves, crushed
⅛ teaspoon ground black pepper
1 medium tomato, coarsely chopped

Wash eggplant and cut in half lengthwise. Remove pulp, leaving eggplant shell about ¼ inch thick. Cut pulp into ½-inch cubes. Set shells and pulp aside.

In large skillet cook ground pork, green pepper, onion and garlic until pork is browned; drain excess drippings. Add eggplant pulp, water, oregano and black pepper; cover and cook over low heat 10 minutes, stirring occasionally. Remove from heat and stir in tomato. Spoon mixture into eggplant shells. Place in 12×8×2-inch baking dish. Bake in 350°F oven 20 to 25 minutes or until heated through.

Makes 2 servings

Prep Time: 25 minutes
Cook Time: 25 minutes

*Favorite recipe from **National Pork Producers Council***

324 ZESTY ITALIAN STUFFED PEPPERS

3 bell peppers (green, red and/or yellow)
1 large disposable aluminum foil pan
1 pound ground beef, cooked and crumbled*
1 jar (14 ounces) spaghetti sauce
3 to 4 tablespoons FRANK'S® Original REDHOT® Cayenne Pepper Sauce or to taste
1⅓ cups (2.8-ounce can) FRENCH'S® French Fried Onions, divided
½ cup uncooked instant rice
¼ cup sliced black olives
1 cup (4 ounces) shredded mozzarella cheese

Ground beef cooks easily in the microwave. Place meat in large microwave-safe bowl. Microwave on HIGH 5 minutes or until meat is browned, stirring once. Drain.

Preheat barbecue grill. Cut peppers in half lengthwise through stem; discard seeds. Place pepper halves in foil pan; set aside.

Combine cooked meat, spaghetti sauce, RedHot® Sauce, ⅔ cup French Fried Onions, rice and olives in large bowl. Spoon into pepper halves, dividing evenly. Pour cold water into pan to ½-inch depth. Cover pan securely with foil.

Place pan on grid. Cook over hot coals about 25 minutes or until peppers are tender. Uncover. Sprinkle peppers with cheese and remaining ⅔ cup onions. Cook 5 minutes or until cheese melts and onions are golden. Serve warm. *Makes 6 servings*

Prep Time: 15 minutes
Cook Time: 30 minutes

325 EULA MAE'S CABBAGE ROLLS

½ pound ground pork
½ pound ground beef
1 can (8 ounces) tomato sauce
½ cup chopped green pepper
¼ cup finely chopped onion
2 tablespoons uncooked regular rice
2 teaspoons salt
½ teaspoon TABASCO® pepper sauce
½ teaspoon dried thyme leaves
1 large head cabbage

• In large bowl mix pork, beef, tomato sauce, green pepper, onion, rice, salt, TABASCO® sauce and thyme.

• Place whole cabbage in large pot of boiling water and cook 10 minutes.

• Remove from water, carefully peel off leaves and cut tough core. Place 2 tablespoons meat filling on center of each leaf, fold sides over filling and roll up.

• Place rack in large skillet and add water to depth of rack, about 1 inch. Place cabbage rolls on rack, seam side down. Cover skillet and steam cabbage rolls over gently simmering water 1½ hours. If water evaporates, add additional water.

Makes 28 rolls

326 ZUCCHINI MEAT SAUCE WITH PASTA

1 package (12 ounces) shell macaroni or corkscrew pasta
2 pounds ground beef
2 onions, chopped
2 cans (26½ ounces each) DEL MONTE® Spaghetti Sauce—Garlic & Herb
1 can (14½ ounces) DEL MONTE® FreshCut™ Diced Tomatoes, undrained
2 small zucchini, thinly sliced

1. In 8-quart pot, cook pasta according to package directions; drain. Keep pasta hot.

2. In 6-quart pot, brown meat over medium-high heat. Season with salt and pepper, if desired; drain. Add onions; cook until tender. Stir in spaghetti sauce and tomatoes; cook 5 minutes, stirring occasionally. (Pour half of sauce into freezer container; cool, cover and freeze for another meal.)

3. Add zucchini to remaining sauce; cover and cook over medium heat 7 to 10 minutes or until zucchini is tender. Serve sauce over hot pasta. Sprinkle with grated Parmesan cheese and garnish, if desired.

Makes 4 servings

Prep & Cook Time: 30 minutes

Zucchini Meat Sauce with Pasta

THE MAIN EVENT

327 STUFFED CABBAGE ROLLS WITH YOGURT–DILL SAUCE

1 large head green cabbage, about
    3 pounds, cored
2 tablespoons olive oil
3 large green onions, sliced
2 large cloves garlic, minced
1 pound ground lamb
2 cups plain yogurt, divided
4 tablespoons fresh snipped dill, divided
1½ teaspoons TABASCO® pepper sauce
1½ teaspoons salt

Over high heat, heat large pot of water to boiling. Add cabbage, core end down. Reduce heat to medium. Cover and simmer until leaves are softened, 10 to 12 minutes. Remove cabbage to bowl of cold water. Separate 16 large leaves from head of cabbage. Trim tough ribs on back of leaves so that they will roll up easily. Chop enough of the remaining cabbage to make 3 cups.

In 12-inch skillet over medium heat, in hot oil, cook chopped cabbage, green onions and garlic until tender, about 10 minutes, stirring occasionally. With slotted spoon, remove to bowl. In drippings remaining in skillet over high heat, cook ground lamb until well browned on all sides, stirring frequently. Remove to bowl with cabbage mixture.

In food processor, blend lamb mixture until finely ground. In large bowl toss lamb mixture with ½ cup yogurt, 2 tablespoons dill, TABASCO® sauce and salt; mix well. Place 3 tablespoons lamb mixture at bottom of cabbage leaf and roll up tightly to form a 3-inch-long roll, tucking in ends. Repeat with remaining lamb mixture and cabbage leaves.

Preheat oven to 400°F. Place cabbage rolls on rack in roasting pan. Add 1 cup boiling water; cover pan tightly with foil. Bake 20 minutes or until rolls are hot.

Meanwhile, in medium bowl combine remaining 1½ cups yogurt and 2 tablespoons dill. To serve, remove cabbage rolls to platter; top with yogurt-dill sauce.

Makes 4 servings

328 PORK–STUFFED PEPPERS

3 large green peppers
¼ cup raisins
1 pound ground pork
½ cup chopped onion
½ cup chopped carrot
½ cup chopped celery
¼ teaspoon salt
1 cup cooked brown rice
2 tablespoons sunflower kernels
½ cup plain yogurt

Remove tops, seeds and membranes from peppers. Cut in half lengthwise. Cook in boiling salted water 5 minutes; drain.

Soak raisins in water 10 to 15 minutes; drain and set aside. Combine pork, onion, carrot, celery and salt in medium skillet. Cook over low heat until pork is done and vegetables are tender, stirring occasionally. Drain thoroughly. Add rice, sunflower kernels, yogurt and raisins; mix well. Spoon mixture into peppers. Place in 12×8×2-inch baking dish. Bake at 350°F 30 to 35 minutes or until heated through. *Makes 6 servings*

Prep Time: 20 minutes
Cook Time: 30 minutes

*Favorite recipe from **National Pork Producers Council***

THE MAIN EVENT

329 WILD STUFFED PEPPERS

6 green peppers
1 pound lean ground beef
2 cups cooked wild rice
1 medium onion, chopped
½ cup dried fruit bits
1 cup shredded Swiss cheese
1 teaspoon salt
1 teaspoon ground black pepper
1 teaspoon ground cinnamon

Preheat oven to 350°F. Cut green peppers lengthwise in half and remove stems and seeds. Combine remaining ingredients. Lightly stuff green pepper halves with wild rice mixture. Place in baking dish and loosely cover with foil. Bake 30 minutes. Uncover; bake 10 minutes more or until pepper is tender.   *Makes 6 servings*

Favorite recipe from **Minnesota Cultivated Wild Rice Council**

330 RICE–STUFFED PEPPERS

1 package LIPTON® Rice & Sauce—Cheddar Broccoli
2 cups water
1 tablespoon margarine or butter
1 pound ground beef
4 large red or green bell peppers, halved lengthwise and seeded

Preheat oven to 350°F.

Prepare rice & sauce—cheddar broccoli with water and margarine according to package directions.

Meanwhile, in 10-inch skillet, brown ground beef over medium-high heat; drain. Stir into rice & sauce. Fill each pepper half with rice mixture. In 13×9-inch baking dish, arrange stuffed peppers. Bake covered 20 minutes. Remove cover and continue baking 10 minutes or until peppers are tender. Sprinkle, if desired, with shredded cheddar cheese.

Makes about 4 main-dish servings

331 STUFFED MEXICAN PEPPERS

1 package LIPTON® Rice & Sauce—Beef Flavor
1¼ cups water, divided
½ pound ground beef
1 cup frozen corn, partially thawed
1 cup shredded cheddar cheese (about 4 ounces), divided
1 medium tomato, chopped
1 tablespoon chopped green chilies
4 large green pepper cups

Preheat oven to 350°F.

In large bowl, combine rice & sauce—beef flavor with ¾ cup water; stir in ground beef, corn, ¾ cup cheese, tomato and chilies. Spoon into pepper cups; place upright in 8- or 9-inch baking pan filled with remaining ½ cup water. Cover tightly with aluminum foil and bake covered 45 minutes. Evenly top with remaining ¼ cup cheese and continue baking uncovered 10 minutes or until cheese melts.   *Makes 4 servings*

THE MAIN EVENT

332 MEXICAN STUFFED SHELLS

12 pasta stuffing shells, cooked in unsalted
    water and drained
1 pound ground beef
1 jar (12 ounces) mild or medium picante
    sauce
½ cup water
1 can (8 ounces) tomato sauce
1 can (4 ounces) chopped green chilies,
    drained
1⅓ cups (2.8-ounce can) FRENCH'S® French
    Fried Onions
1 cup (4 ounces) shredded Monterey Jack
    cheese

Preheat oven to 350°F. In large skillet, brown
ground beef; drain. In small bowl, combine
picante sauce, water and tomato sauce. Stir
½ *cup* sauce mixture into beef along with
chilies, ⅔ *cup* French Fried Onions, and
½ *cup* cheese; mix well. Spread *half* the
remaining sauce mixture in bottom of 10-
inch round baking dish. Stuff cooked shells
with beef mixture. Arrange shells in baking
dish; top with remaining sauce. Bake,
covered, at 350°F for 30 minutes or until
heated through. Top with remaining ⅔ *cup*
onions and ½ *cup* cheese; bake, uncovered,
5 minutes or until cheese is melted.

Makes 6 servings

MICROWAVE DIRECTIONS: Crumble
ground beef into medium microwave-safe
bowl. Cook, covered, on HIGH (100%) 4 to
6 minutes or until beef is cooked. Stir beef
halfway through cooking time. Drain well.
Prepare sauce mixture as above; spread
½ *cup* in 12×8-inch microwave-safe dish.

Prepare beef mixture as above. Stuff cooked
shells with beef mixture. Arrange shells in
dish; top with remaining sauce. Cook,
covered, 10 to 12 minutes or until heated
through. Rotate dish halfway through
cooking time. Top with remaining onions
and cheese; cook, uncovered, 1 minute or
until cheese is melted. Let stand 5 minutes.

333 BOLOGNESE SAUCE

1 tablespoon olive or vegetable oil
1 cup chopped onion
½ cup diced celery
3 cloves garlic, minced
8 ounces lean ground beef
1¾ cups (15-ounce can) CONTADINA®
    Tomato Puree
⅔ cup (6-ounce can) CONTADINA®
    Italian-Style Tomato Paste
½ cup beef broth
⅓ cup dry red wine or water
2 teaspoons chopped fresh marjoram *or*
    1 teaspoon dried marjoram leaves,
    crushed
1 teaspoon salt (optional)
1 pound dry pasta, cooked, drained, kept
    warm

In large skillet, heat oil. Add onion, celery
and garlic; sauté for 3 to 4 minutes or until
vegetables are tender. Add ground beef;
cook for 5 to 7 minutes or until evenly
browned, stirring occasionally. Add tomato
puree, tomato paste, broth, wine, marjoram
and salt. Bring to a boil. Reduce heat to low;
simmer, uncovered, for 10 to 15 minutes or
until heated through, stirring occasionally.
Serve over pasta.   *Makes 8 servings*

Mexican Stuffed Shells

THE MAIN EVENT

334 HEARTY SPAGHETTI WITH PORK

3 slices bacon
¾ pound ground pork
¾ pound bulk pork sausage
1 large onion, coarsely chopped
1 green pepper, seeded and chopped
2 cloves garlic, minced
1 cup dry red wine
3 cans (14½ ounces each) Italian-style tomatoes, crushed
1 can (6 ounces) tomato paste
2 teaspoons dried oregano leaves, crushed
1 teaspoon brown sugar
½ teaspoon dried basil leaves, crushed
½ teaspoon dried thyme leaves
2 bay leaves
12 ounces spaghetti, cooked and drained

In large skillet cook bacon until crisp. Remove bacon to paper towels; reserve drippings in skillet. Crumble bacon and set aside. In reserved drippings cook ground pork, pork sausage, onion, green pepper and garlic over medium-high heat until meat is browned and vegetables are tender, stirring occasionally. Drain well. Add wine; bring to a boil. Boil 10 minutes or until liquid is absorbed, stirring occasionally. Stir in bacon, undrained tomatoes, tomato paste, oregano, brown sugar, basil, thyme and bay leaves. Bring to a boil. Reduce heat and simmer, uncovered, 1 hour or until of desired consistency. Remove bay leaves. Serve with hot cooked spaghetti.

Makes 6 servings

Prep Time: 20 minutes
Cook Time: 60 minutes

*Favorite recipe from **National Pork Producers Council***

335 SPAGHETTI SAUCE

1 pound mild Italian sausage, casings removed
1 cup chopped onion
1 clove garlic, minced
½ cup sliced fresh mushrooms
3½ cups (28-ounce can) CONTADINA® Crushed Tomatoes
2 cups (15-ounce can) CONTADINA® Tomato Sauce
½ teaspoon dried oregano leaves, crushed
¼ teaspoon dried basil leaves, crushed
1 pound dry pasta, cooked, drained, kept warm

In large skillet, brown sausage with onion and garlic, stirring to break up sausage. Stir in mushrooms, crushed tomatoes, tomato sauce, oregano and basil. Bring to a boil. Reduce heat to low; simmer, uncovered, for 30 minutes, stirring occasionally. Serve over pasta.

Makes 8 servings

Spaghetti Sauce

THE MAIN EVENT

336 RAVIOLI WITH TOMATOES AND ZUCCHINI

2 packages (9 ounces each) fresh or frozen cheese ravioli or tortellini
¾ pound hot Italian sausage, crumbled
2 cans (14½ ounces each) DEL MONTE® FreshCut™ Diced Tomatoes
1 medium zucchini, thinly sliced and quartered
1 teaspoon dried basil leaves, crushed
½ cup ricotta cheese *or* 2 tablespoons grated Parmesan cheese

1. In 8-quart pot, cook pasta according to package directions; drain. Keep hot.

2. Meanwhile, in 6-quart pot, brown sausage over medium-high heat until no longer pink in center; drain.

3. Add tomatoes, zucchini and basil. Cook, uncovered, over medium-high heat about 8 minutes or until zucchini is just tender-crisp, stirring occasionally. Season with pepper, if desired.

4. Spoon sauce over hot pasta. Top with ricotta cheese. *Makes 4 servings*

Prep & Cook Time: 20 minutes

337 SAUSAGE SPAGHETTI

1 pound BOB EVANS FARMS® Original Recipe or Italian Roll Sausage
1 large onion, chopped
2 cloves garlic, minced
1 (6-ounce) can tomato paste
1 (32-ounce) can whole tomatoes (regular or Italian style), undrained
1 (4-ounce) can mushroom stems and pieces, drained
2 tablespoons Italian seasoning, or to taste
1 tablespoon Worcestershire sauce
1 pound spaghetti, cooked according to package directions and drained
Grated Parmesan cheese

Crumble sausage into large skillet. Add onion and garlic. Cook over medium heat until sausage is browned, stirring occasionally. Drain off any drippings. Stir in tomato paste; cook 3 minutes. Add all remaining ingredients except spaghetti and cheese, stirring well to break up tomatoes. Bring to a boil over high heat. Reduce heat to low; simmer 30 minutes, stirring occasionally. Adjust seasonings, if desired. Pour over hot spaghetti. Serve with cheese. Refrigerate leftovers. *Makes 6 servings*

SERVING SUGGESTION: Serve the sauce hot over any type of pasta.

Ravioli with Tomatoes and Zucchini

338 STUFFED MUSHROOMS WITH TOMATO SAUCE AND PASTA

Tomato Sauce (recipe follows)
1 pound extra-lean (90% lean) ground beef
¼ cup finely chopped onion
¼ cup finely chopped green or red bell pepper
1 large garlic clove, minced
2 tablespoons finely chopped fresh parsley
2 teaspoons finely chopped fresh basil *or* 1 teaspoon dried basil leaves, crushed
1 teaspoon finely chopped fresh oregano *or* ½ teaspoon dried oregano leaves, crushed
½ teaspoon salt
Dash of freshly ground black pepper
12 very large mushrooms
¼ cup (1 ounce) grated Parmesan cheese
4½ cups cooked spaghetti

Prepare Tomato Sauce; set aside.

Preheat oven to 350°F.

Combine ground beef, onion, green bell pepper, garlic, parsley, basil, oregano, salt and black pepper in medium bowl; mix lightly. Remove stems from mushrooms; finely chop stems. Add to ground beef mixture. Stuff into mushroom caps, rounding tops.

Pour Tomato Sauce into shallow casserole dish large enough to hold mushrooms in single layer. Place mushrooms, stuffing side up, in sauce; cover.

Bake 20 minutes; remove cover. Sprinkle with Parmesan cheese. Continue baking, uncovered, 15 minutes. Serve with spaghetti. Garnish with additional fresh basil leaves, if desired. *Makes 6 servings*

TOMATO SAUCE
2 cans (14½ ounces each) tomatoes, chopped, undrained
Dash of hot pepper sauce
1 teaspoon finely chopped fresh marjoram *or* ½ teaspoon dried marjoram leaves, crushed
1 teaspoon fennel seeds, crushed
Salt and freshly ground black pepper

Combine all ingredients except salt and black pepper in medium saucepan. Bring to a boil. Reduce heat; simmer 5 minutes. Season with salt and pepper to taste.

339 PASTA PRONTO

8 ounces linguine or spaghetti, uncooked
1 pound ground beef, ground turkey or mild Italian sausage
1 cup coarsely chopped onions
1 clove garlic, minced
2 cans (14½ ounces each) DEL MONTE® Pasta Style Chunky Tomatoes, undrained
1 can (8 ounces) DEL MONTE® Tomato Sauce
¼ cup (1 ounce) grated Parmesan cheese

1. Cook pasta according to package directions; drain and keep hot.

2. In large skillet, brown meat with 1 cup onions and garlic; drain. Add tomatoes and tomato sauce. Cook, stirring frequently, 15 minutes.

3. Spoon sauce over hot pasta; sprinkle with cheese. Serve with French bread, if desired.
Makes 4 servings

Prep Time: 10 minutes
Cook Time: 20 minutes

Stuffed Mushrooms with Tomato Sauce and Pasta

THE MAIN EVENT

340 BEEF SPAGHETTI PIE OLÉ

PASTA SHELL
  1 package (7 ounces) uncooked spaghetti
  ⅓ cup shredded Monterey Jack or Cheddar cheese
  1 egg
  ½ teaspoon salt
  ¼ teaspoon garlic powder

FILLING
  1 pound lean ground beef
  1 teaspoon garlic powder
  ½ teaspoon salt
  ½ teaspoon ground cumin
  1 can (10 ounces) diced tomatoes with green chilies, undrained
  ¾ cup light dairy sour cream
  1 cup shredded Monterey Jack or Cheddar cheese

1. Heat oven to 350°F. Cook pasta according to package directions; drain well. In large bowl, whisk together remaining pasta shell ingredients. Add pasta; toss to coat. Arrange pasta in 9-inch pie dish, pressing down and up side to form shell; set aside.

2. Meanwhile, heat large nonstick skillet over medium heat until hot. Add ground beef; brown 4 to 5 minutes, breaking up into ¾-inch crumbles. Pour off drippings. Season beef with 1 teaspoon garlic powder, ½ teaspoon salt and cumin; stir in tomatoes. Bring to a boil; cook 3 to 5 minutes or until liquid is almost evaporated, stirring occasionally.

3. Reserve 2 tablespoons beef mixture for garnish. Stir sour cream into remaining beef; spoon into pasta shell. Place 1 cup cheese in center, leaving 2-inch border around edge. Spoon reserved beef mixture onto center of cheese; bake in 350°F oven 15 minutes or until heated through.

4. To serve, cut into wedges.

Makes 4 servings

Total Prep and Cook Time: 40 minutes

*Favorite recipe from **National Cattlemen's Beef Association***

341 PIZZA PIE

  1 pound lean ground beef
  ¼ cup finely chopped onion
  1 jar (15 ounces) pizza sauce with pepperoni
  ¼ cup sliced black olives
  ¼ cup chopped mushrooms
  1 teaspoon Italian seasoning
  1 tube (8 ounces) refrigerated crescent roll dough
  2 cups shredded mozzarella cheese
  ½ cup shredded Cheddar cheese

1. In large skillet, brown ground beef with onion; drain. Add pizza sauce, black olives, mushrooms and Italian seasoning.

2. Unroll crescent roll dough; press into glass pie plate to form a crust. Spoon meat mixture into crust. Bake at 400°F for 20 minutes. Top with mozzarella and Cheddar cheeses. Bake for an additional 10 minutes or until bubbly. Cut into wedges to serve.

Makes 4 servings

*Favorite recipe from **North Dakota Beef Commission***

Beef Spaghetti Pie Olé

THE MAIN EVENT

342 SPAGHETTI PIE

4 ounces uncooked thin spaghetti
1 egg
¼ cup grated Parmesan cheese
1 teaspoon Italian seasoning
⅔ cup reduced-fat ricotta cheese
½ pound 93% fat-free ground turkey
1 teaspoon chili powder
¼ teaspoon crushed fennel seeds
¼ teaspoon ground pepper
⅛ teaspoon ground coriander
1 can (14½ ounces) diced tomatoes, undrained
1½ cups sliced fresh mushrooms
1 cup chopped onion
1 can (8 ounces) tomato sauce
¼ cup tomato paste
1 clove garlic, minced
2 teaspoons dried basil leaves
1 cup (4 ounces) shredded part-skim mozzarella cheese

1. Cook spaghetti according to package directions, omitting salt. Drain and rinse well under cold water until pasta is cool; drain well.

2. Beat egg, Parmesan cheese and Italian seasoning lightly in medium bowl. Add spaghetti; blend well. Spray deep 9-inch pie plate with nonstick cooking spray. Place spaghetti mixture in pie plate. Press onto bottom and up side of pie plate. Spread ricotta cheese on spaghetti layer.

3. Preheat oven to 350°F. Combine turkey, chili powder, fennel seeds, pepper and coriander in bowl. Spray large nonstick skillet with nonstick cooking spray; heat over medium heat until hot. Brown turkey mixture until turkey is no longer pink, stirring to break up meat. Add remaining ingredients except mozzarella cheese.

Cook and stir until mixture boils. Spoon mixture over ricotta cheese in pie plate.

4. Cover pie plate with foil. Bake 20 minutes. Remove foil. Sprinkle with mozzarella cheese; bake 5 minutes or until cheese is melted. Let stand 5 minutes before cutting and serving. *Makes 6 servings*

343 SPAGHETTI PIE

6 ounces spaghetti, cooked and well drained
2 eggs, lightly beaten
8 ounces ground beef
½ cup chopped onion
¾ cup spaghetti sauce
⅓ cup A.1.® Steak Sauce
8 ounces ricotta cheese
2 tablespoons grated Parmesan cheese

Mix spaghetti with eggs until well blended; press on bottom and side of lightly greased 9-inch pie plate with spoon to form crust. Set aside.

In skillet, over medium-high heat, cook ground beef and onion until meat is no longer pink, stirring to break up meat; pour off fat. Stir in spaghetti sauce and steak sauce. Heat to a boil; reduce heat to low. Cook, uncovered, for 1 to 2 minutes or until slightly thickened. Remove from heat.

Spread ricotta cheese into prepared crust; top with meat mixture. Bake at 350°F for 25 to 30 minutes or until hot. Sprinkle with Parmesan cheese; bake for 5 minutes more. Let stand for 5 minutes before serving.
Makes 6 servings

Spaghetti Pie

344 PASTA PIZZA

4 ounces Italian turkey sausage
  Nonstick cooking spray
1 green bell pepper, chopped
1 cup sliced cremini or white mushrooms
½ cup chopped onion
2 cloves garlic, minced
2 teaspoons Italian seasoning
1 teaspoon dried oregano leaves
2 tablespoons reduced-sodium tomato
  sauce
8 ounces thin spaghetti, cooked and kept
  warm
2 egg whites, beaten
1 tomato, sliced
½ of 3-ounce can pitted ripe olives, rinsed,
  drained and halved (optional)
¾ cup (3 ounces) shredded reduced-fat
  mozzarella cheese
2 tablespoons finely chopped fresh basil
  or parsley

Cook sausage in small skillet until browned. Drain well; crumble and set aside. Spray large nonstick skillet with cooking spray. Heat over medium heat until hot. Add bell pepper, mushrooms, onion, garlic, Italian seasoning and oregano; cook and stir 5 to 8 minutes or until vegetables are tender. Stir in tomato sauce. Combine vegetable mixture, sausage and spaghetti in large bowl; mix in egg whites.

Spray same large nonstick skillet with cooking spray. Heat over medium heat until hot. Add spaghetti mixture to skillet; pat into even layer with spatula. Cook, covered, about 5 minutes or until browned on bottom. Loosen bottom and side of pasta with spatula; invert onto large plate. Slide pasta back into skillet. Arrange tomato slices and olives on top of pasta; sprinkle with cheese. Cook, covered, about 5 minutes or until cheese is melted. Sprinkle with basil. Serve immediately.   *Makes 4 servings*

345 KRAUT PIZZA

1¼ pounds bulk pork sausage
1 cup chopped onion
1 teaspoon fennel seed, divided
1 teaspoon dried oregano leaves
1 teaspoon dried basil leaves
1 large clove garlic, minced
1 tube (10 ounces) refrigerated pizza crust
  dough *or* 1 Italian bread shell
  (16 ounces)
1 package (12 ounces) shredded
  mozzarella cheese
  Pizza sauce
1 can (14.5 ounces) FRANK'S or
  SnowFloss Italian Style Diced
  Tomatoes, drained
1 can (14 ounces) FRANK'S or SnowFloss
  Kraut, drained
  Grated Parmesan cheese
  Salt and pepper to taste

1. Preheat oven to 450°F.

2. Sauté sausage with onion, ½ teaspoon fennel seed, oregano, basil and garlic; drain.

3. On pizza crust, sprinkle thin layer of mozzarella cheese then layer remaining ingredients in the following order: pizza sauce, sausage mixture, diced tomatoes and kraut.

4. Sprinkle remaining ½ teaspoon fennel seed over kraut. Top with remaining mozzarella cheese. Sprinkle with Parmesan cheese and salt and pepper to taste.

5. Bake for 18 to 20 minutes or until cheese is bubbly.   *Makes 6 servings*

Prep Time: 25 minutes
Bake Time: 18 to 20 minutes

Pasta Pizza

346 CANADIAN BACON PIZZA

1 tablespoon vegetable oil
¾ cup chopped onion, divided
⅓ cup chopped green pepper
1 clove garlic, minced
2 tablespoons chopped fresh parsley
1 (10¾-ounce) can tomato purée
1 teaspoon sugar
¾ teaspoon dried oregano leaves
¼ teaspoon salt
¼ teaspoon pepper
Packaged pizza crust for 12-inch pizza
2 cups shredded mozzarella cheese
1 cup shredded Cheddar cheese
1 pound ground pork or bulk pork sausage
6 ounces sliced Canadian-style bacon, cut up
6 to 8 fresh mushrooms, sliced
1 green pepper, sliced into rings
¼ cup chopped red pepper

Heat oil in heavy skillet over medium heat. Add ½ cup onion, chopped green pepper, garlic and parsley; cook, stirring frequently, until tender. Add tomato purée, sugar, oregano, salt and pepper. Bring to a boil; reduce heat and simmer about 30 minutes, stirring occasionally.

Spread sauce over pizza crust, leaving ½-inch border around edge. Combine cheeses; sprinkle half of cheese over pizza sauce.

Combine ground pork and remaining ¼ cup onion in skillet; cook over medium heat until meat is browned, stirring to crumble. Drain well on paper toweling. Spoon half of pork mixture onto pizza.

Layer Canadian-style bacon, mushroom slices and green pepper rings on top of pizza. Sprinkle with remaining pork mixture and chopped red pepper. Bake in 450°F oven for 10 minutes. Top with remaining shredded cheese and bake an additional 10 minutes.

Makes 4 servings

Prep Time: 30 minutes
Cook Time: 20 minutes

*Favorite recipe from **National Pork Producers Council***

347 BBQ BEEF PIZZA

½ pound lean ground beef
1 medium green bell pepper
⅔ cup prepared barbecue sauce
1 (14-inch) prepared pizza crust
3 to 4 onion slices, rings separated
½ (2¼-ounce) can sliced black olives, drained
1 cup (4 ounces) shredded cheese (Colby and Monterey Jack mix)

1. Preheat oven to 400°F. Place meat in large skillet and cook over high heat 6 to 8 minutes or until meat is no longer pink, breaking meat apart with wooden spoon. Pour off drippings; remove from heat.

2. While meat is cooking, seed bell pepper and slice into ¼-inch-thick rings. Add barbecue sauce to cooked meat in skillet. Place pizza crust on baking pan. Spread meat mixture over pizza crust to within ½ inch of edge. Arrange onion slices and pepper rings over meat. Sprinkle with olives and cheese. Bake 8 minutes or until cheese is melted. Cut into 8 wedges.

Makes 3 to 4 servings

Prep and Cook Time: 20 minutes

BBQ Beef Pizza

348 RICE CRUST PIZZA

Rice Crust (recipe follows)
1 jar (15 to 16 ounces) pizza sauce
2 teaspoons Italian seasoning
  Choice of toppings: turkey sausage, bell pepper, black olives, mushrooms and hot pepper sauce to taste
2 cups (8 ounces) mozzarella cheese, shredded

Prepare Rice Crust as directed below.

Combine pizza sauce and Italian seasoning in a small bowl and mix well. Spoon sauce over crust, up to 1 inch from edge. Cover with toppings of your choice and mozzarella cheese. Bake at 450°F until cheese melts, about 10 minutes. Cut into wedges and serve. *Makes 8 servings*

RICE CRUST
1 bag SUCCESS® Rice
  Vegetable cooking spray
2 eggs, well beaten
1 cup (4 ounces) shredded mozzarella cheese
$\frac{1}{4}$ cup onion, finely chopped
1 teaspoon salt

Prepare rice according to package directions.

Preheat oven to 400°F. Lightly spray 12-inch pizza pan with cooking spray and set aside. Combine eggs, rice, cheese, onion and salt in medium bowl and mix well. With back of spoon, press mixture evenly onto bottom and sides of pan. Bake 20 minutes or until lightly browned. Remove from oven.

349 CHEX® MEXICAN PIE

1 pound lean ground beef
1 can (10¾ ounces) condensed tomato soup
1 egg, beaten
1 package (1.25 ounces) dry taco seasoning mix
4 cups Corn CHEX® brand cereal, crushed to 2 cups, divided
$\frac{1}{2}$ cup (2 ounces) shredded Cheddar or Monterey Jack cheese
1 large tomato, chopped
$\frac{1}{4}$ cup chopped green onions
$\frac{1}{4}$ cup sliced stuffed green olives
2 tablespoons chopped fresh parsley

Preheat oven to 375°F. Combine ground beef, soup, egg and taco seasoning until well blended; stir in 1½ cups crushed cereal. Press meat mixture evenly onto bottom and sides of 10-inch quiche dish or pie plate, forming a 1-inch-wide rim. Sprinkle remaining ½ cup crushed cereal on top of rim; press gently. Bake 30 to 35 minutes or until brown. Sprinkle cheese over center of pie. Top with tomato, onions, olives and parsley; let stand 5 minutes before serving. *Makes 8 servings*

VARIATION: For loaf shape, follow directions above, except press meat mixture into 9×5×3-inch loaf pan. Make a 2-inch-wide well lengthwise down middle of meat mixture. Sprinkle remaining ½ cup crushed cereal on outer edges of meat mixture; press gently. Bake 25 to 30 minutes or until brown. Sprinkle cheese in well. Top with tomato, onions, olives and parsley; let stand 5 minutes before serving.

Rice Crust Pizza

THE MAIN EVENT

350 EASY BEEF TORTILLA PIZZAS

1 pound ground beef
1 medium onion, chopped
1 teaspoon dried oregano leaves, crushed
1 teaspoon salt
4 large flour tortillas (10-inch diameter)
4 teaspoons olive oil
1 medium tomato, seeded, chopped
   Greek or Mexican Topping (recipes follow)

Cook and stir ground beef and onion in large skillet over medium-high heat until beef loses pink color. Pour off drippings. Sprinkle oregano and salt over beef, stirring to combine. Place tortillas on 2 large baking sheets. Lightly brush surface of each tortilla with oil. Bake in preheated 400°F oven 3 minutes. Divide beef mixture evenly over tops of tortillas; divide tomato and desired topping over beef mixture. Bake at 400°F 12 to 14 minutes, rearranging baking sheets halfway through cooking time.

Makes 4 servings

GREEK TOPPING: Combine 1 teaspoon dried basil leaves, crushed, ½ teaspoon lemon pepper, 4 ounces crumbled feta cheese and ¼ cup grated Parmesan cheese in small bowl.

MEXICAN TOPPING: Combine 1 teaspoon dried cilantro, crushed, ½ teaspoon crushed dried red chilies, 1 cup (4 ounces) shredded Monterey Jack or Cheddar cheese and ⅓ cup sliced ripe olives in small bowl.

*Favorite recipe from **National Cattlemen's Beef Association***

351 MEXICALI PIZZA

   Vegetable oil
2 large flour tortillas *or* 4 small flour tortillas
1 pound ground beef
1 package (1.0 ounce) LAWRY'S® Taco Spices & Seasonings
¾ cup water
1½ cups (6 ounces) shredded Monterey Jack or Cheddar cheese
3 tablespoons diced green chiles
2 medium tomatoes, sliced
1 can (2¼ ounces) sliced ripe olives, drained
½ cup salsa

In large skillet, pour in oil to ¼-inch depth; heat. (For small tortillas, use small skillet.) Fry each flour tortilla about 5 seconds. While still pliable, turn tortilla over. Fry until golden brown. (Edges of tortilla should turn up about ½ inch.) Drain well on paper towels. In medium skillet, brown ground beef until crumbly; drain fat. Add Taco Spices & Seasonings and water; blend well. Bring to a boil; reduce heat and simmer, uncovered, 5 minutes. Place fried tortillas on pizza pan. Layer taco meat, ½ of cheese, chiles, tomatoes, remaining ½ of cheese, olives and salsa on each fried tortilla. Bake, uncovered, in 425°F oven 15 minutes for large pizzas or 7 to 8 minutes for small pizzas. *Makes 4 servings*

HINT: One pound ground turkey or 1½ cups shredded, cooked chicken can be used in place of beef.

Easy Beef Tortilla Pizzas

THE MAIN EVENT

352 TACO PIZZA

CRUST

**6 tablespoons margarine or butter,
softened**

1 egg

¼ teaspoon hot pepper sauce

**2 cups Corn CHEX® brand cereal, crushed
to ⅔ cup**

1 cup plus 2 tablespoons all-purpose flour

½ teaspoon salt

¼ cup water

FILLING

½ pound ground beef

1 cup refried beans

**1 can (4.5 ounces) chopped green chilies,
undrained**

1 teaspoon chili powder

¼ to ½ teaspoon hot pepper sauce

¼ teaspoon ground cumin

2 medium tomatoes, chopped

½ cup chopped onion

1 cup (4 ounces) shredded Colby cheese

**1 cup (4 ounces) shredded Monterey Jack
cheese**

**¼ cup chopped green pepper
Salsa or Taco Sauce (optional)**

To prepare Crust: Preheat oven to 450°F.
Grease 12-inch pizza pan. Beat margarine,
egg and pepper sauce until creamy.
Gradually add cereal, flour and salt; stir until
coarse crumbs form. Add water; mix well.
Form into ball (dough may be slightly wet).
Press onto bottom and sides of prepared
pan. Bake 8 to 10 minutes or until edges are
lightly browned.

To prepare Filling: Cook ground beef over
medium heat until no longer pink; drain. Stir
in beans, chilies with liquid, chili powder,
pepper sauce and cumin; mix well. Spread
evenly over prepared crust. Top with
tomatoes, onion, cheeses and green pepper.
Bake 10 to 12 minutes or until cheese is
melted and filling is hot. Serve with salsa.

Makes 8 servings

353 TURKEY AND BEAN TOSTADAS

6 (8-inch) flour tortillas

1 pound 93% fat-free ground turkey

**1 can (15 ounces) chili beans in chili
sauce**

½ teaspoon chili powder

**3 cups washed and shredded romaine
lettuce**

1 large tomato, chopped

¼ cup chopped fresh cilantro

**¼ cup (1 ounce) shredded reduced-fat
Monterey Jack cheese**

½ cup low-fat sour cream (optional)

1. Preheat oven to 350°F. Place tortillas on
baking sheets. Bake 7 minutes or until crisp.
Place on individual plates.

2. Heat large nonstick skillet over medium-
high heat until hot. Add turkey. Cook and
stir until turkey is browned; drain. Add
beans and chili powder. Cook 5 minutes over
medium heat. Divide turkey mixture evenly
among tortillas. Top with remaining
ingredients. *Makes 6 servings*

Prep and Cook Time: 20 minutes

Turkey and Bean Tostadas

THE MAIN EVENT

354 BEEF TORTILLA PIZZA

1 pound lean ground beef
1 medium onion, chopped
1 teaspoon *each* dried oregano leaves and
   salt
4 large (10-inch) flour tortillas
   Oil
1 medium tomato, seeded and chopped
1 tablespoon thinly sliced fresh basil
   leaves
1 cup shredded mozzarella cheese
¼ cup grated Parmesan cheese

Heat oven to 400°F. Brown ground beef and onion in skillet over medium heat 8 to 10 minutes or until beef is no longer pink. Pour off drippings. Stir oregano and salt into beef. Lightly brush tortillas with oil. Bake tortillas on 2 large baking sheets in 400°F oven 3 minutes. Spoon beef mixture evenly over top of each tortilla; top with an equal amount of tomato. Sprinkle with basil and cheeses. Return to oven and bake 12 to 14 minutes or until tortillas are lightly browned.

Makes 4 servings

SERVING SUGGESTION: Serve Beef Tortilla Pizza with a mixed green salad with Italian dressing.

Prep and Cook Time: 27 minutes

*Favorite recipe from **National Cattlemen's Beef Association***

Beef Tortilla Pizza

THE MAIN EVENT

355 FAJITAS

MARINADE

½ cup chopped onion
¼ cup GRANDMA'S® Molasses
¼ cup oil
2 tablespoons lime juice
2 cloves garlic, minced
2 teaspoons chili powder
½ teaspoon dried oregano leaves

FAJITAS

1 pound ground beef or turkey
10 (8- to 10-inch) flour tortillas, softened
4 ounces (1 cup) shredded Monterey Jack
    cheese
  Refried beans
  Chopped tomatoes
  Shredded lettuce
  Chopped avocado
  Salsa
  Dairy sour cream

In medium bowl, combine all marinade ingredients; mix well. Crumble ground beef into marinade; stir to coat. Cover; marinate 4 to 6 hours or overnight, stirring occasionally.

In large skillet, stir-fry meat mixture 5 minutes or until brown. To serve, spoon meat onto center of each tortilla; top with cheese, refried beans, tomatoes, lettuce, avocado and salsa. Roll up to enclose filling. Serve with sour cream.

Makes 5 servings

NOTE: Serve with a variety of toppings, if desired.

356 SANTA FE BURRITO BAKE

1½ pounds ground beef
1 cup water
1 can (4 ounces) chopped green chiles,
    undrained
1 package (1.25 ounces) taco seasoning
    mix, dry
2 cups Wheat CHEX® brand cereal,
    crushed to ¾ cup
1 loaf frozen bread dough, thawed
1 cup (4 ounces) shredded Cheddar
    cheese
1 teaspoon margarine or butter, melted
  Chili powder
  Salsa, sour cream and shredded lettuce

Preheat oven to 350°F. In large skillet over medium heat cook meat 5 minutes or until no longer pink; drain. Stir in water, chiles and seasoning mix. Add cereal, stirring until well combined; set aside. Roll bread dough into 15×10-inch rectangle. Spread 2 cups reserved meat mixture in 4-inch-wide strip lengthwise down center of dough. Top with cheese. Cover with remaining 2 cups meat mixture. Bring sides of dough up over filling. Seal top and sides well. Place seam side down on ungreased baking sheet. Brush with margarine. Sprinkle with chili powder. Bake 30 to 35 minutes or until golden brown. Slice and serve with salsa, sour cream and lettuce. *Makes 6 servings*

NOTE: To decorate top, cut 1-inch-wide strip from a short side of dough; reserve. Decorate loaf with reserved dough before brushing with margarine.

THE MAIN EVENT

357 BORDER SCRAMBLE

1 pound BOB EVANS FARMS® Original Recipe Roll Sausage
1½ cups chopped cooked potatoes
1½ cups chopped onions
1½ cups chopped tomatoes
¾ cup chopped green bell pepper
¼ to ½ cup picante sauce
½ to 1 tablespoon hot pepper sauce
½ teaspoon garlic powder
½ teaspoon salt
4 (9-inch) flour tortillas
2 cups prepared meatless chili
½ cup (2 ounces) shredded Cheddar cheese

Crumble sausage into large skillet. Cook over medium heat until browned, stirring occasionally. Drain off any drippings. Add all remaining ingredients except tortillas, chili and cheese; simmer 20 minutes or until vegetables are crisp-tender. To warm tortillas, microwave 1 minute at HIGH between paper towels. Place 1 cup sausage mixture in center of each tortilla; fold tortilla over filling to close. Heat chili in small saucepan until hot, stirring occasionally. Top each folded tortilla with ½ cup chili and 2 tablespoons cheese. Serve hot. Refrigerate leftovers. *Makes 4 servings*

358 BEEF & ZUCCHINI QUICHE

1 unbaked 9-inch pie shell
½ pound lean ground beef
1 medium zucchini, shredded
3 green onions, sliced
¼ cup sliced mushrooms
1 tablespoon all-purpose flour
3 eggs, beaten
1 cup milk
¾ cup (3 ounces) shredded Swiss cheese
1½ teaspoons chopped fresh thyme *or*
  ½ teaspoon dried thyme leaves
½ teaspoon salt
  Dash of freshly ground black pepper
  Dash of ground red pepper

Preheat oven to 475°F.

Line pie shell with foil; fill with dried beans or rice. Bake 8 minutes. Remove from oven; carefully remove foil and beans. Return pie shell to oven. Continue baking 4 minutes; set aside. *Reduce oven temperature to 375°F.*

Brown ground beef in medium skillet. Drain. Add zucchini, onions and mushrooms; cook, stirring occasionally, until vegetables are tender. Stir in flour; cook 2 minutes, stirring constantly. Remove from heat.

Combine eggs, milk, cheese and seasonings in medium bowl. Stir into ground beef mixture; pour into crust.

Bake 35 minutes or until knife inserted near center comes out clean.

Makes 6 servings

Border Scramble

THE MAIN EVENT

359 STUFFED PESTO TORTA

2 tablespoons olive oil
1 cup chopped onion
3 cloves garlic, minced
1 can (14½ ounces) Italian-style tomatoes, undrained and chopped
2 tablespoons tomato paste
2 teaspoons dry Italian seasoning
½ teaspoon salt
½ teaspoon crushed red pepper flakes
1 package (3 ounces) cream cheese, softened
½ cup (2 ounces) freshly grated Parmesan cheese
⅓ cup whole-milk ricotta cheese
¼ teaspoon black pepper
1 pound fresh uncooked Italian sausage, casings removed
1 package (17¼ ounces) frozen puff pastry, thawed
½ pound thinly sliced Gruyère or mozzarella cheese
6 tablespoons purchased or homemade pesto
1 egg yolk
1 teaspoon water

Heat oil in medium saucepan over medium-high heat until hot; add onion and garlic. Cook 2 minutes or until onion is tender. Add tomatoes with liquid, tomato paste, Italian seasoning, salt and red pepper; bring to a boil. Reduce heat to low; simmer, uncovered, 30 minutes to reduce to 1⅓ cups. Remove from heat; set aside.

Meanwhile, combine cream, Parmesan and ricotta cheeses and black pepper; beat with electric mixer at medium speed until smooth. Set aside. Brown sausage in large skillet over medium-high heat until no longer pink, stirring to separate meat. Drain on paper towels; set aside.

Preheat oven to 375°F. Roll out 1 pastry sheet to 13-inch square on lightly floured surface with lightly floured rolling pin. Press pastry onto bottom and up side of 9-inch springform pan. (Pastry will *not* completely cover side of pan and will hang over edge in places.)

Layer ½ of cooked sausage on bottom of pastry shell. Top with ½ of reserved tomato sauce mixture, spreading evenly. Drop ½ of cream cheese mixture by heaping teaspoonfuls over tomato sauce mixture. Arrange ½ of Gruyère in pastry shell, forming solid layer. Spread pesto evenly over Gruyère with small metal spatula. Arrange remaining Gruyère over pesto, forming another solid layer. Drop remaining cream cheese mixture by heaping teaspoonfuls over Gruyère. Top with remaining tomato sauce mixture. Layer with remaining cooked sausage. Trim overhanging pastry to an even height with paring knife. Fold pastry over filling.

Roll out remaining pastry sheet to 12-inch square; trim to 8-inch circle. Make decorative pastry cutouts from excess dough, if desired. Beat egg yolk and water in small bowl with fork until blended. Lightly brush beaten egg mixture on pastry around filled torta. Carefully place 8-inch circle of pastry over torta, pressing gently to adhere. Lightly brush top crust with beaten egg mixture and arrange pastry cutouts on top. Brush cutouts with beaten egg mixture.

Bake 1 hour or until pastry is golden. Let stand 15 minutes on wire rack. To serve, carefully remove side of pan; let stand 45 minutes before cutting into wedges. Garnish as desired.

Makes 8 main-dish or 24 appetizer servings

Stuffed Pesto Torta

360 BEEF AND MUSHROOM FILLED GOUGÈRE

½ pound extra-lean (90% lean) ground beef
½ cup chopped fresh mushrooms
1 small onion, chopped
1 clove garlic, minced
1½ teaspoons chopped fresh thyme *or*
    ½ teaspoon dried thyme leaves, crushed
    Salt and freshly ground pepper
¼ cup butter or margarine
¾ cup cold water
¾ cup all-purpose flour
½ teaspoon salt
3 eggs
¾ cup (3 ounces) shredded part-skim mozzarella cheese

Preheat oven to 425°F.

Brown ground beef in medium skillet. Drain. Add mushrooms, onion, garlic and thyme; cook until vegetables are tender. Season with salt and pepper to taste. Set aside.

Bring butter and water to a boil in heavy medium saucepan. Add flour and ½ teaspoon salt, all at once. Beat with wooden spoon until mixture is smooth and forms a ball. Remove from heat. Add eggs, one at a time, beating well after each addition.

Thinly spread dough onto bottom and up sides of greased 10-inch round baking dish; fill with ground beef mixture.

Bake 25 minutes or until puffed and golden brown. Sprinkle with cheese; continue baking 5 minutes. Serve hot.

Makes 6 servings

361 BEEF & CABBAGE PUFF

½ pound lean ground beef
½ medium onion, chopped
3 cups finely shredded cabbage
1 teaspoon caraway seeds
1½ teaspoons chopped fresh thyme *or*
    ½ teaspoon dried thyme leaves
½ teaspoon salt
    Dash of freshly ground pepper
1 tablespoon all-purpose flour
¼ cup plain yogurt or sour cream
½ package (17¼ ounces) frozen puff pastry (1 sheet), thawed

Preheat oven to 375°F.

Brown ground beef in medium skillet. Drain. Add onion; cook until tender. Stir in cabbage, caraway seeds and seasonings. Cook until cabbage is crisp-tender, stirring occasionally. Blend in flour. Remove from heat; stir in yogurt. Cool.

Place pastry on floured surface. Roll to 12×10-inch rectangle. Cut lengthwise in half to form two 12×5-inch rectangles. Spoon ground beef mixture down center of one rectangle to within 1 inch of outer edges. Fold remaining rectangle in half lengthwise; cut crosswise at 1-inch intervals from fold to about 1½ inches from opposite edge. Unfold rectangle. Moisten edges of rectangles. Place cut rectangle over filling, pressing edges of dough together to seal.

Bake 25 minutes or until puffed and golden brown.

Makes 6 servings

Beef and Mushroom Filled Gougère

THE MAIN EVENT

362 CHICKEN PHYLLO WRAPS

Vegetable cooking spray
1 pound ground chicken
1 cup chopped fresh mushrooms
1 medium onion, chopped
3 cups cooked rice (cooked without salt and fat)
1 cup nonfat low-salt ricotta cheese
1 package (10 ounces) frozen chopped spinach, thawed and well drained
1 can (2¼ ounces) sliced black olives, drained
¼ cup pine nuts, toasted*
2 cloves garlic, minced
1 teaspoon ground oregano
1 teaspoon lemon pepper
12 phyllo dough sheets

To toast nuts, place on baking sheet. Bake at 350°F 5 to 7 minutes or until lightly browned.

Coat large skillet with cooking spray; heat over medium-high heat until hot. Add chicken, mushrooms, and onion; cook and stir 2 to 4 minutes or until chicken is no longer pink and vegetables are tender. Reduce heat to medium. Add rice, ricotta cheese, spinach, olives, nuts, garlic, oregano, and lemon pepper; cook and stir 3 to 4 minutes until well blended and thoroughly heated.

Working with 1 phyllo sheet at a time, spray 1 sheet with cooking spray; fold sheet in half lengthwise. Place ¾ to 1 cup rice mixture on one end of phyllo strip. Fold left bottom corner over mixture, forming a triangle. Continue folding back and forth into triangle to end of strip. Repeat with remaining phyllo sheets and rice mixture.

Place triangles, seam sides down, on baking sheets coated with cooking spray. Coat top of each triangle with cooking spray. Bake at 400°F 15 to 20 minutes or until golden brown. Serve immediately.

Makes 12 servings

Favorite recipe from **USA Rice Council**

363 TOSTADAS WITH PORK

1 pound lean ground pork
1 cup chopped onion
1 jar (8 ounces) taco sauce
1 teaspoon salt
½ teaspoon chili powder
¼ cup ripe olives, sliced
4 corn or flour tortillas (7-inch diameter), heated
2 to 4 cups shredded lettuce
½ cup shredded Monterey Jack or Cheddar cheese (optional)
1 medium tomato, cut into thin wedges
½ cup sour cream
Additional taco sauce (optional)

In skillet, lightly brown ground pork with onion; drain any drippings. Add taco sauce, salt and chili powder; cover and cook over low heat 15 minutes or until flavors blend. Stir in ripe olives.

For each tostada, place heated tortilla on plate. Top with layer of lettuce, then hot pork mixture (about ⅔ cup). Sprinkle with cheese, if desired. Garnish with tomato wedges and dollop of sour cream. Serve with additional taco sauce, if desired.

Makes 4 servings

Prep Time: 25 minutes

Favorite recipe from **National Pork Producers Council**

Chicken Phyllo Wraps

THE MAIN EVENT

364 HEARTLAND CROWN ROAST OF PORK

- 8- to 9-pound crown roast of pork
- 1 pound ground pork, cooked, drained
- 5 cups dry bread cubes
- 1 can (14½ ounces) chicken broth
- 1 cup walnut halves, toasted
- ½ cup chopped onion
- ½ cup chopped celery
- 1 teaspoon salt
- ¼ teaspoon *each* ground cinnamon and allspice
- ⅛ teaspoon pepper
- 2 cups sliced fresh or thawed frozen rhubarb
- ½ cup sugar

Place roast in shallow pan. Roast at 350°F until temperature on meat thermometer reaches 155°F, about 2½ hours. Remove roast from oven. Let stand 10 minutes before slicing to serve.

Meanwhile, combine ground pork, bread cubes, broth, walnuts, onion, celery and seasonings; mix well. Combine rhubarb and sugar; bring to a boil. Pour over bread mixture; mix lightly. Spoon into buttered 2-quart casserole. Cover; bake at 350°F for 1½ hours.   *Makes 16 servings*

Prep Time: 20 minutes
Cook Time: 2½ hours

Favorite recipe from **National Pork Producers Council**

365 STUFFED PORK LOIN GENOA STYLE

- 4- to 5-pound boneless pork loin roast
- 1 cup fresh parsley, chopped
- ½ cup fresh basil leaves, chopped
- ½ cup pine nuts
- 6 cloves garlic, peeled and chopped
- ½ cup grated Parmesan cheese
- ½ pound ground pork
- ½ pound Italian sausage
- 1 cup dry bread crumbs
- ¼ cup milk
- 1 egg
- ¼ cup fresh parsley, chopped
- 1 teaspoon ground black pepper

In food processor or blender, blend 1 cup parsley, fresh basil, pine nuts, garlic and Parmesan cheese. Set aside.

Mix together ground pork, Italian sausage, bread crumbs, milk, egg, remaining ¼ cup parsley and pepper.

Place roast, fat side down, on cutting board. Spread with the herb-cheese mixture; place ground pork mixture along center of loin. Fold in half; tie with kitchen string. Roast on rack in shallow baking pan at 350°F for 1½ hours or until temperature on meat thermometer reaches 155°F. Let stand 10 minutes. Slice to serve.
Makes 10 servings

Prep Time: 15 minutes
Cook Time: 90 minutes

Favorite recipe from **National Pork Producers Council**

ACKNOWLEDGMENTS

The publisher would like to thank the companies and organizations listed below for the use of their recipes and photos in this publication.

Alpine Lace Brands, Inc.
American Lamb Council
Birds Eye
Blue Diamond Growers
Bob Evans Farms®
California Table Grape Commission
Canned Food Information Council
Chef Paul Prudhomme's® Magic
  Seasoning Blends®
Christopher Ranch Garlic
Cucina Classica Italiana, Inc.
Dean Foods Vegetable Company
Delmarva Poultry Industry, Inc.
Del Monte Corporation
Filippo Berio Olive Oil
The Fremont Company, Makers of
  Frank's & SnowFloss Kraut and
  Tomato Products
Grandma's Molasses, a division of
  Cadbury Beverages Inc.
Guiltless Gourmet, Incorporated
Healthy Choice®
Heinz U.S.A.
The HVR Company

Kellogg Company
Kikkoman International Inc.
The Kingsford Products Company
Kraft Foods, Inc.
Lawry's® Foods, Inc.
Lipton
McIlhenny Company
Minnesota Cultivated Wild Rice Council
Nabisco, Inc.
National Cattlemen's Beef Association
National Onion Association
National Pork Producers Council
National Turkey Federation
Nestlé Food Company
Newman's Own, Inc.®
North Dakota Barley Council
North Dakota Beef Commission
Ralston Foods, Inc.®
Reckitt & Colman Inc.
Riviana Foods Inc.
Sunkist Growers
USA Rice Council
Wesson/Peter Pan Foods Company
Wisconsin Milk Marketing Board

INDEX

INDEX

INDEX

METRIC CONVERSION CHART

VOLUME MEASUREMENTS (dry)

1/8 teaspoon = 0.5 mL
1/4 teaspoon = 1 mL
1/2 teaspoon = 2 mL
3/4 teaspoon = 4 mL
1 teaspoon = 5 mL
1 tablespoon = 15 mL
2 tablespoons = 30 mL
1/4 cup = 60 mL
1/3 cup = 75 mL
1/2 cup = 125 mL
2/3 cup = 150 mL
3/4 cup = 175 mL
1 cup = 250 mL
2 cups = 1 pint = 500 mL
3 cups = 750 mL
4 cups = 1 quart = 1 L

VOLUME MEASUREMENTS (fluid)

1 fluid ounce (2 tablespoons) = 30 mL
4 fluid ounces (1/2 cup) = 125 mL
8 fluid ounces (1 cup) = 250 mL
12 fluid ounces (1 1/2 cups) = 375 mL
16 fluid ounces (2 cups) = 500 mL

WEIGHTS (mass)

1/2 ounce = 15 g
1 ounce = 30 g
3 ounces = 90 g
4 ounces = 120 g
8 ounces = 225 g
10 ounces = 285 g
12 ounces = 360 g
16 ounces = 1 pound = 450 g

DIMENSIONS

1/16 inch = 2 mm
1/8 inch = 3 mm
1/4 inch = 6 mm
1/2 inch = 1.5 cm
3/4 inch = 2 cm
1 inch = 2.5 cm

OVEN TEMPERATURES

250°F = 120°C
275°F = 140°C
300°F = 150°C
325°F = 160°C
350°F = 180°C
375°F = 190°C
400°F = 200°C
425°F = 220°C
450°F = 230°C

BAKING PAN SIZES

Utensil	Size in Inches/Quarts	Metric Volume	Size in Centimeters
Baking or	8 × 8 × 2	2 L	20 × 20 × 5
Cake Pan	9 × 9 × 2	2.5 L	22 × 22 × 5
(square or	12 × 8 × 2	3 L	30 × 20 × 5
rectangular)	13 × 9 × 2	3.5 L	33 × 23 × 5
Loaf Pan	8 × 4 × 3	1.5 L	20 × 10 × 7
	9 × 5 × 3	2 L	23 × 13 × 7
Round Layer	8 × 1 1/2	1.2 L	20 × 4
Cake Pan	9 × 1 1/2	1.5 L	23 × 4
Pie Plate	8 × 1 1/4	750 mL	20 × 3
	9 × 1 1/4	1 L	23 × 3
Baking Dish	1 quart	1 L	—
or Casserole	1 1/2 quart	1.5 L	—
	2 quart	2 L	—